PLAYING AT ACQUISITIONS

PLAYING AT ACQUISITIONS

BEHAVIORAL OPTION GAMES

HAN SMIT AND THRAS MORAITIS

Princeton University Press

Princeton and Oxford

press.princeton.edu

Cover design by Jessica Massabrook

First paperback printing 2017
Paperback ISBN 978-0-691-17641-3

Cloth ISBN 978-0-691-14000-1

British Library Cataloging-in-Publication Data is available

This book has been composed in Kabel LT Std & Adobe Caslon Pro.

Printed on acid-free paper. ∞

Printed in the United States of America

CONTENTS

LIST OF FIGURES   vii
LIST OF TABLES   ix
PREFACE   xi
  About This Book   xi
  Who Should Read This Book?   xii
  A New Strategic Valuation Approach as a Bridge between
    Theory and Practice   xiv
  Academic Contribution and Features   xvi
  A Guide through the Book   xviii

CHAPTER 1. LEARNING TO SEE, TO ADAPT TO,
AND TO VALUE UNCERTAINTY   1
  Learning to See Uncertainty   3
  Learning to Adapt to Uncertainty   8
  Learning to Value Uncertainty   11
  Summary   15

PART I. LEARNING TO SEE UNCERTAINTY   17
CHAPTER 2. HOW TO DE-BIAS VALUATION
OVER THE CYCLE   19
  Problem Diagnosis: Why Acquisitions Occur in
    Go/No-Go Waves   20
  Avoiding Irrational Infection of the Valuation Analysis   22
  A Remedy for Uncertainty Neglect: Broaden Your Narrow View 25
  Examples of Appropriate Real Options Thinking in Hot
    and Cold Deal Markets   32
  Conclusions   41

CHAPTER 3. PLAYING AT SERIAL ACQUISITIONS:
THE CASE OF VODAFONE   43
  Six Potential Pitfalls in the Execution of a Serial
    Acquisition Strategy   44
  Can Rational Analysis Discipline Strategy?   57
  Dual Valuation of Growth Option Value to Avoid
    Irrational Infection   61
  How to Use Option Games to Overcome Bidding Pitfalls   65
  Conclusions   68

PART II. LEARNING TO ADAPT TO UNCERTAINTY 73

CHAPTER 4. STRATEGY AS OPTIONS GAMES 75
Classifying Acquisition Options under Competition 78
Expressing a Buy-and-Build Strategy as an Option Portfolio 81
Competition in the Bidding Game 87
Play Poker against Rivals Who Overshoot or Fall Asleep 93
Conclusions 95

CHAPTER 5. DUAL REAL OPTIONS VALUATION: THE XSTRATA CASE 101
Illustrative Example of the Dual Approach: Xstrata's Journey 103
Bottom-Up Framework: Xstrata's Serial Acquisitions 106
Top-Down Framework for Listed Companies: How Finance Can
    Enlighten Strategy 112
General Implications and Limitations 117
Conclusions 118

PART III. LEARNING TO VALUE UNCERTAINTY 121

CHAPTER 6. OPTION GAMES VALUATION 123
Designing and Solving an Option Bidding Game 124
Quantifying the Optionality of the Falconbridge Episode 133
Conclusions: How Option Games Can Deliver Their Potential 147

CHAPTER 7. CONCLUSION AND IMPLICATIONS 151
Biases and Options Are Everywhere 152
The Problem: Selected Pitfalls in Acquisition Decision Making 154
The Solution: How Executives Can De-bias Their Acquisition
    Decisions 158
Selected Implications to Deal Rationally with One's Own Biases,
    Financial Markets, and "Irrational" Rivals 163
Empirical Evidence 166
Promising Future Research Directions 169
Broaden Your View with Option Games 171

BIBLIOGRAPHY 173
INDEX 185

LIST OF FIGURES

Figure 1.1 The Ponzo Illusion: How Perspective Can Bias Vision   4

Figure 1.2 Perceived Uncertainty in the Payoff of Acquisitions (Inner Distribution) Is Lower Than Actual Uncertainty (Outer Distribution)   5

Figure 1.3 Learning to Adapt to Uncertainty: Optionality Generates a Positively Skewed Distribution   10

Figure 1.4 Components of Company Value   11

Figure 2.1 A DCF Valuation That Derives a Significant Part from Its Horizon or Terminal Value May Reinforce Hot and Cold Deal Framing   23

Figure 2.2 A Real Options Analysis May Promote Cautious Venturing   28

Figure 2.3 How a Real Options Approach Can Counter Executive Framing Biases   33

Figure 2.4 Decision Tree for Offshore Oil Development   37

Figure 2.5 Restructuring a Business as a Portfolio of Options   40

Figure 3.1 Staged Decisions in Vodafone's Buy-and-Build Acquisition Strategy   59

Figure 4.1 The Real Options Approach to Classifying Acquisitions   80

Figure 4.2 Staged Decisions for a Buy-and-Build Strategy   85

Figure 4.3 Different Competitive Strategies Following "Buy" or "Build" Expansion in a Value Enhancement or a Value Capture Game   90

Figure 4.4 Timing Strategies Based on the Consolidator's Market Position   93

Figure 4.5 Executive Summary: Conceptual Implementation of Bottom-Up Option Games   99

Figure 5.1 Xstrata's Market Value as It Evolved into a Major Mining Company   104

Figure 5.2 Xstrata's Acquisition Paths as a Series of Platform and Asset Options   111

Figure 5.3 Summary for Implementing Top Down Valuation   119

Figure 6.1 Simultaneous versus Sequential Bidding   141

Figure 6.2 Strategic Option Value of a Minority Stake   145

Figure 6.3 New Players Scramble for Global Mining Assets   146

Figure 7.1 Potential Biases, Pitfalls, and Solutions at Each Phase of the Acquisition Process   155

Figure 7.2 Summary Scheme of Behavioral Option Games   159

LIST OF TABLES

Table 3.1 Biases That Affect Company Strategy 49

Table 3.2 Biases That Affect Company Valuation 52

Table 3.3 Biases That Affect Bidding 54

Table 3.4 Summary of How to Overcome Pitfalls in
Serial Acquisitions 69

Table 5.1 Xstrata's Rapid Growth Trajectory through M&As
in Early Years 105

Table 5.2 Common Corporate Real Options in Acquisitions 108

Table 5.3 Global Diversifieds Have a Higher Proportion of
Growth Option Value (PVGO) to Equity 115

Table 6.1 Scenarios Influencing the Shared or Proprietary Nature
of the Option 140

Table 7.1 Industry Average of the Market Value of Growth
Opportunities, Modified Growth Opportunities, and Mispricing 167

PREFACE

We have a very narrow view of what's going on.
—Daniel Kahneman

ABOUT THIS BOOK

Merger and acquisition (M&A) decisions are among the most crucial CEO and board deliberations, but empirical research reinforces a common belief that a large proportion of such transactions fail to deliver their expected value. This book is designed to support the M&A practitioner—such as the corporate CEO or private equity fund manager—in improving these odds by providing novel tools that are based on fundamental economic theory. Specifically, we offer a new perspective on valuing an acquisition strategy aimed at addressing obstacles we encountered when applying existing tools, obstacles as varied as our own behavioral decision biases, high uncertainty, and competitive bidding situations. We help practitioners move beyond intuition-based acquisition decisions.

What does it take for a CEO to make a "good" acquisition decision? Widely used valuation tools, such as net present value (NPV) and multiple-based approaches, are relatively simple and clear—but they provide only limited protection against the inherent biases any decision maker tends to display. Decision-making processes are further complicated by a web of considerations in sophisticated acquisition settings—such as executing serial acquisitions in consolidating industries or performing valuations of targets in contexts of high uncertainty or fierce competition. Traditional valuation tools may provide little secure guidance in these settings, so objective decision making becomes a challenging endeavor. How can one make wise acquisition decisions about targets, timing, valuation, price, partners, and so on? What is the right mix between analytical and intuitive approaches? What should one do if intuition and rational valuation approaches—such as discounted cash flow (DCF) analysis—point in different directions?

Correct decision-making practice demands that you make your decision only after you understand why intuition and systematic valuation analysis do not match. We argue that acquisition decision making is something that can be improved by making use of new, much richer valuation methods than those currently applied. Because the context in which acquisitions are pursued today is becoming more complex—a result of globalization, consolidation, the entry of new types of competitors with differing objectives, and the changing characteristics of modern business environments—we require new valuation tools to provide the necessary insights to ensure high-quality acquisition decisions. This book makes a significant contribution to providing both implementable tools and novel insights in acquisition strategies.

Between the covers of this book you will find new tools and metrics that will help you determine when a bid premium is justified to improve your company's strategic position or, conversely, when raising your bid may result in overpayment. The strategic valuation analysis we promote goes way beyond currently available models, such as standard DCF or even real option analysis.[1] We offer a *synthesis* of the newest developments in psychology, corporate finance, strategic management, and related fields and use behavioral theory, real options, and game theory to modify traditional approaches to company valuation.

The new perspective on valuation offered here will support the CEO in integrating conceptual strategic intuition and quantitative finance tools and considering objectively the elusive but true value components of a target beyond directly measurable cash flows. At the same time, these approaches can caution and discipline executives' intuition in competitive bidding and strategic decision-making situations, giving them the confidence to bid, but not the overconfidence that could lead to them paying over the odds.

WHO SHOULD READ THIS BOOK?

We hope the book fulfills a function for *practitioners* and has *academic* value for scholars in strategic management and corporate finance in its development of new valuation methods. Empirical evidence shows that shareholders in target firms gain significantly on the acquisition's announcement, while the wealth effect on the shareholders of acquiring firms is much lower. There is a strong argument for adopting new types of quantitative valuation analysis to prevent bidding companies from adding to the low return statistics of corporate M&A.[2] We combine our academic learning and practical experience to synthesize cutting-edge ideas on strategic valuation and communicate them in an accessible and practical manner. We take advantage of findings in the human behavioral

---

[1] The impressive volume of work by Lenos Trigeorgis has helped develop the field of real options. For early papers in the field of real options, see Baldwin (1982), Black and Scholes (1973), McDonald and Siegel (1985, 1986), Dixit (1989), Dixit and Pindyck (1995), Mason and Merton (1985), and Kester (1984).

[2] See, for instance, Asquith, Bruner, and Mullins (1983), Brouthers, van Hastenburg, and van den Ven (1998), Bruner (2002), Chatterjee (1986, 1992), Fuller, Netter, and Stegemoller (2002), Haleblian et al. (2009), and Jarrell and Poulsen (1989) for the failure statistics, synergies, and returns to acquiring firms.

experimental literature to help identify inborn acquisition biases or to anticipate rivals' biases toward various bidding strategies, and propose an integrated
real options and game theory valuation approach to counteract and mitigate
the pitfalls in acquisition strategies. We apply this new valuation methodology
to examples in mining, telecom, and private equity to illustrate how these modern valuation techniques work in practice. Moraitis and the Xstrata executive
team have worked with Smit to apply this thinking and some of these tools
within Xstrata, with some success, as the story of Xstrata attests. Xstrata was a
$500 million mining junior in 2001, but by applying options thinking to parts
of its acquisition strategy, the company managed to reach its ultimate endgame—the merger with Glencore in 2013, creating one of the largest global
diversified natural resource majors.

Playing at Acquisitions will be of interest to executives pursuing transactions
across the globe and to consultants, private equity partners, and financial analysts. The academic framework we present can assist executives of acquiring
companies by helping to discipline their strategy and increase their ability to
value and to bid for target companies successfully. Financial market analysts
can also benefit from the improved understanding these new tools provide for
identifying potential targets and valuing companies in consolidating industries.
When properly applied, the strategic option perspective we present can help
identify when takeover premiums for certain platform acquisitions are justified
and clarify the relationships between the restructuring of fragmented markets
and the strategies and market values of specific companies.

These new and richer valuation tools are better able to address practical
questions of acquisition strategy: What is the value of an acquisition in a new
location? When is it attractive to invest early to preempt competitive entry, and
when is it better to wait? When may a target justify a premium and when is a
bidder likely to overpay? For which companies are rivals likely to bid, and how
much might they be prepared to pay? What is the strategic value of minority
stakes and platform acquisitions beyond that implied by the DCF, and what is
the value of alliances or clubs in bidding? These and other relevant questions
are addressed and brought to life in this book through real-world examples and
stories from the battlefield.

The book also fulfills an *educational and didactic* function, being of interest to
educators in MBA and executive MBA programs and teachers of courses in
corporate finance and strategy, as it presents practical case studies within an
academic framework reflecting current thinking on acquisition strategies.
Playing at Acquisitions invites readers to explore a series of real-life examples
and guides them through the novel tools that are available to them, as well as
the advantages and pitfalls of their use. The book employs modern and interactive educational methods, such as hands-on spreadsheets of real option valuation tools that practitioners can adapt to their situations. We also include
boardroom experiments that executives can play to reveal their own and their

groups' cognitive biases when making decisions. Slides and software tools for executive education complement the book (links to which can be found on the book's Princeton University Press website: http://press.princeton.edu/titles /10333.html).

A NEW STRATEGIC VALUATION APPROACH AS A BRIDGE BETWEEN THEORY AND PRACTICE

Fundamental economic theory provides the building blocks for the new valuation approach proposed in this book, and these building blocks—based on behavioral economics, real options, and game theory—have gained significant academic credence in recent times. In 2002, Daniel Kahneman and Vernon Smith shared the Bank of Sweden Prize in Economic Sciences—the "Nobel Prize" for Economics—for integrating insights from psychological research, especially concerning human judgment and decision making under uncertainty, into economic science. The 1997 Nobel Prize was awarded to Myron Scholes and Robert Merton for their role in the development of options pricing. Their option models opened up a new way to value investment opportunities under uncertainty—also named *real* options.[3] Game theory offers insights into the competitive forces that come into play in bidding contests, and can be used to inform the behavioral dimensions of competitive acquisition situations. In 1994, John Nash, Reinhard Selten, and John Harsanyi shared the Nobel Prize for their work on applying game theory to noncompetitive games, and in 2005 the prize was awarded to two more game theorists—Robert Aumann and Thomas Schelling—for their contributions on conflict and cooperation. Behavioral finance, real options, and game theory form the three components of the new approach to valuation presented here.

Drawing on a combination of the fundamentals of academic theory, metrics developed by the authors, direct experience, and examples from telecom, private equity, banking and mining, *Playing at Acquisitions* guides companies through novel acquisition challenges requiring greater sophistication than those of traditional valuation techniques. The novelties find application in situations including the development and execution of buy-and-build strategies; the value of bidding for a minority stake as an option toward gaining ultimate control; dealing with contested acquisitions and company auctions; and determining the optimal timing and the correct price of a bid depending on the relative behavior, size, or capabilities of the bidder to its competitors. Executives analyzing such strategic situations with existing tools will encounter obstacles. We address such obstacles by modifying conventional valuation tools and provide practical illustrations in the following ways.

---

[3] See Merton (1998) for a brilliant overview of applications of option-pricing theory.

DE-BIASING COMPANY VALUATION ANALYSIS

In this book we show that behavioral theory has significant potential to improve company valuation—in the same way it has impacted many other fields. One aspect that is often overlooked in the acquisition process is how the CEO's *own personal* biases are likely to affect the valuation analysis and the acquisition decision. Using various examples from the telecommunications industry and private equity we illustrate when and why many acquirers seem both to overshoot in hot deal markets and then hold back irrationally in cold ones, shying away from purchases that might bring them important growth opportunities. The traditional methods used for making acquisition decisions are often not sufficiently objective. With lessons from psychological experiments we offer managers a helpful guide to assembling a toolkit to "de-bias" their valuations. It is preferable to improve managers' ability to recognize and guard against their psychological biases rather than to succumb to the tendency to adjust simple quantitative valuations inappropriately, for example by increasing discount rates to account for overoptimistic cash flow estimations.

INTEGRATING VALUATION AND STRATEGY ANALYSIS

The second improvement to valuation we offer is that we move from the valuation of companies considered as isolated projects to an integration of valuation and acquisition strategy. While executives and financial analysts may occasionally overestimate *interproject* synergies in their valuation analyses, they often also overlook the *intertemporal* synergies and path dependencies which are generally present. Path-dependent acquisitions can open up new opportunity routes in uncertain environments, and so can have significant long-term implications. Intertemporal synergies encompass the new optionality resulting from an acquisition, which provides the acquirer with options to capture value sometime in the future, if and when certain conditions arise. Just as good college grades improve the chances of being admitted to an MBA program at a top school, which, in turn, improves future job opportunities, so does the accumulation of strategic assets, in new geographies or with new capabilities, change the spectrum of future opportunities and thus the strategic position and future path of the company.

Examples we employ in this book range from resource accumulation strategies of large mining corporations such as Xstrata, to the globalization strategy of Vodafone, minority stake bidding games, platform acquisitions in emerging markets, and Pan-European consolidations in private equity. We document the experience gained at Xstrata.plc from its founding in 2001 to its ultimate sale in 2013: the strategic deliberations involved in its journey—and those of various other consolidators—underpin many of our academic components and the tools we offer to support the design and execution of acquisition strategies. Our examples illustrate both when such path dependencies are overlooked in valuation analysis and when they are overestimated.

ANALYZING PRICE IN COMPANY AUCTIONS AND BIDDING SITUATIONS

The third improvement we introduce to company valuation in a competitive context is a price analysis. Good acquisition management demands understanding the price, as well as the true value, of a target. While executives often put great effort into valuing their target companies, using DCF analysis, the next step to improve acquisition decision making is the development of applied tools for establishing optimal pricing in competitive bidding situations and company auctions. Academic studies have shown that while, generally, acquisitions create value, overpayment is one of the key factors that results in most of that value flowing to the target's shareholders.[4] Part of this discrepancy between value and price can be ascribed to price analysis being deficient or absent in competitive or game situations—including neglecting the presence or impact of competitors—or the failure to assess the target's true value rigorously (and its value to potential competitive bidders), leading to an unrealistic expectation of synergies, overcommitment, or under some circumstances even underbidding. This book uses examples of fierce acquisition battles—such as Falconbridge and Mannesmann—to provide new quantitative option game frameworks to illustrate the links between acquisition-led corporate strategy and shareholder value, and the role of bidding strategies in ensuring success in both dimensions.

ACADEMIC CONTRIBUTION AND FEATURES

Equally, beyond its value for practitioners, the book provides scholars a contribution to streams in the academic literature in corporate finance, strategic management theory, and related fields. Normative research that advances company valuation tools receives little attention in academic literature despite its significant implications for professionals. The complexities of corporate acquisitions—such as the influence of decision biases and accounting for uncertainties and potential long-term implications—demand more sophisticated methods that integrate strategic management theory and corporate finance models. This books aims to bridge the research gap between strategic concepts and quantitative valuation tools.

---

[4] See, for instance, Andrade, Mitchell, and Stafford (2001), Black (1989), Barney (1988), and Golbe and White (1988).

THE CONTRIBUTION OF BEHAVIORAL OPTION GAMES TO COMPANY VALUATION

Real option theory has been developed to support rational decisions under uncertainty, promoting staging investments, and contingencies such as the use of minority stakes to acquire control, largely following economic assumptions of rationality. A more realistic descriptive theory of real options—one that explicitly assumes only bounded rationality and, by extension, allows for cognitive biases—has received little attention in the academic literature, but we feel it may hold considerable promise for the strategy and company valuation fields.

Here we integrate two views of decision making under conditions of uncertainty: behavioral finance and real options. We distinguish between various potential pitfalls in valuation and develop a framework to mitigate them, which will allow executives to correct and rationalize their intuitive decisions. For instance, behavioral experimental studies suggest judgment biases can distort perceptions of uncertainty when considering a potential acquisition. In the same way as overoptimism and the neglect of the potential downsides of uncertainty may result in overexcitement for deals in hot markets, underestimating the potential upside—e.g., when participants cannot envision that growth options will recover—may create a disincentive to invest in cold deal markets. As a consequence, behavior-induced uncertainty neglect explains the low adoption of real options concepts and its recommendations in practice, and extends the contexts where strategic option thinking is relevant. Such behavioral biases result in suboptimal acquisition decisions, with the potential for errors likely to be exacerbated in consolidating industries, where consolidators design serial acquisitions strategies and fight escalating takeover battles in their efforts to acquire rare platform targets that may determine their future competitive positions.

QUANTIFYING ACQUISITION OPPORTUNITIES TO OPERATIONALIZE VALUE CONCEPTS FROM STRATEGIC MANAGEMENT THEORY

The book also provides a distinctive contribution to the strategy literature in its integration of corporate finance (options games) and strategy paradigms, in this case in the context of acquisition strategies. Although extant management theories (e.g., the resource-based, dynamic capabilities, and knowledge-based views)[5] deal with aspects of sources of value creation through acquisitions, they

---

[5]   See, for instance, Barney (1986, 1995), Dierickx and Cool (1989), Grant (1991), Penrose (1959), Prahalad and Hamel (1990), Rumelt (1984), Teece (1980, 1982, 1984), Teece, Pisano, and Shuen (1997), Wernerfelt (1984), Wernerfelt and Karnani (1987), Winter (1987), Zack (1999), and Zahra and George (2002).

are not explicit about which valuation approach they recommend. We advocate that option games valuation in a competitive context is crucial to operationalizing existing theories in terms of valuation for strategic acquisition decisions, and has the potential to be applied to the broader context of strategic development in an increasingly uncertain environment.

Although the combined theory of options and games has the potential to provide tremendous value for practitioners faced with acquisition decisions, the existing methodologies are not yet in practical, usable forms.[6] This book makes a normative contribution to the quantitative financial analysis of acquisition strategy. This means that we do more than making option games practical: our examples and experiences make the option game framework *implementable* in the context of a consolidation strategy. We draw heavily on our experience to give practical examples that highlight the key flaws evident in acquisition decision making, and develop and illustrate novel valuation techniques that can help mitigate behavioral pitfalls, while capturing the competitive dimensions of acquisition situations.

A GUIDE THROUGH THE BOOK

Chapter 1 provides an overview. By linking strategy to the market value of investment opportunities, we review the basic concepts and foundations of three important academic building blocks of company valuation: behavioral finance, real options, and game theory. Our synthesis of these mechanisms provides a toolkit to reduce the risks for companies embarking on ambitious M&A journeys. The book is structured in three parts:

In the first part—"Learning to See Uncertainty"—chapters 2 and 3 introduce the reader to the practical use of insights from behavioral corporate finance theory to modify valuation analysis to mitigate rather than reinforce the effects of managerial biases. Drawing on behavioral theory, chapter 3 warns managers about a range of behavioral pitfalls in acquisition decisions. This chapter offers a series of boardroom experiments that lecturers, advisors, and consultants can use to make their audience aware of their biases. Using Vodafone's strategy as an illustration, the chapter demonstrates common biases in acquisition decision making, and recommends the use of real options and a market valuation of growth options and games as practical tools to counteract action-oriented biases. The following chapters illustrate how to use these tools.

Part II, "Learning to Adapt to Uncertainty," builds on the previous section by adding real options to the strategic analysis to avoid acquisition pitfalls

---

[6] Elegant and rigorous continuous-time models of competitive exercise strategies have been developed by, among others, Bart Lambrecht, Erwan Morellec, Flavio Toxvaerd, Peter Kort, Sebastian Glyglewicz, Steven Grenadier, and others. Here we show how option games can be implemented to company valuation.

brought about by biases. It develops a dual toolkit that allows managers to account properly for the interplay among uncertainty, growth options, and value creation. Chapter 4 demonstrates the appropriateness of a real options mind-set when valuing and selecting from strategic merger and acquisition alternatives as part of a serial buy-and-build strategy. In chapter 5, our case study example of how a simple market quantification of growth option value can work in practice is based on the strategy of the mining group Xstrata, and cites the strategic games involved in the acquisitions of Falconbridge, MIM, Tintaya, and other targets.

The salient feature of part III, "Learning to Value Uncertainty," is how it makes practical use of the combined option game valuation framework viable. More extensive and sophisticated price analysis is the next step in deal execution. In chapter 6 the reader is introduced to quantifying options games, explained through a series of real-life cases involving strategic bidding and investment problems of increasing complexity

The final chapter pulls all the concepts together. It reviews the strategic framework that integrates options and competitive games to de-bias decision making, and recaps the main conclusions and strategy implications. It provides empirical evidence that acquisitions are driven by growth options and behavioral economics, discusses examples of option game applications beyond acquisitions, and lists promising directions for future research. Most important, it provides a decision framework for directly integrating finance and acquisition strategy in uncertain environments.

PLAYING AT ACQUISITIONS

CHAPTER 1

LEARNING TO SEE, TO ADAPT TO, AND TO VALUE UNCERTAINTY

Life can be understood backward, but ... it must be lived forward.
—Søren Kierkegaard

Suppose there are two types of CEOs who differ in how they approach their investment decisions. The first we call the *designers*.[1] These executives have a clear view of their desired competitive positioning and of the means and metrics of success in their chosen competitive playing field, and intend to design and execute premeditated strategic paths. The others—named *opportunists*—may also have a clear view of how value is created in their chosen playing field, but are not committed to a master plan, preferring instead to continuously take advantage of any opportunities that fit their value criteria as they emerge and when conditions are favorable to them.

Both of these CEO types have their shortcomings. For designers, successfully executing an envisioned acquisition strategy without any apparent mistakes will be a difficult task. The flaw in their logic is that the world—including their competitors—will sit back and permit them to execute their planned strategy unhindered. In the real and uncertain competitive world, macroeconomic change, evolving customer needs, or competitor preemption may render apparently realistic targets unavailable or unattractively expensive. At the same time, a pure opportunist approach cannot provide an organization with the strategic and organizational direction it requires to function successfully, or even to survive in the long term.

We have often seen these seemingly opposing views competing in the boardroom at the moments when key decisions are made—sometimes even in the

---

[1] With a series of articles in the *Harvard Business Review* and several books, Roger Martin developed new ways of thinking on business design. For instance, see Martin (2009, 2013) and Lafley and Martin (2013).

mind of a single decision maker when deliberating an acquisition, for example. Indeed, there appears to be a recurring dilemma when designing and executing acquisition strategies: for designers, on the one hand, designated targets embody the risk of overpayment, which may be founded on unconscious irrational justifications—such as neglecting uncertainty, overoptimistically expecting synergies or growth opportunities, or becoming trapped in an escalating bidding contest. The designer, however, is aware that acquisition opportunities that fit the value criteria and the strategic pathway are limited—especially in consolidating industries—and the missed chance is a very real threat to a company's future competitive position. On the other hand, for the opportunist, the risk lies in waiting for a better deal or even in underbidding—failing to pay the price required to secure a critical target. Pure opportunists may frame an opportunity too narrowly—may tend to consider it in isolation, and so fail to recognize the impact of new long-term growth options the target may bring, or to fully appreciate its value as part of a broader strategy. This applies equally to organic growth and other options available to an organization.

Successful resolution of this CEO acquisition conundrum—especially in the context of uncertainty—can determine the firm's future success, market value, and even survival. Yet too often managers make these decisions based on intuition and experience alone, leaving them vulnerable to the pitfalls of cognitive biases when making them under uncertainty, with little guidance from objective tools to analyze and assist their investment decisions.

In this book we offer a set of approaches and tools that resolve the conundrum, bringing together the best aspects of *design* and *opportunism* in a way that recognizes the need for organizational objectives; a clear strategic framework, which includes the selection of where the organization will elect to compete; value metrics; and even one or more strategic paths aimed at moving the organization toward their desired goal—while at the same time accounting for the inherent uncertainty which the future represents.[2] *Strategic opportunism*—as we have elected to call this new approach to strategy—represents melding the two CEO caricatures of designer and opportunist into a single powerful methodology for designing and executing strategy at the corporate, business unit, and operational levels by augmenting the existing strategic tools and frameworks with those from behavioral and corporate finance and from decision science.

In this book, we illustrate our approach to strategic opportunism by focusing on the design, valuation, and execution of an acquisition strategy. So how can you know whether a deal is beneficial? Given the uncertain future, you can't. Fortunately, both the designers and opportunists among us are biased in predictable ways. You can stack the odds in your favor by limiting the degree to which your own biases influence your valuation analysis and your decisions. For

---

[2] For instance, see Alan G. Lafley and Roger L. Martin (2013) in their book *Playing to Win: How Strategy Really Works*.

this purpose this book integrates insights from behavioral finance with (rational) decision models—such as real options and game theory—to counter these biases in an effort to estimate uncertainty in strategic value and price rigorously and objectively.

In this overview chapter we provide the reader with a helicopter view of a quantitative value-based framework. A key argument in this book is that volatility is always present, and rather than ignoring it in our analysis, we acknowledge its inevitability—even embrace it to our advantage—and adjust our approach to decision making accordingly. Uncertainty means that today's successful CEOs and their executive teams need to be able to act simultaneously as strategists—that is, designers of corporate strategy—and opportunists—with the ability to grasp opportunities that meet their value criteria as they arise. In essence, this requires the setting of clear strategic goals, but—given the reality of uncertainty—also being willing to revise intended decisions, seeking to continually maximize the organization's options to appropriate value. While uncertainty generally deters investment, executives who reframe their roles as strategic opportunists can actually benefit from uncertainty. Once you learn to see uncertainty, you can learn to adjust to uncertainty and benefit by reducing exposure to specific sources of uncertainty, effectively limiting downside vulnerability, while fully exploiting opportunities presented by high uncertainty and change. The goal of valuing uncertainty in an acquisition strategy using option games is to improve the organization's decision making so as to counter known biases and, by enhancing the value of optionality within and external to the organization, to allow for flexibility to revise intended decisions.

LEARNING TO SEE UNCERTAINTY

Consider the two lines in the picture of Figure 1.1. Which one is longer? For most of us, the line on the right seems longer. But if you measure them you will see they are exactly the same length—it is the background perspective that can deceive your objective vision. If perspective can affect our objective visual judgment, it is not hard to imagine how easily we can be deceived in the much more elusive judgments involved in acquisitions. The length of estimation horizons, the sheer complexity of deals, and the uncertainties and ambiguities inherent in valuing targets can make executives' acquisition decisions vulnerable to their personal biases.[3] Grounded in psychology, behavioral theory describes how bounded rationality and personal-level behavioral limitations can distort how we perceive the uncertainty that surrounds our decisions.[4] Interestingly, psy-

---

[3] Dan Lovallo and Daniel Kahneman illuminate the impact of biases on practical acquisition decision making: see, for instance, Lovallo and Kahneman (2003); Kahneman and Lovallo (1993); Koller, Lovallo, and Williams (2011).

[4] See Cyert and March (1963).

Figure 1.1 The Ponzo Illusion: How Perspective Can Bias Vision
Source: Walt Anthony, 2006, used with permission. The Ponzo Illusion: http://opticalillusions4kids.blogspot.nl.

chological experiments have highlighted some stereotypical deceptions to which we are inherently vulnerable. For instance, experimental and empirical studies have repeatedly found that bidders tend to overpay in hot markets, synchronously execute deals, and are—too often—influenced by high stock market valuations. It is also likely that individual framing infects objective valuation analyses.

Psychology has been applied to managerial practices to test the existence and implications of managerial biases in real-life business situations. Although, traditionally, we expect decision makers to make decisions founded on rational arguments—accurately portraying and weighing the possible benefits and risks—there is evidence of deviation from rationality that results in the under-

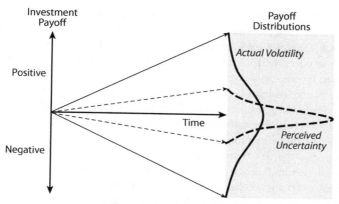

Figure 1.2 Perceived Uncertainty in the Payoff of Acquisitions (Inner Distribution) Is Lower Than Actual Uncertainty (Outer Distribution)
Source: Kil and Smit (2012).

estimation of uncertainty.[5] Schematically presented by the two rotated bell-shaped distributions in Figure 1.2, perceptions of uncertainty (inner distribution) can differ from true volatility (outer distribution) from person to person, depending on how each frames the opportunity, explaining the differences in competing firms' strategic actions. Cognitive biases such as executive overconfidence can result in underestimating firm-level uncertainty, which may otherwise be controllable and resolvable through corporate actions (endogenous uncertainty). This includes overconfidence in the potential realization of synergies or ignoring the threat of rival bidders. Biases can also distort our perception of uncontrollable environmental uncertainty (exogenous uncertainty), such as uncertainty in demand, macroeconomic shocks, and financial crises.[6] Furthermore, self-attribution can bias our perception of the controllable. In hindsight we often attribute successful corporate actions to our unique insight, but blame exogenous uncertainty when transactions fail. To see uncertainty-related biases in a broad perspective, behavioral theory offers three warnings for CEOs and management teams who aim to pursue acquisitions.

1. YOUR INTENDED STRATEGIC PATH IS MORE UNCERTAIN THAN YOU PERCEIVE

When CEOs project the future, like most of us they tend to rely too heavily on their familiarity with the status quo, and underestimate uncertainty: this per-

---

[5] See Garbuio, Wilcox, and Lovallo (2011).
[6] Uncertainty can be endogenous or exogenous (Miller 1992). Endogenous, firm-level uncertainty is controllable and can be resolved through corporate actions, while resolution of exogenous, environmental uncertainty is uncontrollable on a personal or firm level. Industry-specific uncertainty incorporates competitive influences (Miller 1992; Miller and Waller 2003).

spective may limit their awareness of optionality. Macroeconomic or industry demand uncertainty is easily underestimated, in particular because managers have trouble predicting potential low-probability, high-consequence events,[7] such as the potential for and impact of the global financial crisis. Not only do we tend to ignore exogenous extreme events, but we are also prone to underestimating controllable uncertainty—such as uncertainty regarding the realization of synergies or the existence of latent claims, which could be mitigated. Success and confidence can easily become overconfidence and influence CEOs' perception of the uncertainty inherent in their strategic plans. *Overconfidence*—ignoring uncertainties that might influence the potential for success, postacquisition synergies, and target company value—is only one of the biases that executives need to overcome in executing transactions. In particular, when there is groupthink in the management team, executives may suffer from *confirmation bias* and seek data to confirm their prior convictions of the desired strategic path, and subconsciously resist actively seeking disconfirming data. As a result of these biases, the strategic paths they envision are likely to be more uncertain than they think.

2. THE TARGET VALUE YOU OBSERVE IS MORE UNCERTAIN THAN YOU MIGHT PERCEIVE

Bubbles, overpriced financial markets, and the deviation of prices from fundamental values have been with us for centuries. The tulip mania of 1636—often used to illustrate the first recorded economic bubble—was a period in the Dutch Golden Age during which contract prices for bulbs of the (then only recently introduced) tulip reached extraordinarily high levels compared to their intrinsic value, before suddenly collapsing. The price of some single tulip bulbs skyrocketed to 10 times the annual income of a skilled craftsman, close to the price of an Amsterdam canal house, until, suddenly, in February 1637, the buying frenzy instantly turned into a selling stampede.[8]

When people make decisions under uncertainty, they use familiar positions or known anchors—but they often make insufficient adjustments to their valuations from such starting points. When the value of an asset is hard to assess—as in high-tech, dot-com, or biotech ventures, for example—executives and financial analysts base estimates on relative or multiple valuations. As with many things, company or asset beauty is in the eye of the beholder. As a consequence, when comparable valuation methods are used, assets that are acquired for unique strategic reasons—and which, hence, command higher prices—can

---

[7] See March and Shapira (1987).
[8] Dutch dealers started tulip bulb options trading, so that producers could buy the rights to purchase tulip bulbs in advance and secure definite prices.

contribute to the misperception of the value of opportunities in an entire sector.

At times, stock prices in financial markets can reflect a common misperception phenomenon, when valuations may result from expectations of how others will perceive the value of a specific target who, in turn, also based their value on multiples. Anchoring is innate in human nature, and can cause the price of a single commodity or asset to soar to unsustainable heights as long as the expectation remains that it can be sold to a "greater fool" at a higher price. In such cases, prices deviate from fundamental value across the board, as happened in the tulip mania or the dot-com bubble that shook financial markets in the early 2000s. While executives seem to underestimate the volatility in a target's value, irrational investors may cause exuberance, resulting in excess volatility of financial market prices.[9]

3. WINNING THE BIDDING PROCESS ON GOOD TERMS IS MORE UNCERTAIN THAN YOU THINK

Behavioral economists have illustrated that participants in company auctions are vulnerable to the *winner's curse* when they underestimate uncertainty, because they don't possess all the necessary information to value the target accurately or, alternatively, rivals have access to private information on the assets being sold. By definition, the auction mechanism selects the cursed winning bidder as the one who overvalues the asset the most.

The chances of successfully appropriating a target may also be overestimated initially before it becomes apparent that rival bidders may enter the field. CEOs can tend to overestimate their firm's role and influence in the industry,[10] and this may result in an initial bid that is too low. However, once bidders are committed to acquiring the target, a competitive bidding situation can cause irrational bidding as they feel trapped by their pride or aversion to take a loss in an escalating bidding contest, with excessive premiums being paid to secure the target. Auctions structured over several rounds, common in private equity, venture capital, and privatizations, can increase the potential for bidders to become overcommitted once they have participated in the early rounds. This dynamic is mimicked in competitive bid situations for traded companies. The financial, emotional, and reputational costs escalate as the process unfolds, making it difficult for executives to back down. Even when management makes proper use of sophisticated valuation methods before entering an auction or contest, competitors may still base their decisions on irrational heuristics, or be subject to psychological biases and outbid them.

[9] See, for instance, Schiller (1981).
[10] See Zajac and Bazerman (1991).

LEARNING TO ADAPT TO UNCERTAINTY

The first record of an option on a real asset can be found in chapter 11 of book 1 of Aristotle's *Politics*.[11] The chapter, which tells the story of the philosopher Thales of Miletus (624–547 BC), is often quoted by professors in business schools who use it for the same purpose as Aristotle: to refute the view that scholars are unable to turn their theories into real-world success: "If you are so smart why aren't you rich?"

People had been telling Thales that his philosophy was useless, since it had left him a poor man. In response, Thales raised a little capital and used it to pay deposits on all the oil presses in Miletus and Chios. Thus, instead of buying the main asset (the olives), he bought the cheaper right to hire olive presses, whose value would go up and down with that of the olive harvest. Thus, he was effectively securing an option on the olive press capacity. As it was still winter and outside the olive pressing season, there were no other bidders and he acquired these options cheaply. The owners of the olive presses, who were exposed to the uncertainty of the size of the harvest, secured profits through the sale of the options to Thales irrespective of how the harvest might turn out.

For Thales, however, the payoff looked quite different: uncertainty over the quality of the harvest would actually work in his favor. In other words he would benefit from volatility. By controlling the option rights to using the olive presses, Thales had the right to either use these olive presses when harvest time came (exercising the options) or suffer a small loss (his deposit) on a bad harvest. Like all call options, the greater the uncertainty, the greater the potential upside (profit) potential, whereas the downside risk is limited to the premium of the option. In the case of a big upward move in the market rental price for presses—due to a large harvest—the owner of the option exercises it and receives the difference between the prevailing rental price at that time he or she took out the option and the exercise price. In the case of a downward move the option expires unexercised and the owner of the option loses only his or her initial deposit, that is, the option premium. In fact Thales was a classical strategic opportunist. Having cornered the market at a time when there were few bidders for oil presses, Thales further enhanced the value of the option by using asymmetric information—his knowledge of the stars, which pointed to a good olive crop. After proving his point—by making a fortune—he exited the olive pressing business and went back to being a philosopher.

The parallel risk mitigation mechanism at the corporate level is the creation of real options. Thales's experience represents one of the first documented real option games. Real options refer to choices on whether and how to proceed with business investments. Nowadays real options, combined with game theory, offer a formal framework through which decisions relating to capital in-

---

[11] See, for instance, Copeland and Antikarov (2003).

vestment, minority stakes, technology investments, international operations, and the firm's ability to adapt to a changing competitive landscape under uncertain conditions can be considered. In a way, each opportunity to acquire a target is analogous to obtaining a call option. A strategic buyer acquiring a firm in a new geography as part of a serial strategy, seed financing by a venture capitalist, and a platform acquisition by a private equity investor in a new sector all create new options to execute follow-on investments as soon as the initial deal is set. As such, these are examples of managerial decisions that establish a firm's ability to appropriate future options in an uncertain future.

ANALYZING REAL OPTIONS PREVENTS UNCERTAINTY NEGLECT IN STRATEGY

Modeling the real options in a strategy can force executives and analysts to focus explicitly on alternative trajectories and contingencies, options that are likely to arise when the path evolves differently than expected. Moves to develop a new platform with new capabilities can open up follow-on moves that enable the company, due to its accumulated assets to date, to exploit such platforms by exercising growth options that are unique relative to those held by competitors. We further argue that—when properly applied—rational tools such as real options and games may help to overcome several psychological biases in decision making with respect to uncertain opportunities, and can help guide objective managerial judgment to find the best strategic route, given the industry environment. The methodology developed here can structure acquisition trajectories by helping management decide when to pass on opportunities and when to bid aggressively. Expressing an acquisition path as a series of options with clear go or wait intersections puts the focus on the economic logic of the *conditionality* of future strategic decisions. In a real option view within a long-term strategy, acquisitions by and of industry players can no longer be viewed as stand-alone investments, but rather should be seen as options on future options—as links in a chain of interrelated investments.

ANALYZING REAL OPTIONS PREVENTS UNCERTAINTY NEGLECT IN VALUATION

Using NPV analysis alone to analyze opportunities creates the illusion of greater clarity for the decision maker, with the organization's objectives seemingly being met according to a defined scenario of targets and cash flows. However, these approaches do little to account for the impact of the acquisition itself on the organization's future growth path. This contrasts with the strategic opportunist's instinct that some acquisitions can shape the uncertain future of the firm by creating new opportunities and, hence, improve the firm's ability to appropriate further options as they arise over time. Figure 1.3 illustrates the

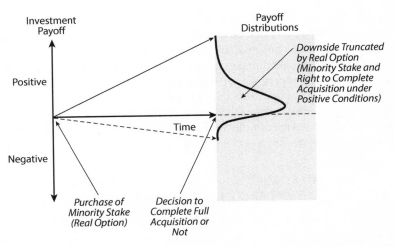

Figure 1.3 Learning to Adapt to Uncertainty: Optionality Generates a Positively Skewed Distribution
Source: Kil and Smit (2012).

acquisition of a minority stake as a real option that may potentially lead to a full acquisition if the conditions are right. Real options permit the holder of a minority stake to perceive volatility and learn to limit losses on the downside by not exercising the full acquisition option in an unattractive environment, exercising caution and effectively truncating the downside in the distribution of Figure 1.3. The holder of such a stake can thus avoid very low payoffs involved in an immediate full acquisition and unfavorable economic development. At the same time, optionality preserves the upside potential of the option to make the full acquisition under more favorable conditions. When investments create growth options—i.e., real options that can be exercised when conditions become conducive—they skew the upside in Figure 1.3, creating an asymmetric risk profile favorable to the holder of the real option.

ANALYZING THE GAME PREVENTS RIVAL NEGLECT

While a firm might acquire another company to increase its growth options, it does not necessarily follow that the acquirer will be able to appropriate all (or even any) of that value. Part of such discrepancies between strategic intentions and financial outturns can be ascribed to deficient or absent price analysis in competitive or game situations, including the failure to rigorously assess the target's true value to competitive bidders. In addition to the growth options embedded in the target company's value, the *price*—what the successful bidder ultimately pays—depends on the intensity of competition in the bidding. To

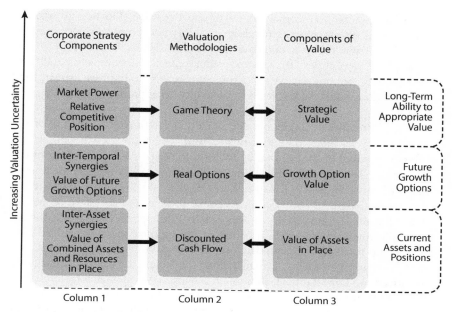

Figure 1.4 Components of Company Value
Source: Based on Smit and Trigeorgis (2004).

prevent underestimating the uncertainties in the bidding process, the winner's curse, or the escalation involved in being overcommitted to intended targets, valuation analysis is more effective in decision making if combined with insights from game theory.

LEARNING TO VALUE UNCERTAINTY

In addition to learning to see and adjust to uncertainty, executives need to appreciate its value. Figure 1.4 positions components of company value in relation to both the traditional constituents of corporate strategy and the proposed approaches to valuing each element.[12] It illustrates the essence of the link between corporate strategy and company value that we seek to strengthen through the behavioral option game approach proposed in this book. Column 1 illustrates the potential strategy components of a merger. The value of the new company is not just the net present value of the future cash flow generated by its assets in place and its interasset synergies. The value of the merged entity in

[12] We here extend the earlier work of Smit and Trigeorgis (2004) on option games with insights from behavioral theory.

financial markets also incorporates the prospective value of its new growth options, and its intertemporal synergies—its ability to capture new opportunities over time despite the uncertain environment due to its scale, market positions, or acquired capabilities. The strategic value reflects the company's ability to exercise these options relative to its competitors so as to improve its own strategic position—and, hence, its *relative* ability to appropriate value into the future.[13]

While interasset synergies are occasionally overestimated at the top of the economic cycle, intertemporal synergies and long-term growth options are often overlooked at the bottom. In addition to the psychological biases of the decision maker, acquisition decisions can be influenced by the bounded rationality of *investors*, who may cause share prices to soar or plunge without any fundamental changes in underlying company value. We therefore propose a dual—bottom-up and top-down—approach to real option valuation, with various adjustments to prevent distortion of the rational analysis involved. The bottom-up fundamental analysis (column 2) should help avoid potential acquirers relying too much on financial market values that can occasionally be mispriced. An important contribution of the top-down approach (column 3) is that it mitigates executive biases when the value of investment and acquisition opportunities along the acquisition path can—in principle—be quantified and related directly to value creation in financial markets.

COLUMN 2: USE BOTTOM-UP OPTION GAMES VALUATION TO AVOID ANCHORING ON EXCESSIVE MARKET PRICES

The primary components of a target's value that lend themselves to being incorrectly valued are those of growth option value and strategic value, as it is relatively easier to value existing assets and the associated interasset synergies. When growth expectations—as reflected in financial market prices—become excessively high, we strongly recommend the use of fundamental valuation techniques (such as option games) to rationalize value and price estimations, and to complement market methods. The bottom-up or fundamental method attempts to value all the growth opportunities of the target company as a portfolio of options and bidding games. While DCF methods are well suited to estimating the value of company assets in place and any interasset synergy, none of the currently popular valuation methods explicitly analyze the effect of uncertainty or rival bidders on value creation. In practice, the acquisition price is determined by the value perceptions of others—in particular rival bidders.

---

[13] The value of a firm can be viewed as consisting of assets in place and growth opportunities. See, among others, Miller and Modigliani (1961), Myers (1977), and Pindyck (1988). A series of articles by Tony Tong shows empirically various insights related to a firm's growth option value. For empirical implications, see Kester (1984), Chung and Charoenwong (1991), Tong and Reuer (2006), Tong et al. (2008), and Tong and Reuer (2008).

Tools such as real options and games can help management teams focus on the rational economic logic of strategic planning, and so provide an interactive link between strategic and financial valuation. Indeed, we can best view the real options game approach to general acquisition strategy valuation, when applied properly, as an attempt to subject the strategic intuition of acquisitions to the discipline of a more rigorous analytical process.

Executives and private equity partners pursuing strategic opportunism should estimate various uncertainties, discuss the most important acquisition options in detail, and identify possible causal links between them. Which acquisition options are mutually exclusive, which can create growth, and which divestment options can limit losses? Which acquisition options are likely to create synergies and which to function as a platform and even spawn new acquisition options? These conditional trajectories—and the potential impact of the resolution of the identified uncertainties on each of them—can point to specific targets and include execute, wait, or abandon intersections at several junctures over time, as well as identify the limited number of possible outcomes for the industry endgame.

COLUMN 3: EMPLOY TOP-DOWN VALUATION TO MITIGATE EXECUTIVE VALUATION BIASES

The market values of targets and bidders encompass, in part, the value of the *potential* future options that a company may enjoy as its strategic position advances. The implied value of a company's growth options can be observed by adjusting the current stock price for the present value of future earnings generated by those assets that are already in place. In fact, depending on the industry and the specific company, the present value of these growth opportunities (PVGO) can constitute a significant part of a company's market value and thus explains any differential from competitors with apparently comparable collections of assets and future cash flows. Since the market value of the target is known,[14] we can tease out the market's perception of the value of its growth options by subtracting the value of assets in place. The gap between the company's market value and the present value of the earning capacity of its assets in place represents the value placed on the firm's strategy to appropriate profitable corporate growth opportunities (PVGO) and includes *growth option value* and *strategic value*. The top-down or market method is commonly used in empirical research for estimating a company's growth option value, but we develop and apply an extension—named the market method for acquisitions (MMA). As well as estimating the PVGO of firms, this method looks at the relative difference between the growth option value and the value of assets in place of large

---

[14]   Based on the stock price before announcement of the transaction, or an average of the market value over a reasonable period of time preceding the announcement.

firms compared to the portfolios of smaller firms. Thus, for consolidation to make sense from a shareholder perspective, an efficient financial market should assign a higher value to leading companies' assets in place and growth opportunities than to those of smaller firms (potentially, the sum of the parts of a future consolidated entity). In chapter 5 we describe how in the mining and metals industry, the pursuit of growth, scale, and scope coupled with how industry leaders outperformed midsize and smaller players—due to diversification or size premiums—created momentum for consolidation toward a few power-houses that came to dominate the industry. These majors created preferential access to growth options due to their global presence and their financial power to undertake significant capital investments. This relative appreciation explains the intention to create similar relative power structures and various merger attempts in consolidating industries.

By contrast, if the differential in PVGO is significantly smaller for the majors (often conglomerates) than for smaller companies, this may point to the need for restructuring strategies. When a management team has a static and biased view and cannot envision the full range of their divestment options or feel reluctant to terminate operations or abandon assets into which they have invested in the past, their companies attract a discount to the company's underlying assets value, estimated simply as value difference, with the value of their individual subsidiary units on a stand-alone basis. This "conglomerate discount," often due to an expensive corporate center, can make them vulnerable to hostile takeovers, and the company risks falling prey to opportunistic investors such as private equity buyers and hedge funds. For instance, in chapter 2 we provide an example of a leading private equity fund that acquired a diversified retail company because it saw divestment options the retail company management did not. The private equity fund could immediately put a floor on their investment by a sale and leaseback of the fashion business's property portfolio, immediately recouping a significant part of its initial equity investment, and subsequently released further value by exercising its options to divest various of the conglomerate's retail elements.

While corporate raiders were notorious for such restructuring strategies in the 1980s, constructive strategies based on a premium for larger companies compared to small firms—such as the buy-and-build and serial acquisitions discussed in this book—have received little attention. Private equity supports—and in some instances leads—strategic players in driving inexorable consolidation trends by restructuring inefficient conglomerates and consolidating fragmented industries through roll-ups and buy-and-build strategies. Based on metrics such as the growth option-to-price ratio and the price-earnings ratio of large global firms and local firms in the same industry, these players see the logic of consolidation and the multiple-arbitrage opportunities involved—assembling local companies together increases the market appreciation of the combined entity and improves overall valuation multiples, resulting in a rerating of the combined entity's cash flows. The metrics developed in this book can also be used to identify the best target companies and industries. For instance, in general, the best target industries for consolidation are those that are fragmented for noneconomic reasons—often including former nationalized companies that have the potential to operate globally: examples include former national airlines and telecom, banking, and mining companies.

SUMMARY

The tools you will discover in this book are of interest to anyone involved in acquisitions—from executives of companies desiring growth through acquisitions to investors, financial analysts, and private equity partners who follow active investment or divestment strategies. In a rapidly evolving and highly competitive business world, designers' plans are likely to have ever shortened life spans. Executive teams should, therefore, be careful of committing rigidly to their chosen courses of action, effectively underestimating uncertainty. Today's successful CEOs and their executive teams need to act as strategists—i.e., designers of long-term corporate strategy—as well as opportunists, embracing new opportunities, dealing with uncertainty, and showing willingness to revise their decisions accordingly. This mind-set requires management to be active in restructuring and rebuilding their companies, setting clear and effective strategic goals, defining distinctive competitive boundaries, identifying and mitigating risks, and putting the right metrics for success in place, while at the same time continually seeking to maximize the organization's options to appropriate value within its strategic framework.

To deal with the growing uncertainty in the world, decision makers need improved approaches to recognizing and adjusting to volatility, supporting their ability to exercise opportunism appropriately, for example, in executing acquisition strategies. The new tools we offer in this book enable practitioners to quantify the value of an entire acquisition strategy in ways that account for changes in strategic position and new optionality resulting from acquisitions, while at the same time mitigating their own biases and accounting for the potential impact of rival bidders' actions.

SUGGESTED READING

Baker, M., R. Ruback, and J. Wurgler. 2004. "Behavioral Corporate Finance: A Survey." In *The Handbook of Corporate Finance: Empirical Corporate Finance*, ed. E. Eckbo et al. New York: Elsevier: 351–417.

Martin, R. L. 2009. *The Design of Business*. Cambridge, MA: Harvard Business Review Press.

Smit, J. T. J., and L. Trigeorgis. 2004. *Strategic Investment: Real Options and Games.* Princeton: Princeton University Press.

Trigeorgis, L. 1996. *Real Options: Managerial Flexibility and Strategy in Resource Allocation.* Cambridge, MA: MIT Press.

SUGGESTED MATERIALS, TOOLS, AND GADGETS

For links to webcasts, tools, and presentations in this book, see http://press .princeton.edu/titles/10333.html.

For webcasts and presentations of the chapters in this book and related books, see http://companyvaluationtools.com/materials.

For game theory resources for educators and students, including lecture notes, textbooks, interactive game theory applets, and online games, see http://gametheory.net.

PART I

LEARNING TO SEE UNCERTAINTY

CHAPTER 2

HOW TO DE-BIAS VALUATION
OVER THE CYCLE

Men of ill judgment ignore the good that lies within
their hands until they have lost it.

—Sophocles

In 2000–2001, overexuberant valuations at the peak of the market induced
decision makers to frame deals for "new economy" (dot-com and telecom) targets as desirable.[1] Similarly in 2007, private equity funds competed heavily in
company auctions, their bids bolstered by high leverage. In contrast, the fall in
public financial markets in 2008 initially led some observers to predict a burst
of M&A activity, in which cash-rich companies would snap up undervalued
businesses. Paradoxically, that never came to pass.

It is puzzling that companies seem to rush into acquisitions during global
economic booms—even when they are aware of the dangers of overpaying—
but appear to lose all interest in dealing when the global economy is sluggish
and the market invariably offers bargains. Certainly there may be good and
rational reasons to invest during procyclical acquisition waves[2]—but many acquirers seem to both overshoot in hot deal markets and hold back unreasonably
in cold ones, shying away from making purchases that might bring them important growth opportunities.

Deal framing in executives' analyses[3]—the way they perceive and model
their acquisition or divestment opportunities—can cause them to overestimate
acquisition opportunities in hot deal markets, when their share prices are at
their peak—or when they may have experienced recent acquisition success—
while their dismay in cold markets often induces them to frame deals as repre-

---

[1] Some of the ideas of this chapter are further developed in Han Smit and Dan Lovallo (2014).
See Smit and Lovalo (2014) for checklists for valuation in hot and cold deal markets.
[2] See McNamara, Haleblian, and Dykes (2008).
[3] See Tversky and Kahneman (1981), Loewenstein (1988).

senting too high risk, so they hold back from making viable new acquisitions or delay divesting loss-making divisions.[4] Decision biases can play surprisingly strong roles in the valuation analyses of even experienced executives.[5] We focus on this particular problem: how rational analyses can become infected and lead executives to manipulate their analyses—inadvertently or knowingly—to get the answers they expect or require.

The remedy we propose goes beyond currently applied valuation models.[6] The solution—using the *behavioral real options* approach—promotes the idea of making adjustments to prevent such "irrational infection" of rational valuation analysis. A dynamic valuation approach, which considers acquisition decisions in terms of options, can force executives to consider uncertainty and widen their perspective by analyzing potential acquisitions as part of their long-term strategies.

PROBLEM DIAGNOSIS: WHY ACQUISITIONS OCCUR IN GO/NO-GO WAVES

Psychological studies show that, even with feedback, it is very difficult for decision makers to recognize their *own* biases. We can address this obstacle to acquisition decisions by asking executives to look at something they can observe much more easily than their own minds: whether they are operating in hot or cold deal markets. Perceiving deal markets as hot or cold can be quite easy and is often reflected by boards' sentiment, rivals' aggressive (or inactive) acquisition behavior, or the exuberance (or pessimism) of investors in financial markets.

HOT MARKETS: WHY MANAGERS VALUE DEALS TOO HIGHLY

In hot deal markets, executives pursue acquisitions driven by high market valuations, overoptimism, and overconfidence, and may end up overpaying for targets for various reasons.[7]

[4] This resembles the disposition effect noted by Shefrin and Statman (1985) and Duhaime and Schwenk (1985).

[5] The extensive and relevant work of Dan Lovallo and Daniel Kahneman has illuminated the impact of biases on practical acquisition decision making: see, for instance, Lovallo and Kahneman (2003), Kahneman and Lovallo (1993), Koller, Lovallo, and Williams (2011).

[6] The academic literature on strategic management views real option theory as a formal and rational framework through which capital and technology investments, risk management, international operations and the firm's ability to adapt to a changing competitive landscape can be considered under conditions of uncertainty—see, for instance, Amram and Kulatilaka (1999a), Bowman and Hurry (1993), Bowman and Moskowitz (2001), Dixit and Pindyck (1995), Kester (1984), Kogut and Kulatilaka (1994a, 1994b), Bettis and Hitt (1995), McGrath (1997), Petersen, Welch, and Welch (2000), Kogut and Kulatilaka (2001), Maklan, Knox, and Ryals (2005), Miller and Waller (2003), Kogut and Kulatilaka (2004), and Trigeogis (1996).

[7] See Smit and Lovallo (2014).

1. *Aggressive rivals create a perception of urgency about deals.* In consolidating industries, a shrinking pool of available deals can greatly strengthen executives' perceptions about the urgency of making acquisitions, inducing them to adopt a now-or-never approach to justify full acquisitions. Such herding behavior can promote frenzied waves of mergers that may continue to go on even long after they have become economically suboptimal. It is precisely in this context that a staged (option-like) approach would be preferable.[8]

2. *Exuberant investors.* Overexuberant stock prices at the peak of the market can influence companies' valuation analyses, when their value estimates are based on or influenced by familiar positions they observe in financial markets. Executives tend to make insufficient adjustments in their valuation models relative to these known starting points, or anchors. Such value misperception becomes more common when the anchors of the relative valuation benchmarks themselves—the financial market values of an industry—are based on each other's inflated relative valuations.

3. *Groupthink lowers perceptions of uncertainty and reinforces personal-level biases.* Supported by deal-incentivized advisors and investment bankers, managers are tempted to look for signs of project success, endorsing their *conformation bias* with valuation analyses that include unrealistic calculations of potential synergies and cash flow expectations, but which fail to identify uncertainties or ignore the potential for shocks or other extreme events. *Groupthink* and team decisions tend to accentuate the danger of managers having unwarranted confidence in their abilities to take acquisition decisions accurately, and of their analyses underestimating the risks involved in negative scenarios. Executive confidence is a critical factor in a company's success—but it has its dangers when executives become overconfident and overoptimistic about the outcomes of their decisions. In particular, value creation in successful previous acquisitions may increase an executive's personal confidence in his or her ability to execute future acquisitions effectively, leading the executive to underestimate the possibility of scenarios that involve failure to realize the intended value.

COLD MARKETS: WHY MANAGERS FREEZE THEIR DEALS

A cold market attitude among executives—easily observable by stalled acquisitions—can arise from the following:

---

[8]   See also Scharfstein and Stein (1990) on herding behavior in investment.

1. *Passive rivals creating a perception that deals can wait.* In cold markets, the threat of preemption from rivals seems low, so executives feel they can afford to wait without risking losing their targets. The limited competition for deals often leads decision makers to behave too cautiously and to delay making investments that could offer them valuable growth options.

2. *Personal-level executive biases focused on risk instead of long-term growth options. Loss aversion* refers to the bias of being more conscious of potential losses than of potential gains—of fearing them more acutely than desiring equivalent or even greater benefits—which can cause CEOs to hold back in cold markets.[9] Loss-averse executives will feel reluctant to pursue M&As and other strategic projects during down-cycles, because they believe they must be riskier when weaker markets have reduced the value of their own companies. CEOs may also underestimate the long-term strategic importance of acquisitions when they analyze (i.e., frame) them too narrowly,[10] because the target's value is much easier to understand in isolation than in the overall context. As a consequence, when environments are uncertain, executives may suffer from *short-termism*, and do not perceive the full potential added value of long-term contingencies.

3. *Anchoring on market valuations.* Anchoring in cold deal markets can involve acquirers basing their valuations on unduly low financial market prices, while the target's management may be anchoring on past transactions in their (higher) valuations of their prospective divestment, resulting in markedly different valuations.

AVOIDING IRRATIONAL INFECTION OF THE VALUATION ANALYSIS

Clearly, in the presence of such potential biases, it is necessary in the first instance to amend traditional valuation analysis to mitigate their possible detrimental impacts in hot and cold deal markets.[11] DCF analysis—the leading

---

[9] See Koller, Lovallo, and Williams (2011). Daniel Kahneman and Amos Tversky have shown that the psychological impact of a loss is about 2 to 2.5 times that of a gain.

[10] Experimental evidence shows that people who are offered a new gamble tend to evaluate it in isolation from other risks. For instance, see Barberis and Hang (2008).

[11] Indeed when bidders do take on acquisitions, they tend to acquire in short succession, and overpay for their acquisitions, depending on whether buying a private firm or purchasing a public firm (Fuller, Netter, and Stegemoller, 2002). We believe acquisitions should be viewed in an acquisition program perspective, where investments are staged rather than to rush or freeze deals. Laamanen and Keil (2008) find that for active acquirers, a high variability of the rate is negatively related to performance. Schipper and Thompson (1983) show that for serial acquirers the anticipation

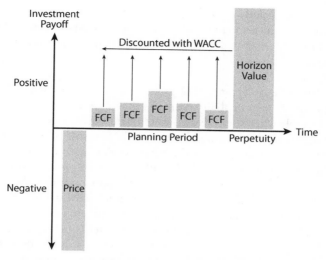

Figure 2.1 A DCF Valuation That Derives a Significant Part from Its Horizon or Terminal Value May Reinforce Hot and Cold Deal Framing

valuation approach—suggests that firms should execute a deal as soon as its NPV becomes positive. The DCF enterprise valuation method involves first estimating the total value of a company by discounting its net free cash flows from existing operations (FCF) at the weighted average cost of capital post-tax (WACC), and then subtracting the market value of any company debt to arrive at the value of its equity. There is a variety of related methods, in which the calculation of company value—as illustrated in Figure 2.1—is usually split up into the value expected to be generated by the transaction during the estimation or planning period, and its horizon or terminal value—the amount it will be worth at the horizon.[12]

CHECKS ON DCF OVERVALUATION IN HOT DEAL MARKETS

Much of the value in a DCF calculation derives from horizon or *terminal value estimates*, which are often quite uncertain. To mitigate overconfidence in the accuracy of the valuation itself, executives can calculate the proportion of value that is determined by the estimation period versus the proportion determined

---

of future acquisitions is reflected in stock prices. See Andrade, Mitchell, and Stafford (2001), Black (1989), Barney (1988), Golbe and White (1988), Gort (1962), Melicher, Ledolter, and D'Antonio (1983), Nelson (1959), and Mitchell and Mulherrin (1996), Singh and Montgomery (1987) on the performance of M&A activity.

[12]   See also Penman (1998) for the estimation of the horizon value.

by the horizon value. In hot deal markets, executives must perform checks and corrections of the estimations of each of the variables making up the horizon value to guard against overvaluation. Several important checks include the following:

- *Top-of-the-cycle profitability, growth expectation, or cost of capital.* Top-of-the-cycle profitability estimates should be adjusted for the phase of the cycle when they are used to estimate the horizon value. A temporarily high growth rate or temporarily low cost of capital can easily result in overvaluation of the horizon value when not corrected to reflect the point in the cycle. By taking the averages of profitability estimates and growth rates over the cycle, horizon values should not inflate the DCF valuation. For instance, executives can use over-the-cycle profitability averages (e.g., three to five years) to estimate horizon values. Even in those cases where high long-term growth estimations are justified, the terminal value formula should still be adjusted for the additional capital invested required to realize this growth.

- *A consistency check on the entry and exit (horizon) multiple.* This check—commonly used in private equity valuations—relates the exit multiple of the DCF calculation (horizon value/future profitability measure) at the horizon date at which the company can be sold (or beyond which it is assumed the business will grow at a constant rate), to the entry multiple for which it will be acquired (estimated value/current profitability measure). Multiple arbitrage (that is entry multiple < exit multiple)—i.e., the assumption that the company can be sold for more than it is acquired for—is unlikely if deal markets are already hot and pricing is at its peak, unless there are clear options for improving the inherent value of the acquired business, for example, through restructuring or the creation of new growth opportunities, or new sources of value for a buyer at exit.

- *Extrapolation of cash-flow growth during the estimation period.* After a recent period of high growth, it is tempting for executives and analysts to become overoptimistic and overestimate the expected growth of operational cash flows and underestimate the impact of increasing competition or technical changes on high margins.

CHECKS ON DCF UNDERVALUATION IN COLD DEAL MARKETS

An overly pessimistic DCF valuation in cold markets can prove just as problematic, and can often result in stalled acquisitions or divestments. When employing a DCF calculation, useful checks for ensuring that executives don't miss out on valuable opportunities in cold markets include the following:

- *Bottom-of-the-cycle correction of horizon (terminal) value.* Cold deal markets require a correction in the estimation of each of the variables of the horizon value. Bottom-of-the-cycle profitability estimations, temporarily low growth rates, or high cost of capital should not be used to assess the long-term horizon value of a target. Instead, a measure of average profitability over the cycle (e.g., three to five years) should be used to estimate horizon value, and the long-term growth rate should typically be greater than the average growth during the estimation period.

- *An entry-exit (horizon) multiple check of the DCF.* In cold deal markets, there is potential for higher exit multiples relative to those paid (multiple arbitrage), justified by future growth options or economic recovery (entry multiple < exit multiple).

Finally, after the DCF analysis is completed, executives should use the prices of similar transactions—called "transaction multiples"—as estimates when valuing a target at hand, and then adjust this value on the basis of the target's particular characteristics. However, this "reality test" against corrected multiples over the cycle needs to be performed after the DCF valuation, so it does not influence the valuation. To consider consistency of the horizon value with observed multiples, analysts can relate the growth rate and cost of capital used in the constant growth annuity formula in a DCF to valuation multiples observed in financial markets. As noted, low (or high) multiples in cold (or hot) deal markets should average out over the cycle, usually using three to five historical years.

A REMEDY FOR UNCERTAINTY NEGLECT: BROADEN YOUR NARROW VIEW

Even when executives correct their DCF analysis, seeing acquisition decisions as simple go/no-go choices based on expected cash flows seems to make them either rush into action even more readily, or to choose to freeze deals. This illusion of the greater clarity of a cash flow scenario can bolster executives' feelings of false confidence, can justify or confirm incorrect prior beliefs about their level of control over the realization of synergies, and can create perceptions that volatility is lower than in reality.

How can executives avoid the illusion of clarity and control inferred from overly static valuations? To integrate uncertainty meaningfully within a holistic framework so as to provide managerial guidance, we propose the notion of expanded "strategic NPV." Besides the standard DCF value of direct expected cash flows from present operations and strategies (direct NPV), strategic NPV also incorporates the dimensions of staging investment flexibility and future growth options. A dynamic analysis of acquisition decisions in terms of options can force executives to consider uncertainty and contingencies by setting up explicit milestones that can indicate when decisions need to be reviewed and alternative actions can be taken where necessary. This expanded analysis requires executives to consider staging deals or deferring acquisitions, pursuing alternative targets for long-term growth, seeking expansion and exit options, discussing the most important growth options in detail, and identifying possible causal links between acquisitions.

In a sense, considering options in acquisitions involves two opposing arguments: a *caution* argument (e.g., considering the options to defer, stage, or recoup the investment) and a *venturing* argument, which encourages the rapid appropriation of the growth option value embedded in an acquisition's horizon value (i.e., its exit value or its future growth option value). To consider which argument should be included in the acquisition analysis, we propose CEOs correct their valuation analyses with a synthesis of two theories for decision making under uncertainty: real options and behavioral economics.

THE CAUTION ARGUMENT: STAGING, DEFERRING, OR RECOUPING AN INVESTMENT

In hot deal markets the analysis of the real options should focus on *staging, deferring*, or *recouping* the investment. The purpose of real options analysis is to force management to think about timing their investments under uncertainty, or alternatively recouping capital early through divestments, as well as accounting for the effects of possible extreme positive or negative events.[13] Examples of potential optionality include the following:

- *Option to defer the investment.* Suggesting something quite different from seeing acquisitions as now-or-never investment propositions, the caution argument (in real options theory) recommends when companies should respond cautiously by staging investments and wait to react to changes in demand, or a more general economic recovery, before executing the next step or, alternatively, should recoup their initial investment by abandoning their interest in the business early.

---

[13] To some extent, a real options analysis can counter attribution bias, defined as attributing success to personal qualities and failure to bad luck. When managers are held (or feel) responsible for a division's failure, they tend to be more retrospectively oriented than those who have not been so closely associated with that division. Providing an exogenous cause for failure—the changed state of the environment—makes it easier for managers to justify abandonment: the decision can be shown to result from using the model correctly, not from their personal failure—so further reducing problems of overcommitment.

This cautious wait-and-see approach—known as the option to de-fer—is applicable to many acquisition decisions, and is based on the typical characteristics of any investment—their irreversible nature and uncertain value. In essence, making the investment (that is, exercising the acquisition option) can be seen as irreversible; if it turns out to be a bad decision, it may not be possible to recover the price and premium by subsequently selling the company. So any irreversible acquisition decision should be made with caution in light of the uncertainty of external factors that may influence future value.[14] Thus real options guide management not to invest in an irreversible project if it can be expected to earn only the opportunity cost of capital, in contrast to what an NPV analysis advocates. Uncertainty gives management the incentive to adapt the timing of investments in concert with external factors. In practice, we often see strategic intuition and real options analysis coincide when executives or other decision makers take this security margin on their net present value into account, to help them feel more comfortable with a deal.

- *Minority stake or staged investment options.* Instead of a full acquisition, a company can first acquire a minority stake as a real option to possibly move to acquire full control later (as in panel A of Figure 2.2). Such a minority stake is a relatively small investment that can be seen as a call option on the remaining stake in the company. This option is exercised only if positive economic developments increase the payoff from the full acquisition. In particular, when rivals are also not exercising their acquisition options, there is no reason to hurry: it will make sense to execute the full transaction (exercise the real option) only when the potential value creation is large, requiring a premium over a zero NPV to compensate for the lost option.

- *Option to exit or divest early to recoup the investment.* In addition to call real options—e.g., to defer or stage—put real options also exist—to divest part of the company early. When restructuring a company, an investor may consider company assets as a portfolio of put or exchange options, and exercise some of them early to recoup (some of) their investment. When the present value of the remaining cash flows of part of a business falls below the resale value to a potential buyer, the asset may be sold—effectively exercising the owner's put option.

- *Avoid options that inflate the hot deal valuation.* Actions such as includ-ing in the valuation hard to specify growth options and sector growth (which in reality will be shared with rivals) can dramatically inflate horizon and company values, and should raise red flags. Similarly, op-

---

[14] See, for instance, Gryglewicz, Huisman, and Kort (2008).

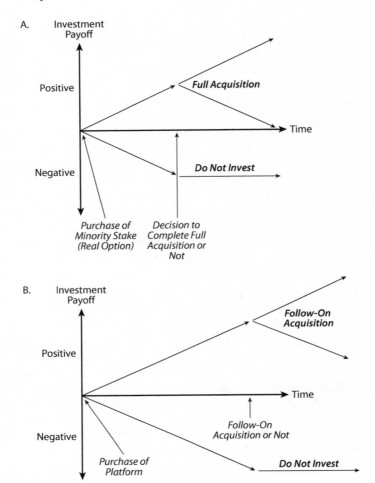

Figure 2.2 A Real Options Analysis May Promote Cautious Venturing. (A) Staging the Acquisition Investment Creates Caution in Hot Deal Markets. (B) Modeling Long-Term Growth Options in the Horizon Value Generates Opportunism in Cold Deal Markets

tions to expand that are embedded in a company valuation analysis can be shared, so there may be no clear advantage in appropriating them. Also, uncertain long-term favorable exit options, such as a trade-sale option premium in the horizon value, should be viewed critically. To correct a hot market valuation, an objective analyst should look for real options that caution the initial investment, either staging or deferring it, and avoid options that amplify the growth option value.

THE VENTURING ARGUMENT: CONSIDERING HORIZON GROWTH OPTION VALUES

Taking the argument further, real options theory also explains why and how investments may be linked over time. In contrast to the caution approach, this venturing argument is based on options in the horizon value of the acquisition—or even beyond. Venturing real options bring long-term contingencies that perceive the acquisition as part of a dynamic long-term strategy, and include the following:

- *Appropriable growth options beyond the horizon.* This venturing real options approach focuses on long-term growth, and includes the value of identifiable new opportunities beyond the acquisition itself—options that can be exercised when conditions become more conducive. Following this approach, new growth options and uncertainty can actually move investment forward. As panel B of Figure 2.2 illustrates, the investment forms the underpinning factor that provides the optionality to proceed to the next stage, if and when it becomes beneficial to do so. Such new follow-on options may include organic growth or access to a new emerging market or geography, perhaps later leading to an exit on favorable terms via a trade sale.

- *Option to expand at (or before) the horizon.* Here the target's infrastructure gives it capacity in excess of its expected output level, so that it can produce at a higher rate if needed. Once the target is acquired, management has the option (but not the obligation) to expand—i.e., exercise the option—should conditions turn out favorable. In cold markets, a target's embedded option to expand if the cold market recovers is equivalent to a call option on a fraction of the value of the business.

- *Long-term favorable options to exit at the horizon.* Similarly, in cold deal markets, a short-term focus by executives may cause them to forgo the importance of favorable options to exit the business or exercise operational options to contract output and assets. The options to exit the business or abandon its assets are American-styled put options and can be exercised early.

In the valuation in cold markets, analysts should avoid real options that may justify static behavior, such as options to defer.

REAL OPTIONS INPUT PARAMETERS

Indeed, professional deal makers (such as venture capitalists) intuitively use both cautious and venturing arguments in their staged approaches to resolve the uncertainty inherent in the start-up ventures they support. Small initial investments limit the potential downside, and can even mean the company can afford to explore several such opportunities in different targets simultaneously. Investments made in earlier financing rounds effectively incorporate venturing options to proceed to the next stage when it becomes beneficial to do so, or to decide against further investment if things turn out worse than expected. While the caution argument limits downside risk by staging or recouping investments, recognizing and—at the right time—realizing these long-term growth options skews the value distribution to the upside.

Drug development in the pharmaceutical industry is also a staged process with various uncertainties. Box 2.1 illustrates how the finance group at Merck defined the option parameters. One should however be alert to the possibility of biases in the estimation of these parameters. Given the similarity in valuation approaches, the input parameters required for modeling real options correspond, generically, to those required for a financial option valuation.

- The option's *underlying value* depends on the type of the option in question. It can be the value of the company or part of the company (e.g., option to defer, minority stake option, option to divest) or the operating value of specific company assets, such as real estate (option to abandon). In these applications a current value is required and is usually based on management's "best estimation" as to the gross value of the business's operational cash flows.

- Estimated *volatility* is a measure for uncertainty in value over time and can be endogenous, requiring investment to be resolved (e.g., technical uncertainty in R&D or exploration uncertainty in mining), or exogenous (e.g., macroeconomic growth). The volatility can be estimated via Monte Carlo simulation of the investment problem, or from the uncertainty in earlier periods' cash flows. In mining, for example, some analysts use a listed security as a proxy (e.g., commodity prices), using either its volatility of returns (historical volatility), or, if financial options exist on this security, their implied volatility. The possibility of extreme economic shocks should also be incorporated in financial models—despite their low probability—helping to remain aware of the chances of the shock materializing, thereby fostering more cautious behavior, especially in hot markets.

- The *strike price* of an option corresponds to any (nonrecoverable) investment outlays or price, typically the prospective price to acquire the targets (call real option) or the resale price of part of the business or specific assets such as real estate (put real option). In general, management would proceed (i.e., the call option would be in the money) if the present value of expected cash flows exceeds this amount. Equally,

BOX 2.1 OPTION ANALYSIS AT MERCK

Merck's finance group used an option-pricing model to determine the project's option value. Existing option models use five factors that influence an option's price, and the finance group defined those factors as follows:

The exercise price is the capital investment to be made approximately two years hence.

The stock price, or value of the underlying asset, is the present value of the cash flows from the project excluding the above-mentioned capital investment to be made and the present value of the up-front fees and development costs over the next two years.

The time to expiration varied over two, three, and four years. The option could be exercised in two years at the earliest, and was structured to expire in four years, by which time Merck thought that competing products would make market entry unfeasible.

A sample of the annual standard deviation of returns for typical biotechnology stocks was obtained from an investment bank as a proxy measure for project volatility. A conservative range for the volatility of the project was set at 40% to 60%.

A risk-free rate of interest of 4.5% was assumed, which roughly represented the U.S. Treasury rate over the two- to four-year period referred to in the model's time to expiration.

The option value that the Financial Evaluation and Analysis Group arrived at from the above factors showed that this option had significantly more value than the up-front payment that needed to be invested.

—Gary L. Sender (Executive Director of Financial Evaluation)

Source: Reprinted by permission of *Harvard Business Review* from Nichols, N. A. 1994. "Scientific Management at Merck." *Harvard Business Review* 72, no. 1: 88–99. Copyright © 1994 by the Harvard Business Review School Publishing Corporation; all rights reserved.

management would divest if the resale price sufficiently exceeds the operating value (i.e., the put option would be in the money).

• *Option term or maturity* corresponds to the life of the option, and is the time during which management may decide to act, or not act on that option. Examples include the time to the expiry of a patent, or the term of the mineral rights for a new mine.

- *Threshold levels* are a sign to take alternative actions—such as deferring a planned acquisition, or pursuing an alternative target. Clear ex ante thresholds that trigger investment or divestment—such as demand levels or critical commodity prices in mining, for example—can help executives discipline any personal-level execution biases and adjust their decisions to avoid overcommitment. In this way, real options can also make it easier for them to forgo intended targets when conditions are unfavorable without such reversals implying personal defeats.

EXAMPLES OF APPROPRIATE REAL OPTIONS THINKING IN HOT AND COLD DEAL MARKETS

We suggest (in Figure 2.3) a simple categorization that illustrates those situations in which more caution is called for, and those that require a more adventurous stance toward strategic planning. The figure relates the modifications a real options toolkit can introduce (in the rows) to potential framing effects of valuation analyses in hot and cold markets (in the columns). In the rows we distinguish between real options tactics suited to acquisitions (call options) or to divestments (put options). Real options to stage investments or growth options embedded in the horizon or terminal value are typically analyzed as call options (in the upper row), while opportunities to abandon, divest, or exit (lower row) are analyzed as put real options. Note that both call and put options can increase caution or venturing behaviors, depending on whether they defer or stage the investment, or increase the long-term value, in a manner similar to growth options, or exit via a trade sale.

In hot deal markets, a real options modification of a DCF analysis typically focuses on the investment outlay, and should encourage executives to take a cautious attitude to entering into bidding wars, either changing the timing and amount of investment in the light of uncertainty or recouping the investment. In contrast, in cold deal markets—when negative framing places excessive focus on risk, and executives freeze because they have an aversion to taking a certain loss—the valuation modifications should promote *opportunism* in the horizon value. Indeed, experienced deal makers facing the changes between hot and cold deal markets adjust their valuations contrariwise. We provide four practical examples of cautious and venturing mind-sets below.

I. KEEP YOUR FEET ON THE GROUND: USING MINORITY STAKES TO EXERCISE CAUTION

Consider the situation in the upper-left box in Figure 2.3. After a successful series of acquisitions in a rapidly consolidating industry, the chief executive of

Framing Effect

		Hot Markets	Cold Markets
Real Options	**Acquisition Options** (Call Options)	**i) "Keep Your Feet on the Ground"** ✓ Options to defer or stage the initial investment introduce caution into the DCF analysis ✗ Expected but elusive growth options post-acquisition can inflate target valuations	**ii) "Look Beyond the Nearby"** ✓ Introduce overlooked long-term growth options beyond the deal into the modified DCF analysis's horizon value ✗ Risk aversion results in seeking options to defer investment
	Divestment/Exit Options (Put Options)	**iii) "Recoup the Investment"** ✓ Put real options to exit early, introduce consideration of negative shocks into a DCF analysis (recoup the investment) ✗ Long-term exit options in the horizon value should raise red flags as they inflate valuations and reinforce a focus on growth instead of on uncertainty	**iv) "Learn When to Let Go"** ✓ Introduce long-term divestment or abandonment put options in the horizon value of the modified analysis ✗ Focus on risk of the investment may put too much emphasis on short-term exit options, while anchoring on high historical values can cause deals to stall

i) In 2008 a major miner described its aggressive tilt at a specialized platinum target at the top of the cycle as "one deal too many." The modified analysis shows the advantage of staging the acquisition to deal with uncertainty.

ii) In 1995 an oil company valued its potential North Sea reserves in a license area on the Dutch Continental Shelf. The modified analysis can expose contingencies and reveal long-term potential growth beyond the acquisition.

iii) The modified analysis should help managers time exits optimally (e.g , divestments or IPOs). In the case cited, a private equity fund exercised it divestment option in a hot private equity deal market in 2007.

iv) In 2004 a leading private equity fund acquired a diversified retail company. Considering divestment options is an important step in triggering decisions about restructuring and repositioning the firm to adjust to demand changes.

Figure 2.3 How a Real Options Approach Can Counter Executive Framing Biases

a major mining venture described his company's aggressive tilt at a specialized platinum target at the top of the cycle as "one deal too many."[15] The acquirer had made an offer in the hot deal market of early 2008, but after the acquirer's last share purchase in that year, the target's shares were trading at far below the offer price. Indeed, with hindsight, the acquirer could have paid significantly less if it had waited. But, as signs grew that the global economy was grinding to

[15] This example is also used in Smit and Lovallo (2014).

a halt, the acquirer avoided overcommitting to the deal by withdrawing its cash offer for the balance of the shares in the face of market uncertainty, a move that caused the target's share price to drop by 50%. At this point—taking options thinking further—the acquirer returned to the market and purchased another 14% of the target, taking its holding to the maximum (without being forced to make an offer for the entire company) of 25%, so ensuring it now owned a "blocking" stake in the target that would represent a very valuable option if and when the market revived. This example reflects the value of staging an acquisition in a hot market (that was cooling rapidly). The financing was already in place, advisor costs had been incurred, and reputations were on the line—but this company learned a valuable lesson from option theory, as the cost of a full hot market acquisition would have put its very survival at risk. Deferring the offer represented a more cautious strategy, which both was less expensive and turned out to be safer, given the continuing economic uncertainties of the time.

The traditional NPV method recommends an instant response to the opportunity of a deal—prosecute the transaction if the NPV is positive or, failing that, walk away. By explicitly acknowledging the presence of uncertainty, a real options perspective offers an alternative approach—that of staging investments and waiting cautiously until uncertainty resolves before making the next move. In a hot deal market, rather than acquiring the entire company at once, a firm can first acquire a minority equity stake and—meanwhile—discover valuable information about its target's future prospects or the resolution of key uncertainties, which then supports its further decision making as to whether and when to complete the acquisition.[16] As with the maturing of an option, this means the full acquisition takes time to complete, during which the economic environment may change and the acquirer can review its intentions.[17] So—like options—minority stakes are more valuable when exploring distant domains or future options with high growth potential, and in periods of high exogenous uncertainty.

II. LOOK FOR GROWTH OPPORTUNITIES BEYOND THE NEARBY IN COLD MARKETS

Now consider the cold markets investment category in the upper-right-hand box in Figure 2.3. In 1995 an oil company conducted a valuation of its potential North Sea reserves in a Dutch Continental Shelf license area. Developing the

---

[16] When—despite clear signals—decision makers fail to withdraw their bids or alter their strategies in other ways (e.g., limiting the acquisition to buying a blocking stake) due to the sunk costs involved in trying to complete the hostile takeover and the associated regret they feel, they are said to fall to prey to the "sunk cost fallacy." The personal considerations of "empire-building" executives may also result in overcommitment. See Bowman and Hurry (1993), Folta and Miller (2002), Adner and Levinthal (2004b), Zardkoohi (2004), and Folta (1998).

[17] This is similar to a call option on the value of synergistic benefits, where the exercise price is the cost of the merger.

reserves would have entailed making substantial sequential investments in test drilling, evaluation drilling, and production capacity, with the exploration phase of drilling test wells—the first link in that chain—typically yielding low returns. This sequence of project stages can be viewed as a set of nested call options. Market prices were very low—only $14 per barrel—and it was hard to imagine they would ever increase to the levels we see today. But, with the project's horizon at over 30 years, and annual oil price volatility estimated at around 30% to 40%, the real options approach teaches managers to consider making certain investments today—even if their NPV appears negative—to access valuable opportunities in the future, especially since such opportunities are contingent on an uncertain future.

Valuations using classical DCF approaches can be affected by cold deal framing and typically ignore such contingencies. The Box 2.2 example illustrates how an analysis was modified to incorporate contingent growth options. Introducing options thinking into organizations, and specifying conditional actions (e.g., acquire or wait) as real options can counter decision makers' tendencies to focus on short-term profitability and help identify multiple potential long-term growth options, of which only the most profitable are then ultimately exercised.[18] Such growth options have call option characteristics, and encompass the broad spectrum of investments undertaken for growth and expansion purposes. Examples include how pharmaceutical companies often acquire R&D ventures and how private equity funds invest in platform buy-and-build acquisitions that can open new acquisition trajectories in new and/or uncertain markets or geographies.

III. AND IV. SEEING EXIT OPPORTUNITIES IN HOT AND COLD MARKETS

The lower half of Figure 2.3 considers exits (as put options) in hot and cold deal markets.[19] Private equity investors behave like natural *opportunists*, continuously seeking to reposition their investments, and management teams should adapt a *cautious venturing* attitude if they want to avoid falling prey to such opportunistic investors. For instance, in 2004 a leading private equity fund (together with a consortium of private equity partners) acquired a diversified Dutch retail company for €2.4 billion, partially financed by an €850 million loan from three banks. As Box 2.3 describes, the acquisition was opportunistic: the company was due to report poor fourth quarter sales results in two weeks, which were likely to encourage shareholders and management to accept a cash offer, especially as the recovery of Dutch consumer demand was uncertain. However, the fund saw *opportunities* in the cold market that the retailer's share-

---

[18] Duhaime and Schwenk (1985).
[19] An excellent overview and discussion of biases in exit decisions can be found in Horn, Lovallo, and Viguerie (2006).

BOX 2.2 LOOK FOR OPPORTUNITIES BEYOND THE NEARBY IN COLD MARKETS

STAGED DEVELOPMENT OF OFFSHORE PETROLEUM DEVELOPMENT ON THE DUTCH CONTINENTAL SHELF

A major advantage of real options analysis over an NPV analysis is that it highlights an appropriate procedure for analyzing geological and oil price uncertainty and supports management's ability to react to that uncertainty. Naturally, better informed decisions can be made over time, as uncertainty becomes resolved. For example, the decision to invest in production facilities is contingent on the quantity of reserves found during the exploration phase and the oil price at that time.

OPTIONS

The various contingent decisions are illustrated in the decision tree shown in Figure 2.4. We start solving at the right side of a more complex and detailed tree, valuing a producing field, and then work backward in time to value the exploration phase. Management has the following contingent decisions or options:

The Option to Start Test Drilling. Geological and geophysical studies help to identify prospective locations for drilling, based on which management can apply for an exploration license and start test drilling.

The Option to Invest in Appraisal Wells. If oil is found during test drilling, further drilling can ascertain whether the reserves are large enough to be suitable for commercial production.

The Option to Invest in Development. Following the exploration phase, and having determined the amount of exploitable reserves in the field, the firm has to decide whether to start development to exploit them, or to abandon operations. As this stage requires the largest capital expenditures, this is where option valuation is most important. Management must determine whether and when it is optimal to invest in production facilities, given the quantity of reserves and the uncertainty of future oil prices. At the production phase of the investment program, uncertainty regarding the quantity of reserves is resolved and the production profile for the field's useful life has been determined. There is no option value to temporarily shut down (mothball) North Sea oil drilling operations, since pipelines and facilities deteriorate very rapidly in that environment. The end of the project's life will involve certain abandonment costs, which management must also take into account.

UNCERTAINTIES

Thus different types of uncertainties or risk are resolved at different stages.

Uncertainty about the Quantity of Reserves. Test drilling for exploration wells maximizes information about the geological section and helps resolve uncertainty about the presence of hydrocarbons. Evaluation drilling via additional appraisal wells can ascertain the extent of exploitable reserves in the well.

Uncertainty about Oil Prices. After the uncertainty of the quantity of reserves is (partly) resolved, the risks of the project are largely associated with fluctuations in oil prices. The quantity of reserves found, in combination with the expected range of future oil prices, will determine whether the field is suitable for commercial exploitation.

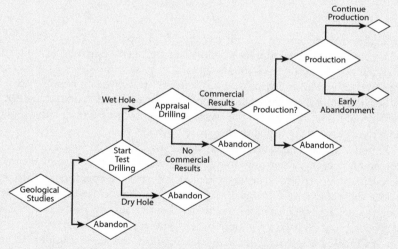

Figure 2.4 Decision Tree for Offshore Oil Development

INSIGHTS

Real options implementation illustrates that oil price uncertainty is important in the valuation of the exploration phase, and challenges the idea that uncertainty provides a disincentive for investment. The valuation re-

BOX 2.2 (CONT.)

sults show that exploration investments in speculative blocks are more effective in resolving the inherent uncertainty, and hence are more valuable than otherwise similar investments in investigating low-uncertainty blocks. This result, which may seem surprising at first glance, hinges on the fact that if the exploration phase fails, the enormous costs of follow-on investments for the production phase can be saved (in some instances the leases can be sold to recoup all or some of the investment). In other words, if the block turns out dry, then only the relatively small exploration investment is lost. On the other hand, the drilling company stands to gain more from a speculative block if it has exceptionally high values in the production phase. The strategies observed in large oil companies support the idea that exploration investments are more effective, and hence more valuable, in more uncertain areas. Large exploration firms have decided to leave the Dutch Continental Shelf and explore unknown and uncertain areas in the Soviet Union, China, and Australia, where there are believed to be better opportunities for larger—i.e., more profitable—discoveries.

holders and management did not see: it could put a floor on its investment by selling and leasing back the fashion business's property portfolio (estimated at €1.5 billion), instantly recouping a significant proportion of its equity investment, effectively affording it "deal caution" (see deal situation iv in Figure 2.3). When there are likely to be future potential buyers, real estate assets can be considered a put option, with the exercise price equal to the trade value and the underlying asset value equal to the current owners' value.[20]

When a management team has a static view of their business, it makes it a vulnerable target. When they find it hard to envision the full range of their divestment opportunities, or feel reluctant to terminate operations or abandon assets, their company's financial market value is often close to a DCF standalone value, implying little or no embedded optionality. In contrast, seeing the same company through a real options lens can help focus managerial attention toward turning assets to alternative uses: in short, this view considers the target's businesses as a portfolio of divestment, abandonment, and exit options.[21] In the case cited above, after the property sale and lease-back, the fund exercised several of its divestment options, including exiting the low-end retail element for €1.1 billion in 2007 (as an example of situation iii in Figure 2.3);

[20] For a business for which both value and price are uncertain, this actually resembles an exchange option.
[21] See also O'Brien and Folta (2009).

BOX 2.3 SITUATIONS III AND IV: EXIT AND DIVESTMENT IN HOT AND COLD MARKETS

The example business here is a leading nonfood retailer in the Benelux region which, by 2004, operated 11 formats across the department store, DIY, fashion, and restaurant segments. The group had 1,400 stores spread across the Netherlands, Belgium, Luxembourg, France, Spain, Germany, and several other markets. Figure 2.5 illustrates the various contingent decisions in the decision tree.

OPTIONS

The Option to Exit Real Estate. One option for the firm is to abandon specific operations, divisions, or even entire businesses, moves that can add significant value to capital-intensive companies with large tangible assets. Like all options, this can be especially valuable in highly uncertain markets, particularly if those assets can easily be switched to alternative uses, or traded in such secondary markets as real estate or land. If demand turns out to be weaker than originally expected, management can contract in various ways: by operating below capacity or reducing the scale of its operations (so saving part of its variable costs), or it can seek to gain some value by selling assets. The option to contract can be seen as a put option on the part of the business that could be sold, with an exercise price equal to the resale value of the associated assets. So when we consider this deal via a real options lens, the equity fund was actually buying the company with a put option—an exit option for the real estate. The selling price almost covered the total price the fund paid to buy the company.

The Option to Divest Various Business Formats. On a business portfolio level, following the divestment of the property portfolio in 2005 (€1.5 billion), the sale of the low-end retail chain in 2007 (€1.1 billion), and the subsequent sales of the fashion formats in 2010, the company is now focused exclusively on its options in its market-leading DIY businesses in the Netherlands and Belgium.

INSIGHTS

When a management team has a static view and cannot envision the full range of their divestment opportunities, or when they feel reluctant to terminate operations or abandon assets, the company can fall prey to opportunistic investors. Although the investor may not have explicitly valued

BOX 2.3 (CONT.)

its real options, considering contraction options is an important step in triggering decisions about restructuring and repositioning the firm to adjust to demand changes.

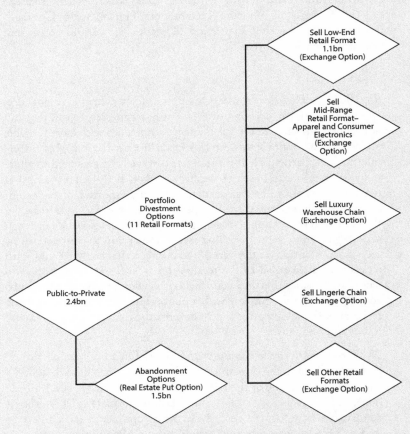

Figure 2.5 Restructuring a Business as a Portfolio of Options

selling the midrange department store and apparel and consumer electronics sectors in 2011; followed by divesting other fashion segments, including the lingerie and luxury warehouse chains.[22]

---

[22] Indeed, empirical research confirms that public offerings appear to cluster in hot markets, when investors place relatively high values on both new issues and firms that are already publicly traded. See Lowry and Schwert (2002), Burch, Nanda, and Christie (2004).

CONCLUSIONS

The behavioral literature shows it is extremely hard for individuals to mitigate their *own* biases. Given that it is difficult for executives to analyze their own minds, we suggest they consider something they can observe much more easily than their own minds: whether they are operating in hot or cold deal markets. A behavioral real options–based valuation checklist can help them temper their natural focus on growth options in hot markets and refocus it on staging their investments: and, in contrast, it can help divert their natural attention from short-term risk to long-term growth options in cold deal markets.[23] Perhaps countering managers' psychological biases, rather than falsely modifying valuations, may represent the best we can do to make quantitative valuation analysis a more representative and objective decision-making mechanism, helping mangers avoid either rushing headlong into transactions or, alternatively, becoming overly conservative.

SUGGESTED READING

Horn, J. T., D. P. Lovallo, and S. P. Viguerie. 2006. "Learning to Let Go: Making Better Exit Decisions." *McKinsey Quarterly*, no. 2: 64–75.

Koller, T., M. Goedhart, and D. Wessels. 2010. *Valuation: Measuring and Managing the Value of Companies*. Hoboken, NJ: John Wiley.

Lovallo, D., and D. Kahneman. 2003. "Delusions of Success: How Optimism Undermines Executives' Decisions." *Harvard Business Review* 81, no. 7: 56–63.

SUGGESTED MATERIALS, TOOLS, AND GADGETS

Han Smit's page on valuation tools provides DCF spreadsheets as well as real options valuation tools and webcasts. Links to the page can be found on this book's Princeton University Press website: http://press.princeton.edu/titles /10333.html.

Aswath Damodaran's home page is an excellent portal on DCF valuation, and provides references to his books, spreadsheets, and data. See http://pages .stern.nyu.edu/~adamodar/.

---

[23] See also Miller and Shapira (2004), Tiwana, Keil, and Fichman (2006), Tiwana et al. (2007).

CHAPTER 3

PLAYING AT SERIAL ACQUISITIONS

THE CASE OF VODAFONE

Necessity never made a good bargain.

—Benjamin Franklin

In a period of only a few years in the early 2000s, Vodafone's then CEO Chris Gent grew the company from a small UK-based mobile operator into the world leader, with over 240 million customers.[1] He did this via a sequence of 26 strategic transactions, including the acquisition of AirTouch, deals leading to the creation of the Verizon wireless business in the United States, a bitter takeover battle for Germany's Mannesmann, and many Asian alliances such as the China Mobile linkup.

Today's economy is characterized by uncertainty, globalization, and the rapid emergence of significant new markets (most notably in China and India), which boast substantial consumer bases, skills, and low-cost production capacity. The need for increased efficiency in such an environment makes Vodafone's global acquisition strategy enviable. Management teams typically envision a series of transactions based on buy-and-build principles, in which they initially acquire a platform in a new geography or market and then leverage their newly acquired competencies and assets into follow-on acquisitions over a wider geographic and customer base.

---

[1] The views in this chapter are those of the authors and are further developed in their article, "Playing at Serial Acquisitions," published in *California Management Review* 53, no. 1 (2010): 56–89, © 2010 by the Regents of the University of California. Published by the University of California Press. The authors would like to thank the editor of *California Management Review*, David Vogel, Jon Morgan of Paraphrase, and three anonymous referees for their comments and suggestions that have benefited this article.

Judging from Vodafone's acquisition story, Chris Gent played his cards well, while both Vodafone's rivals and the financial markets acted irrationally in some instances. Using Vodafone's shares as a currency for its acquisitions, Gent created a successful global telecom brand, while many of Vodafone's rivals, failing to see the strategic value of such acquisitions, remained imprudently conservative. But even he may have made some typical serial acquisition errors on the road to building the world's leading telecom company: he was sometimes accused of hubris, and some of Vodafone's acquisitions, executed at a time when the deal market became increasingly hot, were thought to be overpriced by the investor community.[2]

Novel company valuation methods (such as real option game valuation) belong to a field that has been hitherto separate from behavioral literature. We argue that a structured and rational quantitative analysis, using a modified option game toolkit, could help mitigate several management biases. This chapter uses the Vodafone story to illustrate how behavioral pitfalls in strategy, valuation, and bidding can be related to various components of the options and game valuation approach. In later chapters we present in-depth applications of each of the concepts discussed here and quantify them in various applications in mining and private equity.

SIX POTENTIAL PITFALLS IN THE EXECUTION OF A SERIAL ACQUISITION STRATEGY

Vodafone's strategy during the early 2000s was an archetypal example of global consolidation.[3] After a successful marketing campaign had secured it a dominant position in its UK home market, acquisitions in the United States, Europe, China, and Japan gave Vodafone a platform from which it created a global telecom brand. It gained a strong position in the United States when it outbid Bell Atlantic to buy AirTouch for $62 billion in January 1999, a merger that created one of the world's largest international mobile telecom companies, with an extensive presence covering most of Europe and the United States. Vodafone considered a number of subsequent options in the United States, includ-

---

[2] See also Bertrand and Schoar (2003) and Aktas, de Bodt, and Roll (2009, 2011) for the impact of CEOs on firm performance.

[3] Serial acquirers are occasionally accused of hubris for engaging in multiple deals (Billett and Qian 2008); however evidence indicates experienced serial acquirers do a bit better in financial markets (Schipper and Thompson 1983; Kil, Smit, and Verwijmeren 2013), even though they pay a premium for their first public deal in a series. Despite these higher average payments, the market reacts more favorably to serial acquirers than to single acquirers, implying its expectations that serial acquirers are better able to identify and extract synergies and to position themselves for future acquisition options.

ing a move to combine the US mobile phone interests of Vodafone AirTouch and Bell Atlantic.[4]

In 2000, the company strengthened its position in Europe when it launched a hostile $205 billion bid for Germany's Mannesmann telecom group in a battle that remains one of the largest hostile takeovers in history. This move secured Vodafone's place as a key European operator, and led to further acquisition opportunities in a European mobile market that was fragmented but rapidly beginning to consolidate.

In China, Vodafone invested $2.5 billion to forge a strategic alliance with China Mobile in October 2000, which gave it a foothold in the world's largest mobile market, and gave China Mobile access to Vodafone's marketing and technical expertise, particularly in third-generation mobile technology. Meanwhile the group's initial investment in Japan followed from the merger with AirTouch and comprised taking equity stakes in nine regional mobile telecom companies. This created the option for further investments, which led to J-Phone Vodafone and the acquisition of Japan Telecom, as well as of Alltel Corp for $28 billion.

However, when a serial acquisition vision overrides rational analysis, it may be vulnerable to cognitive biases that can undermine objective decision making. Extensive psychological experimental studies suggest that there are general human biases in decision making that appear to affect decisions in predictable ways.[5] Serial acquirers should try to mitigate the biases in their boards or of their CEOs that lead to suboptimal acquisition decisions, while at the same time being aware that their rivals, financial analysts, and investors will have their own biases, and can also sometimes act in predictably irrational ways. Such cognitive biases can manifest in irrational strategies, in overheated contests for platform targets, or in the overvaluation of targets.

POTENTIAL PITFALLS IN SERIAL ACQUISITION STRATEGIES

PITFALL 1: OVERINVESTMENT OR OVERCONSERVATISM IN CONSOLIDATING INDUSTRIES

Acquisitions are surrounded by uncertainty, and how they are described or framed is likely to affect the way executives perceive the levels of risk involved.[6] Aversion to losses is a central feature of Kahneman and Tversky's prospect

---

[4] Bell Atlantic later walked away from a partnership agreement with AirTouch. The intended strategic move would have led to an alliance between the two companies' cellular networks that would have given them national reach.

[5] Financial economic and psychological studies confirm that acquisition strategies can be vulnerable to managerial hubris. For instance, see Baker, Ruback, and Wurgler (2004), Barberis and Thaler (2003), Hayward and Hambrick (1997), Roll (1986), Roll (1993), Shefrin (2007), Seth, Song, and Pettit (2000), and Shleifer (2000).

[6] When managers take risks and exhibit risk preferences, they differ from the classical processes

theory (a descriptive theory, based on extensive experimental evidence) of how people evaluate risk. Decisions are determined by gains and losses measured relative to a reference point. Loss aversion—meaning that people are more sensitive to the possibility of losses than to potential gains of the same magnitude—may lead executives to behave in ways that are suboptimal from shareholders' perspectives. Confronted with acquisition decisions in a consolidating industry, executives may exhibit *narrow framing* and *aversion to a certain loss.*

A CEO may tend to avoid taking a certain loss by refusing to abandon bidding contests or to divest assets. For instance, Vodafone was accused of excessive bidding in repeatedly raising its offer (up to a 70% premium) to win its hostile takeover battle against Mannesmann's management. Similarly, when a market entry decision is considered to have been made at a loss relative to a reference point—for instance, where the price paid for a platform acquisition exceeds its stand-alone value—management may choose to continue making risky investments in an unattractive region hoping to gamble their way out, rather than to divest the original platform at a lower but certain loss.

A CEO may also look at a strategic platform acquisition in a too narrow way, because the payoff distribution of the investment is much easier to understand in isolation than it is in the overall context of a serial acquisition strategy that involves interdependent follow-on investments and/or acquisitions in other regions or markets. Clearly, overly narrow framing was one bias that did not affect Chris Gent: while Vodafone was capturing its leading position, some of its rivals remained conservative, unable to appreciate the new growth opportunities in the industry. Vodafone was clearly not in conservative mode and framed its strategy much more broadly, targeting multiple or parallel platform acquisitions—in the United States, Europe, China, and Japan—to position itself to make follow-on acquisitions across multiple geographies.

In summary, aversion to certain losses and overly narrow framing may result in an excessively static acquisition strategy that will deliver suboptimal growth in shareholder wealth. However, while narrow framing may result in an overly conservative acquisition strategy that fails to fully capitalize on upside potential, aversion to sure losses can lead a consolidator to overinvest, increasing losses by continuing to invest when the market signals indicate otherwise—in essence, throwing good money after bad.

PITFALL 2: JUDGMENT BIASES RESULT IN OVERINVESTMENT IN AN ACQUISITION STRATEGY

While the first strategy pitfall can result from how executives *perceive* risk, pitfall 2 results primarily from the way they *estimate* risk. A management team

---

of choosing from among alternative actions in terms of the mean (expected value) and variance (risk) of the probability distributions over possible outcomes. See March and Shapira (1987).

may envision a well-crafted long-term consolidating strategy that involves the selection of a series of targets to secure its strategic position and to capitalize on—or even catalyze—industry consolidation. However, judgment biases reinforced by groupthink and disregard for warning signals can mean that the strategy they envision is based on overoptimistic expectations of synergies and the illusion of control over their targets.[7]

One such judgment bias that CEOs may face—and which can result in unrealistic acquisition attempts—is *overconfidence*.[8] Experimental evidence has shown that people generally tend to be overconfident, a factor that can be particularly prominent—and seductive—in the type of environments that typically surround highly successful executives who may have already executed a string of value-accretive transactions.[9] Such managerial hubris—the often unrealistic belief held by bidding managers that they can manage the assets of a target firm more efficiently than its current managers—goes hand in hand with *excessively optimistic* expectations.[10] In the same way that behavioral corporate finance studies show that start-up entrepreneurs usually have overly optimistic views of their ventures' potential for success,[11] executives involved in serial acquisition strategies can overestimate their company's ability to fully appropriate a target's value, and thus to overvalue its growth potential.[12]

In serial strategies, these kinds of biases may be path-dependent, since the acquiring company's past successes (or recent media praise for its CEO) can increase the risk of overconfidence. Thus, previous successful acquisition efforts can introduce overly optimistic views of the attainability of follow-on targets, and increase the danger of managers trying to take the company a "deal too far." Table 3.1 provides an overview of simple boardroom experiments that can reveal senior executives' sensitivity to cognitive biases that can affect their ability to pursue their acquisition strategies rationally. While experiments such as "Feeling Confident?"[13] ought to cause executives to revisit the rationality of their own belief in their abilities, it is worth remembering that overconfidence

[7] See Barnes (1984), Coval and Shumway (2005), Kahneman and Lovallo (1993), and Lovallo and Kahneman (2003).

[8] Experimental studies show that people hold a variety of self-serving biases, believing that they are more capable than in fact they are. Such biases will lead to overoptimistic planning in the future. For instance, see Larwood and Whittaker (1977).

[9] "Reference group neglect" reflects a tendency to underreact to changes in the reference group one competes with—see, for example, Camerer and Lovallo (1999). Such CEO overconfidence and hubris can lead to ill-advised takeovers—see, for example, Roll (1986).

[10] While overoptimism is reflected in an overestimation of a target's growth options and synergies, overconfidence concerns managers' views as to their abilities to capture these synergies or realize the acquisition.

[11] Cooper, Woo, and Dunkelberg (1988).

[12] The strategy is particularly vulnerable for overinvestment when projects can be internally financed. See also Malmendier and Tate (2005, 2008, 2009).

[13] Svenson (1981).

is a general and self-serving human bias, which, sadly, appears to be only minimally affected by feedback.

In particular, groupthink and team decisions tend to accentuate the risk of unwarranted confidence in acquisition decisions, supporting the underestimation of the risks involved and so leading to the illusion of control. CEOs and top management teams often suffer from self-attribution, when they sometimes unconsciously credit their own actions when they succeed, but blame bad luck when they fail.

A related judgment bias in strategy design lies in a subconscious resistance to critically testing hypotheses. Seeing only what we want to see is labeled *confirmation bias*: experiments show we tend to seek confirmatory data and opinions, leading to systematic overconfidence in favored hypotheses. This type of general bias—investing more energy into looking for evidence that supports a hypothesis than into seeking signals that might contradict it—is illustrated by the "Confirmed!" card experiment described in Table 3.1.[14] Confirmation and overconfidence in strategy can also partly result from (or be reinforced by) other biases, such as groupthink. Group processes are sensitive to *joint confirmation bias*: imagine a group of executives and their consultants evaluating whether a postacquisition integration would realize the synergies they expected when they bid for the company. Just as participants choose cards that they expect will be able to support (rather than contradict) their hypothesis in the Table 3.1 experiment, executives—supported by their business development teams, consultants and investment bankers (who are, after all, incentivized to complete, rather than abort, transactions)—rarely seek or are presented with data that contradict a transaction's essential value proposition.

Where significant decisions that can materially affect the value of the organization are to be made, the benefits of looking for potentially contraindicatory evidence are clear. Nevertheless, executives often persist instead in seeking yet more confirmation, which does not necessarily provide them with any new information.[15]

POTENTIAL VALUATION PITFALLS

In addition to the pitfalls in the process of developing the acquisition strategy, the assessment of value by the executive team (or by the financial market community at large) can present another pitfall for companies seeking to acquire. Although Vodafone was accused of paying too much for its acquisitions in the early 2000s, in fact the entire sector proved difficult to value, with only hindsight confirming that it was overvalued.

---

[14] These experiments and an overview of biases in exit decisions are discussed in Horn, Lovallo, and Viguerie (2006). See also Wason (1968).

[15] See Jones and Sugden (2001).

TABLE 3.1 BIASES THAT AFFECT COMPANY STRATEGY

Pitfall Bias/ Heuristic	Board Room Experiment	Description of Human Biases That Affect Strategy Decision Making
Pitfall 2. Judgment cognitive biases: Overconfidence, overoptimism, illusion of control, and confirmation bias to a business model enforced by board room groupthink	Experiment: "Feeling Confident?" "Rank your driving skills (on a scale of 1 to 5) compared to the average in this group ($n = 3$)." Subjects are asked to write down in a sealed envelope their estimate of their competence as drivers in relation to the group. When the average result is calculated it is almost invariably greater than 3, a statistical impossibility. The majority of subjects regarded themselves as more skillful and less prone to taking risks than the average driver in the group.	Behavioral researchers have identified a tendency to consider ourselves "better than average" on positive characteristics. This may be lead executives be overoptimistic about their assessments of integration plans, about their ability to appropriate targets, and about scenarios in which synergies are realized, and thus to overvalue targets. This overconfidence goes hand in hand with overoptimism and illusions of control, where uncertainty about extraneous factors or strategic uncertainty is underestimated.

Experiment: "Confirmed!"

Four double-sided cards are laid out on the table, each with a number on one side and a letter on the other. Suppose that we can see only the face of the four cards, as shown below. "Which pair would you choose given the opportunity to flip over just two cards to test the assertion 'If a card has a vowel on one side, then there must be an even number on the other side?'"

Problem	E	2	C	3
Response 1	4	K		
Response 2	4			A

The most common response to the question (response 1) is the combination of the E and 2 cards. E confirms the statement by having 4 on its reverse (an uneven number would refute the statement). However, turning over the 2 does not provide new information. A consonant (e.g., K) on the other side would not actually say anything about the statement, while a vowel would appear to confirm the statement, but could not make it necessarily true for all the cards. So turning the 2 over cannot test the

These tendencies tend to lead to systematic executive overconfidence in acquisition situations, resulting in executives selecting evidence that confirms their next intended transaction. Actively seeking and evaluating disconfirming information and factoring such data into their calculations would minimize the risk of confirmation bias. Groupthink situations can lead to collective overconfidence, reinforcing the unwarranted acceptance of confirmatory evidence and disregard for any contraindications, as well as to the danger of boards becoming polarized.

Executives (and their advisors) should be careful not to overestimate their judgment capabilities, overvalue targets, or be overoptimistic about plans and scenarios to realize synergies. They should recognize that a major acquisition in a consolidating sector is likely to invite competitive responses from rival consolidators who do not want to be left in the cold when the industry's "musical chairs" reaches its endgame. The executive team must take a realistic view of its chances of appropriating the target—considering *all* factors such as the ownership structure, management's perspective, the investment community's expecta-

TABLE 3.1 (CONT.)

Pitfall Bias/ Heuristic	Board Room Experiment	Description of Human Biases That Affect Strategy Decision Making
	assertion. The correct answer in this experiment is response 2: the combination of E and 3. Turing over the 3 choice *could* prove that the statement is false if the other side reveals a vowel (as it does: i.e., A). This is a simple example of *actively seeking data that could contradict a hypothesis or assertion.* Not reading the statement carefully enough—in fact, reading an unjustified assumption into it—participants tend to choose the E and 2 cards because they see them as being capable of providing evidence that confirms the assertion. They tend *not* to choose the 3, even though it is the only one that could *disprove* the statement.	tions and competition, and all the available evidence, both positive and negative. If targets seem to be unattainable, executive teams should not pursue them and recognize that this is the right decision.

There are three categories of psychological pitfalls that may cause suboptimal serial acquisition strategy: biases, heuristics, and framing effects.

- A bias is a predisposition to an error of some type.
- A heuristic or a rule of thumb is based on experience, industry standards, or academic constructs. It is not uncommon for managers to rely on heuristics in their valuation of targets, but their unquestioned use as substitutes for rigorous fundamental analysis may affect optimal decision making.
- Framing concerns the way the decision is described and often influences executives' decisions.

When company value is illusive and difficult to quantify—as when trying to assess the growth potential of platform acquisitions—the tendency is to revert to the heuristics of relative values (rules of thumb) that may over- or underestimate target values and rely too little on fundamental valuation methods. Market inefficiencies can lead to financial markets failing to price firms correctly, and the resultant inaccurate valuations inevitably influence acquisition decisions.[16] Irrationality in financial markets influenced both the valuation and the financing of Vodafone's acquisitions.

PITFALL 3: RELATIVE VALUATION WITH INSUFFICIENT ADJUSTMENT

Relative (rather than absolute) valuations, often utilizing simplified heuristics, can introduce flaws into the process of valuing a target. The common human tendency to rely too heavily on one trait or piece of already-known information

---

[16] For instance, see Shiller *(*2000*)*. Evidence shows that high market valuations are strongly related to merger activity (Rhodes-Kropf and Viswanathan, 2004), and managers of overvalued firms buy targets that are less overvalued (Rhodes-Kropf, Robinson, and Viswanathan 2005).

when making decisions represents a cognitive bias that has been described as *anchoring*: once the anchor is set, there is usually a bias toward that value. Take for example an executive deciding to set an offer price for a target. He or she may start from the basis of prices paid for similar companies and then use "multiples" (e.g., enterprise value-to-EBITDA and price-earnings multiples)[17] as the basis for refining their valuation of the company, rather than considering how well the target company and its strategy fit into the bidder's own strategy. The boardroom experiment "Anchor and Adjustment" (presented in Table 3.2) illustrates the dangers of such cognitive drawbacks in valuing target companies.[18] The valuation analysis may suffer from related biases, such as *representativeness*, where the valuation is overly dependent on relative valuation compared to its peers or to a rival bid. A relative multiple analysis should function only as a reality check on a fundamental valuation, utilizing tools such as NPVs augmented with real options to determine the value of a target's current operations and its growth options from the acquirer's perspective.

PITFALL 4: CAN ONE TRUST PRICES IN FINANCIAL MARKETS? BEAUTY IS IN THE EYE OF THE BEHOLDER

The analysis becomes more complex when (already biased) bidders observe rival bidders and attempt to account for their actions and reactions. The "Biased Beauty Contest" game (see again Table 3.2) provides a metaphor for thinking about multiple valuations in financial markets.[19] Sometimes prices seem to be determined by others' perception of beauty—but they in turn may be basing *their* perceptions on *their view* of how *others* perceive the target's beauty. Pricing in financial markets and bidding in the private equity world sometimes work in the same way, with bidders basing their guesses as to a target's value on their perceptions of other bidders' estimates.[20]

In consolidating industries, the dynamics of relative value are markedly more acute than for acquisitions in simpler sectors, since targets take on increasingly strategic meaning as the industry consolidates. Beyond its scarcity value, the same target may play a particular role in the serial acquisition strategies of, or offer unique synergies to, one or more bidders, with the result that different

---

[17] Earnings before interest, taxes, depreciation, and amortization (EBITDA) is an accounting profitability measure that is corrected for the influences of the financing of the company to measure operational performance.

[18] The experiment in the table is based on Tversky and Kahneman (1974). See also Strack and Mussweiler (1997).

[19] This contest was performed in an article on behavioral finance by the renowned behavioral economist Richard Thaler (1997) published in the *Financial Times*.

[20] For instance, private equity investors should be careful with pricing secondaries—i.e., acquisitions from other private equity funds. In private equity, up to 80% of a DCF valuation of a buyout is likely to come from a horizon or exit value that is often based on an exit EBIDA multiple, which in turn is related to the entry multiple. If the entry multiple is incorrect, so is the exit multiple.

TABLE 3.2 BIASES THAT AFFECT COMPANY VALUATION

Pitfall Bias/ Heuristic	Board Room Experiment	Description of Human Biases That Affect Valuation
Pitfall 3. Biases in valuation analysis: Anchoring and insufficient adjustment, representative, available and affect heuristics	Experiment: "Anchor and Adjustment" This experiment shows how we anchor our estimates. A valuation team is asked two questions: *"Is the number of countries in Africa more or less than [a high or low random number]?"* and *"How many countries do you believe there are in Africa?"* Participants given a low random number in the formulation of the first question tend to significantly underestimate the number of countries when answering the second question, while those given a high random number tend to overestimate their second answer.	In relative valuation we base estimates and decisions on familiar positions or "anchors" and often make insufficient subsequent adjustments relative to that starting point. Even in fundamental valuations, we tend to "work to a given value" when uncertainty is involved. A valuation may be biased if it is based on readily available information relative to less salient information (the "availability" heuristic), or when valuation and decisions are based on intuition (the "affect" heuristic).
Pitfall 4. Excess pricing in financial markets: Biased beauty contest	Experiment: "Biased Beauty Contest" *Participants are asked to write down a number between 0 and 100 such that their guess will be as close as possible to 2/3 of the average guess in the group.* Behavioral economists use this experiment to show the bounds of rationality in game theory. A player might think that the average participant is not involved and that the average guess will be 50. So the player guesses 33, which is 2/3 of 50. The next order of sophistication in "thinking how others think" incorporates the view that the other guessers will understand the same first level of thinking and so assume that they will guess 33 on average, and therefore select 22 (as 2/3 of 33). Game theorists search for an equilibrium—that is, a number which, if everyone guessed it, no one would have any incentive to change their guess: in this instance, that number would be 0.	Sometimes prices seems to be determined by the "perception of beauty" of others, who in turn might base their "perception of beauty" on what *they* think *our* perception is. Relative valuation of a target can therefore be risky if the benchmark is itself mispriced and does not rely on fundamental analysis. The relative appreciation of an acquirer can be used as a means of financing its follow-on acquisitions (e.g., Vodafone's market appreciation helped it to acquire targets in bidding contests by paying in shares).

parties may have (perhaps markedly) different views as to its value. When bidding, managers and financial analysts both use comparable methods, but the valuations of assets acquired for specific strategic reasons (which maybe unique to one acquirer) can lead to misperceptions about value of the entire sector. Market prices can also deviate from fundamental values as happened in the dot-com bubble that affected the financial markets during the early 2000s. Given the vulnerability of financial market valuations to environmental turbulence, buyers would be well warned to assess the validity of comparable or relative valuations with a critical eye—unless a particular target has unique strategic value (for example, as part of a premeditated serial acquisition strategy) or offers significant unique synergies.

Financial markets were at the peak of their irrational exuberance at the turn of the millennium and, with "new economy" firms in hot demand into 2001, may have greatly overvalued the telecom industry's growth opportunities. Serial acquirers sometimes choose to finance their acquisitions with shares, thus taking advantage of the relative appreciation within the sector and at the same time hedging against whole-sector mispricing by financial markets. Vodafone countered the anxieties expressed about the costs of its serial acquisition strategy in this period by paying with its own shares, so as to benefit from the general rerating of the telecom industry at the time—in effect, their stock served as a useful currency helping to mitigate the risk that it might be overpaying for its fully priced targets.

POTENTIAL BIDDING PITFALLS

Even if the aforementioned obstacles to their acquisition strategies and valuations have been successfully negotiated, executives face yet another challenge to successful execution: *the bidding contest*, which appears in its starkest forms in bidding auctions and bidding wars. Auctions are seen as efficient ways to match bidders and targets—smooth, swift, and fair. However, when they are structured over several rounds, with only limited time for advisors to plough through information in data rooms (as is common in private equity auctions and privatizations), the threat that bidders can become overcommitted is increased. This process is similar in competitive bid situations for public companies: in either case, the costs—financial, emotional, and reputational—will escalate as the process unfolds.

PITFALL 5: ENTRAPMENT IN AN ESCALATING BIDDING CONTEST

Consider the classic thought experiment "War of Attrition" (described in Table 3.3), which shows how two rivals engaged in a bidding war can end up paying much more than the object is worth to justify their initial bidding expenses, exacerbated by the typical competitive instinct of behavior in auctions.

TABLE 3.3 BIASES THAT AFFECT BIDDING

Pitfall Bias/ Heuristic	Board Room Experiment	Description of Human Biases That Affect Bidding
Pitfall 5. Escalated commitment	Experiment: "War of Attrition" A £5 note is auctioned between two rivals in an English (i.e., ascending price) auction. Bids increase by £1 per round until one bidder gives up and the other wins the £5 note. *However, in this format the loser and the winner still both pay their highest bid.* In practice, the winning bid often exceeds £5, since neither rival wants to give up and have paid his or her bid unnecessarily. The above example is in some sense similar to a company auction, with costs of advisors that are sunk.	Escalation reflects the decision makers' unwillingness to admit they were mistaken to go this far in the first place. It often arises in situations in which the bidding process is costly, but there seems to be a possibility of achieving a better outcome by bidding further. Bidders should ignore the impact of prior investments if they are sunk. *The situation resembles waiting for a friend—if you have already invested 15 minutes, you are more likely to invest another 5; if you have already invested an hour, you are more likely to invest another 15 minutes.*
Pitfall 6. Winner's curse (can result from bias and information asymmetry)	Thought experiment: "The Winner's Curse" An undisclosed amount of small change in a wallet (taken randomly from a group member) is auctioned among the group. Bids are sealed and the highest wins the unknown amount. "What would you bid for an asset with an unknown value?" Participants will want to bid a margin below their estimate (which is inevitably uncertain and made on guesswork rather than evidence) to allow for profit, but high enough to win the auction. However the dynamic created by the combination of the uncertain value and selection of the highest bid often results in the winner being the bidder who most overestimates the target's value—which the winner subsequently regrets.	When the value of the asset being auctioned is uncertain, the winner is likely to overestimate its worth and bid too high. Even relying on a good valuation method can leave some uncertainty. A rational bidder should submit a bid at a price that is lower than his or her uncertain value estimate—and the less accurate the valuation, the lower the bid should be. The main lesson is the importance of gathering as much information as possible about the true fundamental value of the assets being sold.

Irrational escalation of commitment (*commitment bias*) reflects the choices of decision makers who are unwilling to admit that they were mistaken to have gone this far in the first place.[21] Decision makers can too often persist in bidding, even after the price exceeds the target value, simply to justify the actions

---

[21] See also Haunschild, Blake, and Fichman (1994) and Hietala, Kaplan, and Robinson (2003).

they have already taken. This often arises in situations in which the bidding process is costly, but where there still appears to be a possibility of achieving better outcomes by continuing to bid. Vodafone fought several such takeover battles in what was a rapidly consolidating industry: in particular, it had to outbid Bell Atlantic to buy AirTouch for $62 billion and, as noted earlier, was again forced to pay a substantial (70%) premium over the prevailing market price to win its hostile takeover battle for Mannesmann.

Entering a bidding contest is costly—bidders have to pay fees to their bankers, legal advisors, and consultants, whose reputations will often be as much on the line as are those of the focal company and its executives. Executives hate to admit that their past investments were ineffective, and what better way to reaffirm the value of their earlier acquisitions than by displaying even greater commitment to them through further investments? Group dynamics also play a role: executive teams (and even boards) become invested in the bid process, creating rationales to show why walking away would cost more in terms of reputation, momentum, loss of key skills, or even share price pressure. Pressure from their bankers can often reinforce such group logic for pushing on—"one more price increase will do it"—to the point of ignoring dissenting voices or contraindicating data.

This kind of escalation is, at least in part, related to the *sunk cost fallacy*—a phenomenon where increased investments are made mainly to justify cumulative prior investment decisions, even in the face of new evidence suggesting that those original decisions were probably wrong. When previous transactions along the serial acquisition path were justified on the basis of future transactions, it becomes even more difficult for a team to later back off from one of those future transactions, since they have come this far in their serial acquisition strategy.

In such strategies, the premium paid for a platform acquisition acquired as a precursor to the current target can even be seen as a sunk cost—thus acting as a further incentive to overpay. Worse still, powerful arguments can be made that the entire serial acquisition strategy will stall or even fail altogether unless the current target is acquired *at all costs*. Previous expenditures—such as on due diligence, consultancy, or financing, or even on a previous high premium platform acquisition—should *never* be used as arguments *by themselves* to continue bidding: they should be ignored, unless their nature and any associated learning provide real insights into whether it makes sense to continue.

PITFALL 6: THE WINNER'S CURSE—SUCCESSFUL BIDDING ON INACCURATE INFORMATION

Bidders in auctions are vulnerable not just to irrational escalated bidding: inaccurate information can also lead to auction bids that exceed the value of the acquisition. At the time of Vodafone's expansion, the winner's curse was quite common in the telecom industry, in auctions for licenses and acquisition bidding contests.[22]

When several bidders contemplate the acquisition of the same target company, they may not know the target's exact value when they bid. Where "good" information as to the target's value is difficult to come by—or is just uncertain—bidders are obliged to fall back on trying to estimate its value independently. When the company is worth (roughly) the same to all bidders, the *only* thing that distinguishes them will be their respective valuation estimates. The winner will thus be the one that makes the highest *estimate*. If, in fact, the *average* bid is accurate, then the winning bidder will be the one that has *most* overestimated the target's value, and so (by definition) is almost certain to have overpaid—the winner's curse.

Consider a simple numerical example of two different companies being auctioned, one with a well-defined value derived from ascertainable cash flows (A) and the other (B) with an uncertain value based on growth options. Suppose the value of company A is $2 billion: as this value is known, bidders will bid just under that level—high enough to outbid rival bidders, low enough to leave the transaction profitable. The range of bids will, therefore, be quite restricted, since they will be based on "good" information. However, in the company B case, where the asset is of (comparatively) unknown value, the increased uncertainty will mean a much wider distribution of bids, since they are all based (more or less entirely) on estimates. Suppose the bids vary from $1 billion to $3 billion, with an average (measured by the mean of their distribution) of $2 billion. As the auction rules ensure both companies are sold to the highest bidders, it is likely that company A's acquirer will have paid somewhat less than $2 billion, but the acquirer of the uncertain target B *is the one that most overestimated its value*—this "cursed" winner will pay $3 billion.

Imagine now the auctioning of an item of uncertain value when some bidders know more about the item than others—that is, a situation of *information asymmetry*. Anyone who has bought antiques at an auction will know the unpleasant feeling that creeps up on you when you have just outbid a professional trader or collector. They know more than you—you have almost certainly paid too much. Bidders who fail to take the possibility of information asymmetry into account are even more likely to fall foul of the winner's curse.

A situation that illustrates the winner's curse of hard to value assets was the 2000–2001 auction of 62 UMTS (3G) licenses in the European telecom market, which realized a total of €109 billion. Operators trying to consolidate their pan-European markets needed footholds in four key markets: France, Italy,

---

[22] However, in auctions with private value (i.e., when the target has a different value for each of the bidders) the winner's curse does not arise. See also Varaiya and Ferris (1987) and Thaler (1988) on the winner's curse.

Germany, and the United Kingdom. Buying several licenses sequentially would give them economies of scope and scale that would result in stronger strategic positions. The UK 3G network license, therefore, represented a platform investment, and the high prices paid in this auction partly reflected the extra value that was expected to result from follow-on investments in later auctions. The winners would benefit from a full-scale expansion, while those less successful would have a more restricted set of future opportunities. However, like the auctioning of many assets with elusive value, the sale led to a winner's curse. Market misperceptions of the value of these licenses were amplified by operators' overconfidence in their abilities to increase scale and this cumulative overvaluation caused even the average bid to be higher than the true value, further increasing the winning bid and the burden of the winner's curse. A fundamental (e.g., real option) valuation could have resulted in a clearer view of the worth of the optionality, while at the same time incorporating uncertainty into the value estimation model.

Even when a good valuation method is available, uncertainty will remain. A rational bidder should take account of the danger of the winner's curse and submit a bid that is lower than the value estimate; and the more uncertain the valuation, the lower the bid should be.[23] A seller should recognize that bidders' awareness of the winner's curse may lead them to bid more cautiously. Indeed, sellers at private equity auctions can be observed doing everything they can to limit uncertainty for buyers, for example, by providing strategy reports from consultants and approved leverage from financiers.

CAN RATIONAL ANALYSIS DISCIPLINE STRATEGY?

Executives need to be constantly aware of their potential biases if they are to protect themselves from making suboptimal decisions in their strategy, in company valuations, and in their bidding. But awareness alone may not be sufficient to ensure a successful consolidation strategy: psychologists have demonstrated that recognizing our errors and biases does not necessarily lead us to be able to correct them and exhibit more rational decision making.

Quantifications using a rational real options and games analysis may offer further help in mitigating the effects of several cognitive biases.[24] To avoid

---

[23] However, an actual overpayment will generally occur only if the winner fails to account for the winner's curse when bidding (an outcome that, according to the revenue equivalence theorem, need never occur).

[24] For articles on real options, see, for instance, Dixit and Pindyck (1995), Amram and Kulatilaka (1999b). In the strategy literature real options have been used for analyzing technology investments, international operations, and the ability of the firm to adapt to a changing competitive landscape. For instance, see Bowman and Hurry (1993), Kogut and Kulatilaka (1994a), Bettis and

overpayment, executives should use financial market valuations as a top-down, objective view based on growth option value that confirms or disconfirms the added value of consolidation, rather than depending solely on subjective management information or instinct. The advantage of integrating game theory into the options approach is that it explicitly recognizes value erosion and the interaction of rival bidders playing the game of musical chairs for available acquisitions under uncertainty. When a target is offered at an auction, or when multiple bidders make an offer for a publicly traded firm, value can be eroded if other buyers seem likely to bid up the price.

ILLUSTRATION: VODAFONE'S ACQUISITION STRATEGY AS A PORTFOLIO OF REAL OPTIONS

The appropriate way to structure a list of target options into a consolidation strategy is to map alternative *acquisition paths*—that is, to adopt a "lattice" approach, mapping long-term contingent series of acquisitions and organic investments against the key uncertainties that, as they are resolved, will modify the available options. With the help of some hindsight, Figure 3.1 presents a simplified illustration of the staged decision structure of Vodafone's strategy and of the synergistic opportunities arising from its acquisitions or alliances,[25] representing the sequential stages of its acquisition strategy as branches on a tree. Exercising its UK acquisition options gave Vodafone a dominating home market position that provided it with a platform that enabled it to pursue a worldwide network expansion strategy and leverage the competences it gained into follow-on acquisitions, as well as enhancing its cash flows via various cost and marketing efficiencies.

Vodafone executed a series of opportunistic platform acquisitions to position itself for multiple follow-on acquisitions using the buy-and-build principle. Vodafone's platform acquisitions in the United States, Europe, China, and Japan each provided the basis for growth in that region. Such acquisitions derive a significant part of their value by creating new paths for follow-on investment opportunities, altering both the position of the enterprise and its strategic course. For instance, Vodafone pursued a strategy of acquiring follow-on options in existing operations—sequentially increasing its shareholdings in Vodafone Libertel (Netherlands), Vodafone-Panafon Hellenic (Greece), Vodafone Telecel-Comunicacoes Pessoais SA (Portugal), and Europolitan Vodafone AB (Sweden)—the fundamental rationale being the delivery of growth.

Hitt (1995), Fichman, Keil, and Tiwana (2005), Kogut and Kulatilaka (2004), McCarter, Mahoney, and Northcraft (2011), and van Putten and Macmillan (2004).

[25] For articles on real options and acquisitions or joint ventures in the strategic management literature, see Chi (2000), Chi (1996), Chi and McGuire (1996), Miller and Folta (2002), Kogut (1991), Reuer and Tong (2005), and Smit (2001).

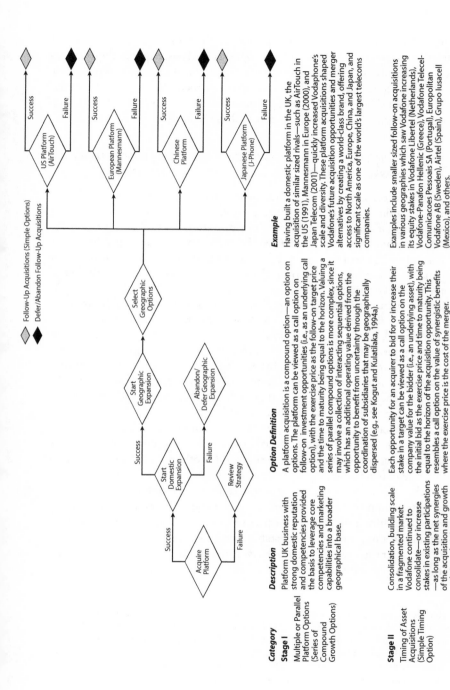

Follow-Up Acquisitions (Simple Options)

Defer/Abandon Follow-Up Acquisitions

Category	Description	Option Definition	Example
Stage I Multiple or Parallel Platform Options (Series of Compound Growth Options)	Platform UK business with strong domestic reputation and competencies provided the basis to leverage core competencies and marketing capabilities into a broader geographical base.	A platform acquisition is a compound option—an option on options. The platform can be viewed as a call option on follow-on investment opportunities (i.e., as an underlying call option), with the exercise price as the follow-on target price and the time to maturity being equal to the horizon. Valuing a series of parallel compound options is more complex, since it may involve a collection of interacting sequential options, which has an additional operating value derived from the opportunity to benefit from uncertainty through the coordination of subsidiaries that may be geographically dispersed (e.g., see Kogut and Kulatilaka, 1994a).	Having built a domestic platform in the UK, the acquisition of similar sized rivals—such as AirTouch in the US (1991), Mannesmann in Europe (2000), and Japan Telecom (2001)—quickly increased Vodaphone's scale and diversity. These platform acquisitions shaped Vodafone's future acquisition opportunities and merger alternatives by creating a world-class brand, offering access to North America, Europe, China, and Japan, and significant scale as one of the world's largest telecoms companies.
Stage II Timing of Asset Acquisitions (Simple Timing Option)	Consolidation, building scale in a fragmented market. Vodafone continued to consolidate—or increase stakes in existing participations—as long as the net synergies of the acquisition and growth options at that time were sufficiently valuable.	Each opportunity for an acquirer to bid for or increase their stake in a target can be viewed as a call option on the company value for the bidder (i.e., an underlying asset), with the initial bid as the exercise price and time to maturity being equal to the horizon of the acquisition opportunity. This resembles a call option on the value of synergistic benefits where the exercise price is the cost of the merger.	Examples include smaller sized follow-on acquisitions in various geographies which saw Vodafone increasing its equity stakes in Vodafone Libertel (Netherlands), Vodafone-Panafon Hellenic (Greece), Vodafone Telecel-Comunicacoes Pessoais SA (Portugal), Europolitan Vodafone AB (Sweden), Airtel (Spain), Grupo Iusacell (Mexico), and others.

Figure 3.1 Staged Decisions in Vodafone's Buy-and-Build Acquisition Strategy

The various types of acquisition options are the building blocks of a serial acquisition strategy. A bottom-up real options analysis requires the team to explicitly identify these types of options (e.g., platform or asset investment or divestment options) and to use option valuation methods (e.g., the binomial model) to value the set of real options embedded in the organization and its businesses. (Figure 3.1 describes several of these acquisition options types.)

OVERCOMING PITFALL 1: REAL OPTIONS CAN MITIGATE EFFECTS FROM NARROW FRAMING OR AVERSION TO CERTAIN LOSSES

Aversion to a certain loss may result in overinvestment, even in the face of contraindications, while narrow framing can mean potential buyers not taking full advantage of acquisition opportunities' upward potential, thus missing the boat in a consolidating industry. When the success of a serial acquisition strategy is redefined in terms of options and uncertainty, it provides a rationale for implementing, altering, or deferring decisions, depending on the evolution of the external environment.

First, as discussed in the previous chapter, a real options approach can mitigate the biases that lead to a conservative strategy that is based on overly narrow framing. A platform acquisition is no longer considered in isolation, but rather as the first link in a chain of investments, where earlier investments are prerequisites for those that follow. Interestingly, according to real option theory, business risk or dispersion of future company values can exert substantial *positive* influence on the value of real growth options, and may justify (staged) acquisition decisions even in uncertain areas.[26]

Second, the appropriate use of a real options approach should help prevent overinvestment due to aversion to certain losses. Real options analysis focuses on flexibility: as information about the success (or otherwise) of a staged acquisition strategy is revealed, management can decide whether (or when) to proceed to the next stage, or to alter or even terminate its future investment plans. A real options approach dictates that it is preferable to increase option value by phasing acquisition processes in uncertain regions (such as emerging markets), first acquiring a minority stake or establishing a joint venture to gain entry into a new market, rather than rolling out investments quickly in (maybe multiple) commitment-intensive acquisitions.

---

[26] This insight, which may be surprising at first glance, hinges on the fact that if the platform entry fails, the follow-on acquisitions need not be made. In other words, if the entry fails, then only the relatively smaller foothold investment is lost. On the other hand, more can be gained from the riskier markets because of the better chance of exceptionally high returns in a growth stage. As a result, the growth option value today of the high-risk markets will be larger than otherwise similar low uncertainty markets (all other things equal).

OVERCOMING PITFALL 2: WHICH JUDGMENT BIASES CAN A REAL OPTIONS FRAME MITIGATE AND WHICH CAN IT NOT?

Judgment biases among the top team will change the way a strategy is conceived and presented, and will tend to implicitly support the assumption that things will turn out exactly as predicted in the strategic plan. An illusion of control may lead to a static strategy that continues to aim at acquiring originally intended targets, irrespective of whether they are no longer attractive or relevant in a changing business environment. Furthermore, confirmation bias enforced by groupthink may render acquisition plans inflexible—real options can help mitigate these problems to some extent.

The real options view does not consider the successful execution of a serial acquisition strategy as being a process that is entirely under the control of the executives, but rather one that is partly conditional on the external uncertainty and subject to extraneous events. A real options approach analyzes the business environment by assigning probability distributions and values to uncertain macroeconomic, industry, or business developments. Explicitly requiring management to model external uncertainty limits self-serving biases, such as where an executive team unconsciously credits its own actions when acquisitions succeed and blames bad luck when they fail.

A warning should be issued at this point. As noted in chapter 2, valuation models—including real options—can be used for self-justification or rationalization. Framing acquisition opportunities as real options can lead executives to see options everywhere, and executives should take care to avoid taking an overoptimistic view of acquisitions' growth options in hot deal markets to justify higher bids. To suppress overvaluation of growth option values, targets should be selected from a comprehensive list, and care should be taken not to overestimate the levels of added value—in terms of either synergies or future options—associated with each one. Judgment biases can also serve to increase the value of growth options so as to justify or rationalize intended investment decisions; this is a weakness of any valuation method, including a real options analysis. One way of limiting overvaluation is to integrate real options analysis with game theory; another way is to check valuations against (presumably more) objective values in financial markets.

DUAL VALUATION OF GROWTH OPTION VALUE TO AVOID IRRATIONAL INFECTION

As with all analyses, the high degree of subjectivity inherent in designing acquisition paths and the variables used in real options analysis mean that the associated techniques can also be used inappropriately to justify a preferred course of action or higher bidding prices. The fundamental valuation of a consolidation strategy should be subjected to a reality test by comparing it with the value of assets and growth options of industry players of different sizes and using various strategies. Shareholder value must be the key criterion in assessing an acquisition, so the value added by a firm's consolidation strategy should ultimately at least equal the amount by which the future value of the consolidating firm exceeds the sum of the costs of its individual acquisitions and of any organic growth it pursues. This top-down analysis can function as a reality check on a fundamental valuation by using option game tools to determine the value of its current operations, their embedded options, and those that might arise from its intended acquisition.

The gap between the company's market value and the present value of the earnings capacity of its assets in place represents the value the market assigns to the firm's strategy to appropriate profitable corporate growth opportunities—or its "implied PVGO,"[27] that is,

$$\text{Implied PVGO} = \text{Market Value (MV)} - \text{Assets in Place (PV)}$$

Consider, for example, an estimation of the proportion of Mannesmann's 1996 stock price made up of the present value of its future growth options (PVGO/P). The (then) present value of its assets in place can be relatively easily estimated. Suppose that its 1996 earnings were DM22 per share and the cost of equity was 11%, and assume that the earnings capacity of its current assets would have been constant under a hypothetical no-growth strategy. The perpetuity equation results in share values of DM200 for the capitalized value of its earnings from assets in place (under a no growth policy). However, since Mannesmann's average 1996 equity price was DM550, the market's assessment of the PVGO embedded in its stock price amounted to DM350—some 64% of its stock market value.

The value imputed from a growth option analysis is most helpful when considering the relative value of possible targets—or the value of a specific target to different potential bidders. For consolidation to make sense, an efficient financial market should assign a higher value to leading companies' assets in

---

[27] PVGO = Market Value − Assets in Place = MV − PV (earnings). See Myers (1977). It is customary to normalize this equation by dividing PVGO by MV. A related version of the equation is suggested by Tony Tong and Jeffrey Reuer (2008), who estimate PVGO using economic value added: PVGO = Market Value − (Capital Invested + Present Value of Economic Value Added). Both metrics measure the difference between market price and a more or less refined accounting value. Growth options value was first empirically studied by Kester (1984). More recently, growth options value has been related to systematic risk (Chung and Charoenwong, 1991), R&D, uncertainty, and the skewness of returns, to the pricing of initial public offerings (Chung, Minsheng, and Yu 2005), to idiosyncratic risk (Cao, Simin, and Zhao 2006), to firm, industry, and country effects (Tong et al. 2008), to downside risk of multinational corporations (Tong and Reuer 2008), and to international joint ventures (Tong et al. 2007).

place (PV) and growth opportunities than to those of smaller firms. The larger firms' lower cost of capital results in an appreciation of their assets in place, and their better growth prospects should be reflected in higher PVGO-to-price (and EV/EBITDA) ratios than those of smaller players. Vodafone's average PVGO-to-price was only slightly higher than those of its largest acquisitions—such as AirTouch (PVGO-to-price of 85%)[28] or Mannesmann (PVGO-to-price of 90%),[29] but considerably higher than its smaller targets (e.g., Libertel had a PVGO-to-price of 69%).

OVERCOMING PITFALL 3: CAN BOTTOM-UP OPTION VALUATION PREVENT OVERRELIANCE ON RELATIVE VALUES AND HEURISTICS?

Since the value of a strategic acquisition derives from its ability to enhance a consolidator's strategic position (including giving it valuable future options to expand and to acquire), the valuation of platform acquisitions requires careful scrutiny and more sophisticated competitive analysis than either that offered by a simple relative valuation or suggested by heuristics. A combined real options and game theory framework can incorporate the elusive strategic value that is so difficult to capture when using anchors as starting points. This analysis is beneficial in quantifying the merits of strategic alternatives and in helping assess trade-offs, so that price tags can be attached to investment decisions.

However, companies should be careful about inferring that rational analysis is "truth"—the misperception that once numbers are attached, data are accurate. Although we argue that analysis can be sensitive to biases, we do *not* therefore suggest that strategic intuition is necessarily flawed. Real options and game techniques can complement the intuitive strategic thinking process in a dynamic way that will be consistent with that strategy's underlying logic and design. It is essential to translate the qualitative discussion of a course of action into a proper options structure and to identify its strategic elements. Game theory, supplemented by options analysis, helps to tackle the complex strategic problem involved in this process and reduce it to a simpler analytical structure. The framework it provides can also offer clear management guidance for executable actions by steering managers' decisions as to whether, when, and under what conditions investments would be appropriate. It also provides the vital link between strategy and the quantification of value creation.

[28] For AirTouch the four-year average (92% in 1995, 89% in 1996, 77% in 1997, and 82% in 1998) is based on yearly average stock price before acquisition and a cost of capital of 11%. For Mannesmann the four-year average is based on 64% in 1996, 99% in 1979, 99% in 1998, and 97% in 1999.
[29] PVGO/Price of an acquisition typically increases compared to the stand-alone PVGO/Price due to the acquisition premium.

OVERCOMING PITFALL 4: CAN FINANCIAL MARKETS PROVIDE AN EXTERNAL VIEW?

The PVGO measure is arguably contingent on market sentiment. Evidence suggests that takeover activity is strongly related to stock market valuations.[30] The relative value of leading companies allows them to acquire serial targets relatively cheaply, taking advantage of their highly valued equity to finance their transactions.[31] A serial acquisition strategy can be based on rational value drivers, but also on the market mispricing specific targets or entire sectors—the case of Vodafone seems to be consistent with these findings: its acquisitions were concentrated in the period 1998 to 2000 when its share price was at its peak.[32] A bidder may try to select a target that offers better value for its higher value equity.

Empirical studies typically separate market value into intrinsic and mispriced elements. We can separate out these behavioral finance arguments in a new decomposition of firm value. Our method "backs out" the value of the growth option set from the firm's equity value, but with the modification that the market value is adjusted for mispricing. The present value of growth options (PVGO) can be estimated from the value of assets in place and the adjusted market value of the firm. This is done by first using a pricing model to estimate the mispricing in overall market value and deducting from the market capitalization (MV) both any excess (mispriced) value (XSP) as well as the present value (PV) component on the same basis as before (i.e., continuing current operations based on past investments or assets in place in a no-growth scenario and estimated using standard NPV techniques). The remaining (residual) equity value is taken to reflect the value of the firm's set of growth options (PVGO).[33] That is,

---

[30] For instance, see Rhodes-Kropf and Viswanathan (2004); Dong et al. (2006).

[31] A popular proxy for mispricing is the ratio of market value to book value. For instance, Rhodes-Kropf, Robinson, and Viswanathan (2005) find that bidders have a larger MV/B than targets, but both have higher MV/Bs than nonmergers.

[32] Empirical studies also show that targets are in general undervalued relative to bidders, or at least less overpriced by financial markets. Shleifer and Vishny (2003).

[33] For an extensive empirical study on growth options value and mispricing, see van Bekkum, Smit, and Pennings (2011). To estimate the fundamental price P, we adopt the methodology as recently applied in a takeover context by Rhodes-Kropf, Robinson, and Viswanathan (2005), who estimate fundamental value (as opposed to observed market value) from an asset pricing model by Fama and MacBeth (1973). In this model, fundamental value is estimated as the predicted value from a series of simple OLS regressions, estimated by year and industry. This procedure is also employed in the accounting literature on value relevance (Penman 1998; Francis and Schipper 1999; Barth, Beaver, and Landsman 2001). One advantage of this computation is that it measures mispricing at the firm level, which serves our purpose in estimating the fundamental value equation. The fundamental value of firm i in an industry j at time t is derived from the regression equation,

$$\ln(\widehat{MV}) = \alpha_{0jt} + \alpha_{1jt}\ln(B)_{ijt} + \alpha_{2jt}\ln(NI)^{+}_{ijt} + \alpha_{3jt}I_{NI<0}\ln(NI)^{+}_{ijt} + \alpha_{4jt}LEV_{ijt}$$

Implied PVGO = Market Value (MV) – Excess Pricing (XSP)
– Net Value of Assets in Place (PV)

Firms in growth industries (e.g., computers, software, drugs) tend, on average, to have a higher growth option value component (PVGO/MV) than firms in annuity-generating industries, for two reasons. First, they operate in more volatile and rapidly evolving environments (characterized by more frequent technological innovations and more intense competition), with this higher underlying volatility translating into higher (simple) option values. Second, they tend to have a higher proportion of compound (multistage or growth) than simple (cash-generating) options, which (since these are options on options) further amplifies their strategic value. This higher growth option value, in turn, is translated into higher market valuations for such high-tech or growth stocks.

HOW TO USE OPTION GAMES TO OVERCOME BIDDING PITFALLS

Vodafone's hostile $205 billion acquisition of Mannesmann in Germany was an example of escalated bidding. The European market was undergoing rapid consolidation and the limited acquisition opportunities in the industry were hotly contested. Vodafone had to secure its place as a key European operator against its main rivals, such as Germany's T-Mobile. The higher valuation of Mannesmann relative to Vodafone stemmed partly from it representing a potential target platform in Germany for those seeking to secure a dominant position in the consolidating European telecom sector.

Suppose that the stand-alone value of Mannesmann could be estimated at $71 billion, the synergies at $2 billion, and the divestment options at $50 billion.[34] The expanded NPV with the additional strategic value component could therefore be calculated as follows:

Expanded NPV = [net stand-alone value of platform + divestment
options – price] + [expected synergies + strategic growth option
value from Mannesmann in European expansion]

$$= [71 + 50 - 205] + [2 + \text{strategic growth option value}]$$

$$= [\text{strategic growth option value}] - 82$$

---

where MV is market capitalization, B the book value, NI^* the absolute value of net income, LEV the leverage of a company defined *as total debt/(market equity value + total debt)*, and $I_{(NI<0)}$ an indicator function for negative income observations. This allows for including firms with negative income so that α_{2jt} can be interpreted as an earnings multiple, while at the same time firm value can be adjusted downward through α_{3jt} if an industry has negative income in a given year.

[34] Vodafone agreed to divest Orange.

So, even though Vodafone's acquisition gained it embedded platforms in two of Europe's most important mobile telecom markets (Germany and Italy), justifying its final bid for Mannesmann involved effectively estimating the value of the strategic growth options at $82 billion—a figure so high it could be considered unlikely. One could surmise, then, that Vodafone's preemptive bid was motivated (at least in part) by its desire to win, rather than fairly reflecting the fundamental growth option value of its acquisition.

Naturally, the growth option value for a consolidator created through potential future acquisitions is the excess value of the targets to the successful acquirer over their acquisition price; that is, the firm's ability to extract synergistic value from those acquisitions beyond what it pays for them. In the option game approach, the potential for making acquisitions is assessed on *both* their value *and* price characteristics. In this context the *value* of such acquisitions is what those targets are potentially worth *to each bidder*, based on the impact on that bidder's accumulation path. *Price*, on the other hand, is what the successful bidder ultimately pays.

OVERCOMING PITFALL 5: CAN ONE AVOID IRRATIONAL ESCALATION IN BIDDING AND PLAY POKER BY BETTING AGAINST RIVALS' PREDICTABLE BIASES?

In the run-up to an auction, a biased rival bidder will behave differently to a rational bidder. Rivals who are biased and/or overconfident may fail to see all the consequences of their actions, so that while rational players perceive the decisions in a game clearly and consistently, rivals who still base their decisions on heuristics or have psychological biases may outbid them in auctions.

Acquisition games are therefore better applied if rationality is combined with insights from behavioral economics, so bidders can predict their rivals' *irrational* behaviors and respond to them *rationally*.[35] The rational bidder should take an opportunistic view, but try to avoid battles that lead to escalating commitment to bidding. As noted, overcommitment arises in situations in which the bidding process is costly, but there still seems to be the possibility of achieving better outcomes by bidding further. This is particularly so when acquisition value is hard to ascertain, when multiple bidders are interested, or when bidders have experienced successes in acquisition battles. While an overconfident and overoptimistic rival is hard to beat in a bidding contest without paying an excess premium, executives must remember that exiting the bidding game can also be a valuable option.

Indeed, rational bidders can "play poker" against biased rivals, aiming to exploit their psychological strategy biases. For instance, in the early stages of industry consolidation, rivals may have too conservative a strategy and frame acquisitions too narrowly, holding them back from making what they perceive

---

[35] Camerer (2003).

as risky consolidating acquisitions. Recognizing this bias allows a canny consolidator to identify where and when to make an early bid to avoid ending up in a bidding contest later in the game. Vodafone's aggressive buildup strategy allowed it to seize the initiative in the growing but still fragmented telecom market by moving before its rivals into an aggressive acquisition growth program that enabled the enlarged firm to gain increasing market share and become an industry leader in a growing sector. The revelation of the success of Vodafone's acquisition strategy triggered a series of mergers and acquisitions in the industry, changing the probability of success of specific strategies. In the endgame, rival consolidators may end up in a negative-sum game, with intense competition for assets, overcommitment, and bidding wars reducing the economic pie by attracting capital into the industry at excessive levels relative to the potential returns.

OVERCOMING BIDDING PITFALL 6: CAN PLAYERS' UNIQUE POSITIONS AVOID THE WINNER'S CURSE?

To avoid the winner's curse, a rational bidder should try to gather information and develop an independent view about the fundamental value of a target, both to the company itself and to its rivals. The winner's curse underscores the importance of relying on fundamental methods for valuing targets in competitive settings. As already discussed, when a target's value is illusive and there are multiple bidders, some may overvalue the assets on sale, and others undervalue them. So it is crucial that a firm makes every effort to improve its information about a target, certainly to try to gain superior information to that available to rival bidders.

Savvy bidders will avoid the winner's curse by "shading" their bid, setting it below their (ex ante) estimation of the uncertain value of the target. The less accurate their valuation (e.g., the higher growth option value it includes), the lower the bid should be. The severity of the winner's curse increases with the number of bidders, and also when the average bid is higher relative to exterior market conditions because of judgment biases.

The winner's curse does not apply to all auctions. In the early stages of industry consolidation there may be occasions when the average bid is too low relative to the target's fundamental value, for example, when biased rivals are too conservative and have not yet recognized the target's potential strategic value to an acquirer. Similarly, bidders from different contexts—for example, a private equity bidder versus a strategic player, or a consolidator versus a nonconsolidating bidder—are likely to assign different values to the same target. When the company has private value (i.e., when it generates unique synergies), the winner's curse also does not arise.

The key question is the extent to which the acquirer can develop a unique and advantaged position in its path to appropriate further growth options compared to other firms involved in similar buy-and-build strategies. The factors affecting each firm's growth options may also differ, generating significant differences in how they exercise and time their bids. It is precisely in these circumstances that the consolidating bidder's ability to assess the strategic value of a target as accurately as possible—within the context of its defined serial acquisition strategy—becomes essential to ensuring it continues to deliver sustained growth in shareholder value.

Company- and context-specific platform path dependencies will mean the value of a specific follow-on target to one potential acquirer is unlikely to equal its value to another, and this will cause a variance between its inherent value and the ultimate price different bidders are willing to pay. Organizational capabilities and their set of corporate real options—and the impact of uncertainty itself—will differ for each firm. Exercising the option to expand, for instance, is going to be more valuable for a consolidator than for a nonconsolidating player, especially if the consolidator is a market leader by virtue of its size, earlier acquisitions, and complementary assets. Naturally, a realistic review of potential interlopers into the bidding process must be performed, as well as an evaluation of the unique incremental value of the target to each rival bidder, taking their different synergies and strategic objectives into account.

The optimal route for consolidators in these circumstances may well be to seize the advantage by taking preemptive action at relatively low prices, and target selection should be based on to securing increasing advantage. If the consolidating company has already established a dominant position in its industry, the threat of preemption by a smaller rival is reduced, unless the rival is able to capture a blocking position—for example by securing a small but decisive stake in a desirable target.

CONCLUSIONS

Many industries are witnessing accelerating consolidation trends—driven by both fundamental economic forces and behavioral biases—that will continue to dictate the value of consolidating companies and their targets. In order to be more successful than their competitors, organizations must seek ways to maximize their ability to identify and capture new opportunities, while also being able to respond appropriately to economic changes, by deferring or abandoning intended acquisitions as industry or economic situations change, or by contracting production capacity to limit losses from adverse market developments. The execution of a serial acquisition strategy is vulnerable to the way managers perceive risk and losses, judgment biases in their strategy, the bidding behavior of rivals, and mispricing in financial markets. Table 3.4 provides a summary of the important pitfalls for firms seeking to execute serial acquisition strategies and how to overcome them.

TABLE 3.4 SUMMARY OF HOW TO OVERCOME PITFALLS IN SERIAL ACQUISITIONS

Pitfall	Behavioral Bias	How to Overcome or Mitigate the Pitfall
1. Overinvestment or overconservatism in consolidating industries	• Loss aversion • Narrow framing	A real options view widens our frame and can help prevent over- (or under-) investment due to loss aversion
2. Judgment biases result in overinvestment in an acquisition strategy	• Overconfidence • Illusion of control	Real options mitigate static scenario thinking and uncertainty neglect
3. Relative valuation with insufficient adjustment	• Anchoring • Representativeness bias	Bottom-up fundamental valuation prevents overreliance on relative values and heuristics
4. Mispricing in financial markets	• Common misperception • Irrational herding	Dual top-down and bottom-up valuation corrects for mispricing
5. Entrapment in an escalating bidding contest	• Over commitment • The sunk cost fallacy	Option thinking allows abandoning escalating auctions and stimulates opportunism in the low cycle
6. Bidding on inaccurate information	• The "winner's curse"	Cautious bidding awaiting resolution of uncertainty

The various behavioral biases at play can make competitive interactions in the acquisition game increasingly complex and sophisticated. The existing toolkit for company valuation and acquisition strategy—present value and traditional strategy approaches—falls short in guarding against such biases. We argue that using more sophisticated analysis tools, applying real options, with extensions based on game theory and modified market valuations, can result in a strategy that is at once more rational and more dynamic.

The decision analysis should be complemented with a top-down PVGO quantification that uses direct information from financial markets to counter irrationality on the inappropriate use of this new tool to justify overpayment.

Vodafone's acquisition history provides various examples of the behavioral problems involved in consolidation acquisitions. Although Vodafone's huge expansion was perceived as being built on the personal ambition of the CEO, without his efforts Vodafone could not have expanded to become the world leader it is today. Analyzing this behavioral dilemma with the approach advocated in this chapter requires

1. Considering the acquisitions strategy through a real options lens

2. Performing a reality check using top-down (PVGO) valuations

3. Using a game theory extension to analyze the price in the competitive bidding situation

First, to look at the growth strategy through a real options lens, while Vodafone's CEO was sometimes accused of managerial hubris (pitfall 2), he framed Vodafone's strategy in a manner consistent with a *real option* view (and much more broadly than some of his conservative [pitfall 1] competitors). From this perspective, Vodafone's Mannesmann acquisition delivered embedded platforms in two of Europe's most important mobile telecom markets (Germany and Italy) as part of a global strategy that targeted platform acquisitions across multiple geographies.

Second, top-down (PVGO) valuation requires that company valuation and financing takes into account financial markets' (biased) appreciations of growth options. Financial markets were at the peak of their irrational exuberance at the turn of the millennium, and may have greatly overvalued the entire telecom industry's growth opportunities (pitfall 4). Following the insights from the top-down or market method, the excess pricing of Vodafone's own shares—a result of the general overrating of the telecom industry at the time—in effect gave it the potential to overpay for its fully priced targets. "New economy" firms were in hot demand into 2001, and it would be going too far to hold Vodafone responsible for the general overvaluation of the telecom industry. Moreover, the costs of its serial acquisition strategy and of building the company to be the world leader it is today were—in effect—borne by those investors who bought Vodafone shares at the top of the cycle in 2001.

Third, the *option game* approach is not only about option values, but also about price and the bidding game. Even though Vodafone's Mannesmann acquisition provided a powerful step into new markets, justifying its final Mannesmann bid effectively estimated the value of the strategic growth options involved at some $82 billion—a figure so high one would consider it unrealistic from an *option game* perspective. One could surmise that Vodafone's bid might have been motivated in part by its desire to win (pitfall 5) rather than fairly reflecting the target's fundamental real option value. The general market context made telecom assets difficult to value—so making auction bidders vulnerable to the winner's curse (pitfall 6)—and estimates were often overly dependent on relative valuation of the target's peers or of rival bids (pitfall 3). In the next chapters we discuss application of these three valuation tools in more depth.

SUGGESTED READING

Copeland, T. E., and P. Tufano. 2004. "A Real-World Way to Manage Real Options." *Harvard Business Review* 82, no. 3: 90–99.

Miller, K. D., and Z. Shapira. 2004. "An Empirical Test of Heuristics and Biases Affecting Real Option Valuation." *Strategic Management Journal* 25, no. 3: 269–84.

Shefrin, H. 2007. *Behavioral Corporate Finance: Decisions That Create Value*. New York: McGraw-Hill.

SUGGESTED MATERIALS, TOOLS, AND GADGETS

Han Smit's site on valuation tools provides executive games. Links to the page can be found on this book's Princeton University Press website: http://press .princeton.edu/titles/10333.html.

PART II

LEARNING TO ADAPT TO UNCERTAINTY

CHAPTER 4

STRATEGY AS OPTIONS GAMES

Price is what you pay. Value is what you get.

—Warren Buffet

In 1996, the European private equity investor HAL Investments agreed to buy Pearle Benelux, a leading optical chain in Belgium and the Netherlands, and made further acquisitions in the same industry in Belgium and the Netherlands as well as in Germany, Austria, and Italy.[1] Some independent financial buyers work with permanent financing, in which the funds invested and any cash flows generated are available for an unlimited time, enabling them to pursue long-term buy-and-build strategies. In contrast to standard roll-ups and quick restructuring strategies—which typically aim to turn investments around in two to three years—a buy-and-build acquisition strategy is a longer-term sequential activity with a typical planning horizon of five or more years.

Similar acquisition strategies to that executed by HAL have been employed by acquirers in other consolidating industries—for example, in telecom, mining and metals, and the retail industry by Vodafone, Xstrata, ArcelorMittal, and various private-equity-backed retail chains. The management team envisions a series of transactions based on buy-and-build principles, in which they initially acquire a "platform" in a sector and then leverage their newly acquired core competencies and assets into follow-on acquisitions over a wider geographic, product, or customer base. However, executing a serial acquisition strategy is a difficult task in the real and uncertain world, where forces such as competitor preemption or unpredictable macroeconomic change may render intended targets unavailable or unattractive.

---

[1] The views in this chapter are further developed in Han Smit's article "Acquisition Strategies as Option Games" (2001). He would like to thank the editor of *Journal of Applied Corporate Finance* Don Chew and anonymous referees for their comments and suggestions that have benefited this article.

Traditional strategy approaches analyze general industry conditions and attractiveness.[2] The sources of competitive advantage and value creation achieved through consolidation result (externally) from an improved, more concentrated industry structure, an improvement in the consolidator's strategic positioning and its potential to make acquisitions and/or (internally) through the leverage of unique competences. Where antitrust barriers form no impediment, fully utilizing the cost advantages of consolidation—such as economies of scale, economies of scope, and learning cost effects—can enhance a company's power to retaliate against possible entrants, or limit the threat of substitution and improving its capacity for making follow-on acquisitions.

The impact of uncertainty is not fully developed in traditional strategy and company valuation approaches, which, as a result, are unable to fully conceptualize important aspects of potential future acquisition decisions and how they might impact the strategy execution path. A traditional net present value (NPV) analysis of a set of forecasted cash flows from a single transaction does not capture the full value of a platform acquisition, since much of its value derives from the acquirer's option to build on its initial acquisition by expanding either organically (internally) or through further acquisitions. Prominent private equity firms such as Hicks Muse Tate & Furst, Warburg Pincus, and Golder Thoma Cressey Rauner—and specialized publicly traded funds—also provide capital and actively pursue industry consolidations. Such investors recognize that pricing the first of an expected series of acquisitions requires a dynamic analysis of the target's synergistic growth potential. One of many buy-and-build examples is Hicks Muse Tate & Furst's acquisition of DuPont's connector systems unit (later renamed Berg Electronics) in 1993. Its buy-and-build strategy included seven follow-on acquisitions, which improved Berg's efficiency in marketing and distribution. In 1996 Berg went public and was eventually acquired by Framatome in 1998, providing a generous return to its shareholders.

This chapter develops a framework for assessing the value generated by both the option-like and competitive characteristics of an acquisition strategy. The conceptual approach is based on real options and principles from game theory. In an illustration of the approach in Box 4.1, Judy Lewent explains how she uses real options and games thinking in her strategic decision making at a major pharmaceutical company. The method treats an acquisition strategy as a package of corporate real options actively managed by the firm in a context of competitive responses or changing market conditions. This framework can help management answer several questions that are important for a successful ac-

---

[2] Acquisitions may change an industry's structural conditions and competitive forces—see Porter (1980). A bid may benefit rivals or invite competitive reactions, and additional strategic value may lie in improving an acquirer's strategic position by changing the industry environment—see Shapiro (1989), Farrell and Shapiro (1990), and Perry and Porter (1985). Consolidation is considered one of the driving forces of acquisitions in the 1990s—see Holmstrom and Kaplan (2001).

BOX 4.1 OPTIONS AND GAMES AT MERCK

Risk, complexity, and uncertainty define the business environment. While there is broad agreement about the need to manage within an ever-changing context, few have suggested a framework for managing risk or a set of tools to help cope with uncertainty. Yet that is precisely what Judy Lewent, CFO of Merck & Co., Inc., and her 500-member finance team have developed to deal with the high-stakes nature of the pharmaceutical industry. [On average, it costs $359 million and takes ten years to bring a drug to market. Once there, seven out of ten products fail to return the cost of the company's capital investment.]

"To me, all kinds of business decisions are options," says Judy Lewent. "I believe strongly that financial theory, properly applied, is critical to managing in an increasingly complex and risky business climate. I think that finance departments can take the nuances, the intuitive feelings that really fine business people have and quantify them. In that way, they can capture both the hard financials of a project and the strategic intent."

"When you are in a situation like this [involving the acquisition of another company like Medco], with many players, I think it is instructive to use game theory analysis. Game theory suggests one optimal strategy if the game ends after one play. However, since this particular game won't be over in one play, game theory forces you to see a business situation over many periods from two perspectives: yours and your competitor's."

"Tremendous spillover benefits arise as a result of scientists' propensity to publish and exchange ideas, particularly at the discovery stage; yet this in no way diminishes the highly competitive nature of the research process."

"On the business end, we also think that sharing information can be more productive than hiding it. And I believe that business is more productively done in an expanding market than in a shrinking market."

"When we came out with our antihypertensive Vasotec, Bristol-Myers Squibb had already launched Capoten. Both drugs have roughly the same method of action. The strategy that we adopted was not to cannibalize the Capoten markets. Rather, we wanted to go after the tenfold additional patients who were on older, less safe and less effective medicines. In that way, we could expand the market for both companies."

"How do we know when to support a rival and when to compete more aggressively? The paradox is that we perform in both modes at the same time. For example, we formed joint ventures such as The Du Pont Merck Pharmaceutical Company and the Johnson & Johnson Merck Consumer Pharmaceuticals Co. We brought together organizations with distinctly different strengths in a financial framework that helps each party achieve

BOX 4.1 (CONT.)

its strategic objectives. The agreements also help each partner diversify risk by sharing future investment and financial gain. The downside is that while we strengthen our own position with these 50% owned ventures, we are also building new competitor companies."

"But the most interesting aspect of this is to think about the nature of innovation in the drug industry. What exactly does it take to make the kind of scientific breakthrough necessary to create a new drug, one with significant therapeutic value? That intangible element of insight makes all the difference in our industry."

Source: Reprinted by permission of *Harvard Business Review* from Nichols, N. A. 1994. "Scientific Management at Merck." *Harvard Business Review* 72, no. 1: 88–99. Copyright © 1994 by the Harvard Business Review School Publishing Corporation; all rights reserved.

quisition strategy: How valuable are the growth opportunities created by the acquisition? How can we best sequence the acquisition options in the strategy? When is it appropriate to grow organically, and when are strategic acquisitions the preferred route? How is the industry likely to respond, and how will that affect the value of our acquisitions and future targets? How do we deal with our own investment biases and the likely biases of rivals? New research makes it possible for such strategic considerations to be analyzed in a formal and rigorous fashion that is consistent with the tenets of both market economics and modern financial theory. The subsequent sections present a series of frameworks to address these questions.

CLASSIFYING ACQUISITION OPTIONS UNDER COMPETITION

In attempting to quantify the value of a buy-and-build strategy, for example, acquisitions are viewed no longer as stand-alone investments, but rather as links in a chain of interrelated investments in which the early investments are prerequisites which set the path for those that follow.

The flexibility of a sequential or staged acquisition strategy can provide great benefits to the investor when there is major uncertainty about industry consolidation. Once uncertainty about the success of the first stage of the consolidation is resolved, management can expand operations or simply decide not to proceed with the next stage (i.e., not exercise the real option or sell the company to another player). This option can be analyzed as an "exchange" option—

a kind of option in which the value to the buyer is traded or exchanged against a future price or value.[3] However, there is an important element missing in the standard real options approach—namely, the competitive setting. Few investment opportunities, whether they are organic investments or acquisitions, exist in a vacuum—other industry players can be expected to react in some way. For example, acquisition of a target could set off a series of acquisitions by competitors, thereby preventing the firm from carrying out the follow-on bids it had planned. Or, the initial acquisition could have the opposite effect—of discouraging would-be competitors and solidifying the firm's first-mover status. The integration of real options valuation from corporate finance with game theory and principles of competition allows for a complete assessment of the flexibility value of an acquisition strategy in an interactive competitive setting.

In a buy-and-build strategy, the trajectory of target options needs to be continuously developed and refined according to the company's current and future portfolio needs, as driven by the potential for increased shareholder returns. For example, a traditional classification for mining acquisitions would be based on size, geographic, or currency diversification and access to new and/or attractive assets or commodities. An option-based classification of targets, based on their growth option value and price nature, can help account for potential growth in the value of an acquisition as it alters a firm's competitive position, its likely future trajectory, and thus its value in financial markets.

In developing its serial acquisition paths, a firm might acquire another company to increase its PVGO, but it does not necessarily follow that the acquirer will be able to appropriate all (or even any) of the acquisition's value. In the context of classifying targets in terms of their option value, therefore, the acquisition *value* is what the target is worth to each bidder, based on the impact acquiring it would have on its future accumulation path. The *price*, on the other hand, is what the successful bidder ultimately pays and depends on whether it is a *proprietary* or a *shared* option.

Classifying investment opportunities based on their real options characteristics, as shown in Figure 4.1, helps focus managerial attention on acquisitions' embedded strategic and growth option value. To identify and sequence potential acquisitions in the strategy, we classify potential acquisition targets based on their *option value* characteristics. Those that are likely to realize their benefits primarily through synergies or expected earnings streams (or operating cash flows) are classified here as *asset acquisition options*. Examples might include the divestiture of an unwanted division or an acquisition used to share assets to achieve more efficient use of production facilities (i.e., to exploit economies of scale), or a late-stage acquisition to manage excess capacity in a mature industry that generates incremental cash flows but lacks potential for synergistic follow-on acquisitions. The fundamental rationale for acquiring them is

---

[3]   For a numerical model of the exchange option in a financial context, see Margrabe (1978).

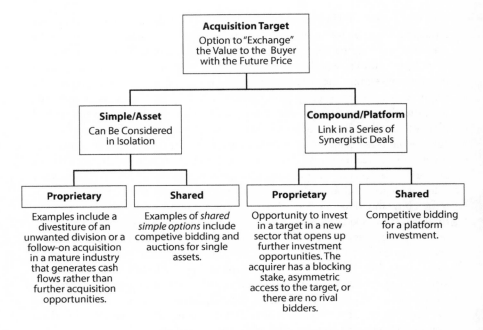

Figure 4.1 The Real Options Approach to Classifying Acquisitions
Source: Based on Kester (1984) and Trigeorgis (1996).

to leverage their perceived complementarities with assets that are already in place—or simply to deliver growth.

A *platform acquisition option*, however, involves higher growth option value than an asset acquisition option, since it involves *an option on options*, or a compound option.[4] A platform acquisition—be it to access an emerging market, a new geography, or a joint venture in which firms combine resources as well as strengthening core capabilities—acts as a beachhead into a new sector. Such an acquisition can be a critical component in a serial acquisition strategy, as it derives a significant part of its value by creating a new path of follow-on investment opportunities. In this sense, a platform acquisition can alter the strategic course and position of the enterprise, and is best seen as the first stage in a sequence of interrelated investment opportunities. The acquirer initially undertakes one or more platform acquisitions in each new related industry or geography, and then leverages its newly acquired core competencies or efficiencies into follow-on acquisitions.

---

[4] See Kogut and Kulatilaka (1994b), McGrath (1997, 1999), McGrath and Macmillan (2000), and McGrath, Ferrier, and Mendelow (2004) for an alternative conceptual framework, which views real options as strategic platform investments and as source of choice and heterogeneity.

In addition to its simple and compound option *value*, Figure 4.1 considers a potential target's *price* characteristics. The primary source of strategic uncertainty in a consolidation game revolves around the firm's ability to appropriate its desired opportunities, which, in turn, is influenced by whether the option might be shared with competitors. Naturally, the value created through an acquisition is the excess value of the target to the successful acquirer over its acquisition price—that is, the firm's ability to extract synergistic value from the acquisition beyond what it pays for it. But this price will depend on the extent to which the option to bid on a target is *shared* with rival bidders.

Proprietary acquisitions, those where the opportunity is exclusive to the bidder, all but guarantee that the synergistic value will flow to the successful acquirer. *Shared acquisition* opportunities (those that are available to more than one rival in an industry) are likely to require a more involved, game theory-based analysis. This situation arises, for example, when the target is offered at an auction, or when multiple bidders make offers for a publicly traded firm. The competitive aspect of shared options makes it difficult for strategic and financial buyers to avoid paying for at least part of the synergistic value and strategic optionality they perceive.[5] It is not always possible to keep one's options open when acquisition opportunities are shared. If there are opportunity costs to waiting—such as early dividends or the opportunity to capitalize on a specific market dynamic—the holder will seek to exercise the option early.

EXPRESSING A BUY-AND-BUILD STRATEGY AS AN OPTION PORTFOLIO

In a buy-and-build strategy, the investor acts as an industry consolidator, with the intent of transforming several smaller companies into an efficient large-scale network. The initial platform acquisition generates the option for future follow-on acquisitions, which can be undertaken (i.e., options can be exercised) after indications have been received as to the likely potential speed of consolidation and as uncertainty about the success of the buildup strategy is resolved over time. Additional value is created through the consolidation of synergistic acquisitions as operations become integrated, cost efficiencies are realized, and

---

[5] Competitive interaction and growth option value have been qualitatively discussed by Kester (1984). New research in finance addresses this embedding of a game of capacity expansion within a dynamic real options–based investment analysis—see, for example, Smit and Ankum (1993) and Grenadier (2000a, 2000b). Elegant and rigorous continuous-time models of competitive exercise strategies have been developed by, among others, Grenadier (1996), Kulatilaka and Perotti (1998), Lambrecht (2001, 2004), Morellec and Zhdanov (2005), Thijssen, Huisman, and Kort (2012), Toxvaerd (2008). For other useful guides to the valuation of expansion, production, or exit options and their option interactions, see Trigeorgis (1996), Copeland and Antikarov (2001), and Smit and Moraitis (2010a).

market share increases. Financial buyers then have several exit strategies available, including sale to a strategic or a larger financial buyer, or an initial public offering.

A buy-and-build strategy unlocks value in several ways. First, in private equity transactions there is frequently a *financial leverage* effect—the investor typically uses a significant amount of debt to finance the acquisition, although since the financial crisis in 2008 the amount of possible leverage has reduced. Besides creating valuable tax shields, the resulting highly levered financial structure strengthens managerial incentives to improve efficiency and cash flow. Second, there are *synergistic* benefits, including those attributable to increases in size. A buy-and-build strategy unlocks synergistic value through economies of scale or scope, and the increased size of the consolidated firm is likely to result in improved market presence and competitive position. Moreover, as the firm becomes larger and more mature, the private equity investor is likely to have more attractive exit opportunities. The value added by the consolidation ultimately equals the amount by which the future (exit) value of the consolidated firm exceeds the sum of the cost of the individual acquisitions and the cost of any organic growth in the component firms.

The platform company should be a respected company that can provide the acquirer with a secure foothold for future growth opportunities and generate this compound growth option value. It should preferably be a leader in quality or service, and have some proprietary technology base or some other characteristics that can differentiate its production process or product, or have geographic advantage or proximity to potential follow-on acquisitions, which can then be successfully leveraged into further acquisitions. Particularly in a competitive bidding situation, the acquisition of a good platform company may require a substantial premium, and the deal can appear to have a low NPV or return based on measurable cash inflows considered in isolation. For instance, Hicks Muse Tate & Furst's 1999 acquisition of Hillsdown, the British foods and furniture conglomerate, required a substantial premium over its market value. The initial bid of 127 pence per share was subsequently raised to 147 pence to acquire full control of the company—but the investor justified this price by arguing that the firm provided a platform for developing its European food business.

The value of an acquisition target depends critically on the buyer's intentions: its value to a buy-and-build investor can be significantly different from its trading value in the financial markets on a stand-alone basis, and it can have significant strategic value when considered as a first step in a series of investments. The synergistic opportunities of the investment, and the premium that might have to be paid to acquire such a company are significant components of its value, and should be incorporated in a bidder's valuation techniques.

From this vantage point, an individual acquisition is a component of a strategic investment plan. Its value should thus be based on an expanded NPV approach that starts with the stand-alone value and takes into account not only the *potential* synergistic effects but also the strategic impact of competitive interactions, as well as management's flexibility to alter planned investment decisions as future market conditions change: in other words, its value should reflect its potential future optionality. Expressed as an equation,

Expanded NPV = (stand-alone value of platform – price)
+ value of future (shared) synergistic opportunities

To measure the value of an acquisition requires first estimating the stand-alone value, after which a real options approach can help to assess the value of any synergistic opportunities, which arise mainly from the firm's flexibility to adapt the strategy if market conditions turn out differently than expected. Finally, principles of game theory (discussed in the next chapters) can be used to assess the likely effect of competitors' responses on the eventual value of the acquisition. For instance, there can be value erosion in a shared compound option if other buyers bid up the price or if the industry responds by expanding capacity and reducing the target's market power. At the same time, the impact on the buyer's future optionality of not succeeding in acquiring the target should also be factored into the decision-making process.

STAND-ALONE VALUE

Stand-alone value can be estimated directly or indirectly. The direct method uses the market value before any merger negotiations, while the indirect method involves first estimating the total company value by discounting its net free cash flows at the weighted average cost of capital (after taxes) and then subtracting the (market) value of debt to arrive at the value of the equity. This value can be subjected to a reality test using competitors' earnings multiples.

ADDED VALUE OF SYNERGISTIC OPPORTUNITIES

The consolidation strategy is partly based on cost advantages that can be gained when one investment can support multiple profitable activities less expensively in combination than separately. One of the key drivers of synergistic value in a buy-and-build strategy is building size in a fragmented market. Highly fragmented markets with no dominant players are ripe for consolidation. Through the resulting economies of scale combined with potential market share leadership, the consolidator pursues investment timing and pricing policies to enable the firm to create facilities of efficient scale. In HAL's acquisition of Pearle, for example, follow-on acquisitions were expected to capitalize on the platform's operational excellence, and the resulting consolidation was expected to create efficient scale facilities. Sectors with potential for economies of scope, important competencies or technologies can cut across geographic boundaries. These cost advantages can result from producing and selling multiple products related by a common technology, production facilities, or sales, distribution and network. The private equity investor can contribute another source of value by providing strategic input regarding acquisitions, financing, and exit: With these functions being handled by the private equity investor, the target company's management can focus on growth, integration, and improving margins.

The elusive value of synergistic opportunities requires an estimate of the present value of the cost efficiencies or margin gains gained through sector consolidation, based on a relative analysis of profitability, market position, and size. For instance, suppose that the potential available follow-on acquisition has a (stand-alone) present value of €750 million, which could be increased by an estimated 10% as a result of cost and marketing efficiencies or improved pricing following the platform acquisition.[6] Thus, based on these expected synergies, the net present synergistic value equals €75 million, assuming the firm is completely committed to a predetermined path of future follow-on acquisitions. However, the future synergistic benefits, just like future demand in the industry, are highly uncertain, and require flexibility to adapt the strategy if the path evolves differently than expected.

As mentioned earlier, the opportunity to acquire the target is more like an option on the buyer's future value. When the price of the target is uncertain, the target is like an exchange option on the buyer's future value (with an exercise price equal to the acquisition price).[7] A firm will continue to consolidate if the net synergies of the acquisition at that time are sufficiently valuable (synergistic effect greater than one); but if sector developments turn out worse than expected, and the net synergistic value falls to zero, management will decide not to continue to build up.

To assess the flexibility value we have to *look forward* to how the industry might evolve and then *reason back* to the point at which follow-on acquisitions are undertaken. This is equivalent to the backward induction principle of option valuation. The dynamics of the synergistic effect can be modeled with a binomial tree over the life of the option, where each branch represents the synergistic effect (ratio of buyer value to price) according to favorable or unfavorable developments in a sector. Starting at the end of the tree and working backward, the option tree assigns values to outcomes such as undertaking the

[6] The average synergistic effect is defined as the ratio of the acquisition value to the buyer to the acquisition price (or to the acquisition price considered in isolation when ignoring any competitive bidding effects). This can be checked based on a multiple analysis or deal experience.

[7] The acquisition can also be seen as providing a call option on the synergistic effect (the ratio of the buyer's value to the acquisition price, here (€750m + €75m) / €750m = 1.1) with a time to maturity equal to the horizon of the build-up, and with exercise price calibrated to one. The "dividend yield" is the yield on the buyer value and the "interest rate" is the yield on the price.

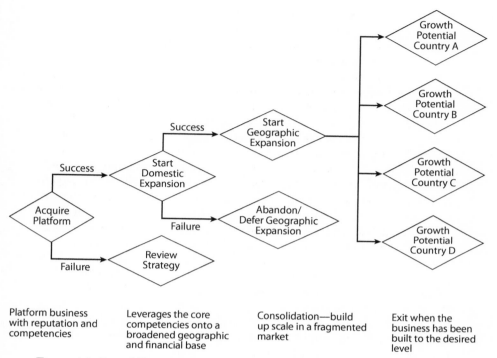

Figure 4.2 Staged Decisions for a Buy-and-Build Strategy

acquisition immediately, waiting to see how the market evolves, or foregoing follow-on acquisitions. The estimated option effect would be higher than the net synergistic effect (which is 10% in our example), since it includes flexibility.

A compound option valuation is often more complex, as it may involve a collection of interacting and sequential real options. Further follow-on acquisitions in several geographical locations could increase cash flows as a result of cost and marketing efficiencies. Figure 4.2 presents a simplified structure of the compound option value of future synergistic opportunities. A strategy may include the timing of asset and platform acquisitions, as well as realizing those options that are embedded in the target—such as restructuring or organic expansion opportunities. An investor wanting to implement a global consolidation strategy will aim to execute *multiple* or *parallel platform acquisitions*, so as to position itself to be able to make opportunistic follow-on asset acquisitions across multiple dimensions—for example, into new commodities, products, markets, or geographies—using the buy-and-build principle. Parallel platform acquisitions are used in related diversified strategies to help acquire follow-on targets to gain new knowledge or to build new competences in related sectors, and to leverage these to diversify further. When the consolidation strategy matures, an *exit option* and *a merger option* with several potential strategic buyers may become possibilities.

It is worth sounding a word of caution with regard to the application of real options theory—the risk of underestimating the effects of *option interaction*.[8] Real-life transactions are often complex and may involve a collection of interacting real options. The valuation of flexible combinations resulting from an acquisition or merger should be based on an assessment of the interactive portfolio of options that captures the value resulting from combining the firms.[9] Often the combined value of a collection of such real options differs significantly from the sum of their separate stand-alone option values, evaluated using ready-made tools such as the Black-Scholes formula, and may not always be greater. Similarly, a platform acquisition in a new geography may preclude platform acquisitions in other locations. For this kind of real option application, a discrete-time binomial analysis might be the most appropriate approach. The initial decision to invest in a platform can be made by first creating a number of industry endgame scenarios and then solving them backward to evaluate all future potential outcomes of a proposed consolidation strategy. The idea is to begin with the growth potential of each platform at the terminal nodes in the decision tree and then reason backward to determine the optimal decision to make at each key point. Clear external thresholds or trigger levels—such as projected demand levels or critical product prices—on which decisions should be based, or which indicate alternative actions (such as deferral or the pursuit of a different target), can make executives adjust their decisions and so help avoid overcommitment due to loss aversion. An ex ante option analysis will probably differ from a biased analysis, and should make it easier for executives to relinquish intended targets without it implying personal defeat. Thus the options view should allow them to take full advantage of the upside potential created when events turn out better than expected, but still limit their losses on the downside.

Often, merger or mature continuing values are modeled as the end node of the binomial tree of a portfolio of options, using binomial option pricing or simulation. Reasoning backward from each scenario and examining each potential juncture at which a platform acquisition and follow-on investments could be made also permit the development of a multitude of path segments

---

[8] See Trigeorgis (1991) and Trigeorgis (1993) for an excellent overview and models with multiple options.

[9] For instance, the option to abandon a company for salvage value may not add much relative to the option to default held by the shareholders of a highly leveraged firm. If the firm declares bankruptcy, most of this value will go to the bondholders.

for each of the company's major competitors, generating valuable insights to what their possible moves might be, and thus into the relative value of each target to each of its rivals.

Starting from the potential acquisition opportunities in each country (as shown on the right of Figure 4.2) the investor can estimate the value of the options portfolio in the consolidation. Suppose that this procedure of working backward results in a value of future synergistic opportunities of €125 million. The expected value of synergistic opportunities was €75 million (continuing our earlier example), which when applied to the available acquisition pool of €750 million (ignoring any competitive interaction effects) resulted in a net synergistic effect of the potential acquisitions of 10%. The additional flexibility value therefore equals €125 million − €75 million = €50 million. Suppose that the expected yearly operating cash inflows of a platform, discounted at the weighted average cost of capital, are worth €450 million and that the price of acquiring the platform is €500 million. The expanded NPV of the strategy could then be calculated as follows:

$$\text{Expanded NPV} = (\text{platform value considered in isolation} - \text{price}) \\ + \text{expected value of synergies} + \text{flexibility value}$$

$$= (€450 \text{ m} - €500 \text{ m}) + (€75 \text{ m} + €50 \text{ m}) = €75 \text{ m}$$

In an increasingly uncertain and dynamic marketplace, the strategic adaptability created by the real options in consolidation strategies is essential. The consolidator should take advantage of favorable future investment opportunities, respond appropriately to threatening competitive moves, and act to limit losses from adverse market developments. Often, the acquisition itself is an option on a package consisting of a flow of expected earnings plus the value of other embedded corporate real options, such as the option to expand, shut down, switch production, or exit.

COMPETITION IN THE BIDDING GAME

Buy-and-build investors do not like to admit that they pay premiums for synergies. However, the competitive forces of shared opportunities make it difficult for them to make acquisitions without paying for at least some of the synergies they expect to enjoy. Indeed, we often see firms paying a premium over its inherent value to acquire a target.

The issue in developing paths is to what extent the acquirer can develop a unique, advantaged position to appropriate further growth options compared to other firms using similar buy-and-build strategies. One source of such uniqueness results from a firm's overall strategic position and from its choice of *acquisition paths* that can facilitate follow-on acquisitions.[10] Platform path dependencies mean that the value of a specific follow-on target to one potential acquirer is unlikely to equal its value to another, causing a variance between its inherent value and the ultimate price different bidders are willing to pay. It is precisely in these circumstances that the consolidating bidder's ability to assess the strategic value of a target critically—within the context of its defined serial acquisition strategy—becomes essential to ensuring that it continues to deliver sustained growth in shareholder value. Where this assessment is positive, acquiring a platform company that really opens up new paths may well involve paying a premium.

A bidding game can arise when players assign different values to an acquisition target than the financial market does. In the battle for Hillsdown, for example, Hicks Muse Tate & Furst outbid an offer by British venture capital firm Candover Investments, with both players' bids representing substantial premiums over the target's market price. The value to Candover, backing a management buyout team, stemmed in part from the management's commitment—while Hicks Muse saw Hillsdown as a platform to develop its food business in Europe.

CHANGING INDUSTRY COMPETITION: ORGANIC GROWTH VERSUS ACQUISITIVE GROWTH

When competing firms can affect each other's behavior, it is often useful to expand the valuation analysis, using game theory principles. This can involve a zero-sum game (when two firms face a shared investment opportunity) in which the value for the players of the game is in strict conflict—that is, the gain of one player is the other player's loss. Alternatively, there may be opportunities for cooperation among firms that can increase the total market. At the same time, more extreme forms of competition can end up shrinking the players' share of the total economic pie.

In a buildup strategy, the company must decide on the optimal mix of organic and acquisitive growth that intends to underpin its expansion, each of which may invite a different competitor response and affect the industry's future competition and profitability in different ways. A key factor in determining an appropriate competitive growth strategy is whether it involves the firm taking an "aggressive" approach to competition (in the sense of increasing market share at the expense of its competitors) or an "accommodating" approach (if the resulting value creation can be shared with—and may even benefit—its rivals). A second important factor is how the competitor is expected to react to

---

[10] A special issue of *Sloan Management Review* (Spring 1999) spans articles on real options and related concepts such as complexity theory, a dynamic view of strategy, or pursuing dual or multiple strategies simultaneously. See, for instance, Williamson (1999) and Beinhocker (1999).

either of these stances, which may depend on industry characteristics, and specifically on whether the competitor's reactions tend to be "reciprocating" or "contrarian"—that is, whether they are similar (playing fair when treated fairly, or competing tit-for-tat) or opposing (taking advantage of the other's accommodating stance). Reciprocating rivals may increase or decrease the economic pie (in win-win or lose-lose patterns), but contrarian rivals will compete for larger shares of a fixed pie (a win-lose scenario).

Competitive reactions are typically reciprocating in terms of price competition: that is, a price move by one firm can be expected to be matched by the competing firm. In contrast, competition for volume or capacity can be regarded as contrarian—capacity expansion by one in a growing demand environment (e.g., capturing a larger market share, so preempting a competitor's growth) results in a lower incremental capacity for that competitor. So we can distinguish between various investment strategies according to their competitive stances (aggressive or accommodating) and the nature of competitors' reactions (reciprocating or contrarian).

Figure 4.3 illustrates four different competitive growth strategies, influencing the intensity of competition in an industry and rivals' market shares. When overall growth in a market is limited, growth by a particular firm is possible only if it takes business away from its competitors (lower row: aggressive) or makes acquisitions that together exploit economies of scale (upper row: accommodating). In this value-enhancement game, firms can increase the total size of the economic pie only if they "accommodate" their competitors through acquisitions that more fully utilize the benefits and cost efficiencies of cooperation within consolidated entities. By contrast, the pie can shrink if firms elect to be aggressive and pursue organic growth strategies that are perceived as a threat to their competitors' market shares, so inviting retaliation and defensive reactions. In mature and low-growth industries, in particular, organic expansion can result in intensified price competition or a "war of attrition" for larger market shares (a lose-lose situation). Strategic acquisitions seem to be the preferred route for firms facing the risk of intense competition, since they deliver synergies that are expressed through quick increases in market share, but also minimize the potential for price wars within the sector (a win-win pattern). Buying existing market share does not cause rivals to retaliate—their existing capacity is not threatened, and increased industry concentration can even limit the intensity of competition.

The competitive landscape is different in times of higher growth, when there is greater opportunity for profitable capacity expansion. In these conditions, the investment opportunities that face industry competitors give rise to what might be viewed as a value-capture game. With higher industry growth, organic capacity expansion by one firm is less likely to take place at the expense of a competitor's existing capacity, thus limiting the risk of intensified competition. The optimal route in these circumstances can be to take the initiative. An ag-

Expected Growth

	Low Growth	High Growth
	Reciprocating Response: Joint value enhancement, e.g., benign price environment versus price war	*Contrarian Response:* Value preemption game, e.g., volume competition
Accommodating Buy: Growth through acquisition—stable or reduced competition	*i)* Win-Win Increase the total size of the pie by accommodating each other—jointly exploit the synergistic effects of the acquiring firm	*iii)* Lose-Win Threat of competitors gaining market share if they preempt organic growth options
Aggressive Build: Growth by organic expansion—intensified competition	*ii)* Lose-Lose: Don't invest/wait—capacity expansions can increase competition and trigger further retaliating reactions (e.g., price war)	*iv)* Win-Lose: Invest early to preempt favorable investment opportunities

(Left vertical axis label: Growth Strategy)

Figure 4.3 Different Competitive Strategies Following "Buy" or "Build" Expansion in a Value Enhancement or a Value Capture Game

gressive buildup strategy can generate a first-mover advantage: if the competition retreats, the expanding firm can gain market share and become an industry leader as the sector grows. While the quadrants in the figure illustrate the extremes, firms can use it to understand how to craft a strategy that balances organic and acquisitive growth.

The total strategic value of a buy-and-build may thus consist of *strategic preemption value* from timing investment opportunities with regard to other players, and a *strategic reaction value* reflecting the impact of the rival's response on profits.

Revisiting our earlier simple example, suppose now that the consolidating firm seizes the initiative in a fragmented and growing market and moves before any of its competitors with a program of early and aggressive acquisitions and organic growth. Suppose that exercising the options prematurely completely erodes its flexibility value. Observing this strategy, other consolidators may choose to stay out altogether or to enter later. Suppose that this *strategic preemption value* can be estimated at €60 million, and that other incumbents reduced the scale at which they expand capacity to avoid a market share battle, generating a *strategic reaction value* of €25 million (based on estimated incremental profits compared to a base-case sequential strategy). The expanded NPV with the additional strategic value component would then be calculated as follows:

Expanded NPV = (stand-alone value of platform − price) + (expected value of synergistic opportunities + flexibility value) + strategic value

$$= €(450 − 500) + €(75 + 0) + €(60 + 25) = €110 \text{ m}$$

By reducing the likelihood of competitive intrusion, the strategic (commitment) value of €85 million more than offsets the loss in flexibility value of €50 million in the sequential strategy.

PREEMPTION VALUE OF INVESTMENT TIMING STRATEGIES

Contrary to options theory, game theory shows us that it is not always preferable to keep one's options open. Sometimes a player can seize a first-mover advantage by making a preemptive investment commitment (i.e., exercising the option prematurely). This framework can be used to shed light on—and in some cases even quantify—the value of a competitive first-mover advantage, depending upon the quality and market power of the platform and the generic or proprietary nature created by bidder's strategic positions.[11]

As described in Box 4.2 (see page 96), when players directly influence rival bidders and their strategic timing behavior (as in a bidding contest or a company auction with two or three bidders), an integrated option game valuation is required, in which the optimization of options—to invest, wait, or abandon under uncertainty—is replaced by an investment subgame, which also introduces competitive interactions. In addition to this technique, Box 4.2 also shows what kind of additional insights a dynamic game analysis could offer. Option games provide fresh insights into the reasons for acquirers investing during procyclical acquisition waves.[12] We could label the different competitive landscapes—described in more detail in panel B of the box—as "Land Grab" at the top of the cycle, "Grab the Dollar" at intermediate demand levels, and "Musical Chairs" when demand growth is low or negative. As the panel shows, when expected demand levels are high at the top of the business cycle, the drive toward industry consolidation may see a scramble for assets (a Land Grab) as cash-rich rivals pursue acquisitions. The Grab the Dollar game describes a situation where the current market prospects are favorable only if one of the players invests, but simultaneous investment results in a battle with negative expected payoffs. When demand reverses, so does this frenetic buying behavior, and the game changes to Musical Chairs: when the music stops, indicating low levels of expected demand, companies prefer to wait and few bids emerge.

---

[11] See also Lieberman and Montgomery (1988) on first-mover advantages and Warner, Fairbank, and Steensma (2006) on acquisition timing.

[12] This view is consistent with suggestions from the empirical literature on merger waves that the timing of the exercise of acquisition options occurs procyclically. See also Lambrecht (2004), Toxvaerd (2008), and Lambrecht and Myers (2007).

Consider a situation in which two firms engage in a bidding contest for a follow-on acquisition. In the classic bidding contest between two equally dominant players, the competitive pressure to acquire the target induces both to bid and pay a premium, eliminating most (or even all) of the target's synergistic option value. When the firms enter the bidding contest simultaneously and the synergistic benefits they expect are also equal, they will be forced to pay a premium almost equal to the total synergistic value in order to capture the company.

Of course, in many—if not most—cases the two players will not be exactly symmetrical; one will have a stronger market position or may perceive more value in the target than the other, and the organizational capabilities and bundle of corporate real options—and, indeed, their levels of uncertainty themselves—will be different for each firm. As a result, the value of a corporate real option may be different for each buyer, depending on each other's resources and assets. Exercising the option to expand, for instance, is going to be more valuable for a consolidator than for another player when the consolidated firm is a market leader by virtue of its size, earlier acquisitions, and complementary assets.

In many industry contexts the synergies are based on timing advantages: a firm or an alliance that can consolidate first can enjoy significant advantages. In addition, the quality of a firm's products and its organizational capabilities are often distinctive, if not unique—assets that can prove to be a source of comparative advantage in the strategic exercise of the firm's acquisition buildup options. The factors affecting each firm's growth options may also differ, generating significant differences in their exercise and timing behaviors. For example, a firm with less cash flow variability or lower investments costs—or one that anticipates earlier competitive entry—is likely to exercise its options early.

Firms' differing abilities to appropriate acquisition options are illustrated in the framework presented in Figure 4.4, which shows that, when competitors' relative market power and asset bases differ—either globally or regionally—their ability to follow optimal investment timing strategies is also likely to vary. The upper row depicts the case where a consolidated company has established a dominant position in its industry or region. The company can safely preserve and nurture its growth options when their NPV is low (quadrant i). As there is little threat of successful preemption by smaller rival bidders, targets become proprietary (or at least semi-proprietary) opportunities for such dominant companies. When it becomes likely the economy will grow (quadrant ii), the higher value of the options to all players may encourage a company to invest early, although for a dominant company there is still only a limited threat that its acquisition targets will be preempted. The natural growth path is mostly organic, since the company already has a strong, mature platform position.

The lower row depicts the situation of a local or smaller company in a weaker strategic position. During the low cycle when the NPV is low, such a company

NPV from Immediate Investment

		Low NPV Expected High Option Value from Waiting	High NPV Exected Low Option Value from Waiting
Consolidator's Market Position	**Dominant** Global Player	i) • Low value of marginal projects favors optimized timing—can always react to competitive bid. • No threat of preemption—can wait.	ii) • High value favors early investment. The natural accumulation path is mostly organic, since industry majors have mature positions in regions and commodities. • Limited threat of preemption of acquisition opportunities by others.
	Weak Local Player	iii) • Deferment and organic growth until the market develops sufficiently. • Threat of preemption of opportunities by larger competitors induces relatively early investment when the market recovers.	iv) • Ambitious companies develop a presence through acquisitions in multiple regions and multiple resources to capture new projects. • Risk of preemption of opportunities—early mover strategy. Industry minors risk becoming targets.

Figure 4.4 Timing Strategies Based on the Consolidator's Market Position

must be mindful that a stronger competitor might come in and erode its option value (quadrant iii), and the potential competitive damage to its growth options such a move would represent may force it to take risks and invest relatively early in future growth (e.g., through taking minority stakes in platform companies). When demand increases (quadrant iv) more ambitious medium-sized companies will seek to develop a presence in multiple regions and multiple resources and create positions for future organic growth by making early acquisitions to prevent erosion of their value and to counter the threat of preemptive competitor moves. Less ambitious industry minors are likely to become targets.

PLAY POKER AGAINST RIVALS WHO OVERSHOOT OR FALL ASLEEP

Although real options may help to see and appreciate uncertainty, the real options analysis itself can be irrationally infected. For instance, real option exercise biases—a tendency to exercise options suboptimally (that is, invest either prematurely or belatedly based on personal predispositions and risk profile)—

can result in real options being exercised too early or too late. Trigger-happy executives can destroy option value by exercising acquisition options hastily, especially when they also overvalue targets, underestimate uncertainty, or fear being left out of a transaction frenzy in hot deal markets. Equally, value can be lost or missed when conservative decision makers pass up opportunities to exercise well-priced acquisition options in cold markets. Thus, whether option holders exercise their options precipitously in hot deal markets or fall asleep at the wheel in cold deal markets affects the value of those options. The costs of mismanaging options may vary depending on the volatility of the underlying asset—but they can be substantial.[13]

But, while executives may be vulnerable to exercise biases, their rivals may be too. Acquisition option games are better applied if rationality is combined with insights from behavioral economics, enabling bidders to predict and respond rationally to rivals' irrational behaviors. The extent to which rational bidders can play poker against biased rivals, and take advantage of their psychological strategy biases, depends on the context of the bidding game and the level of demand.

AVOID OVERSHOOTING IN HIGH-DEMAND, TOP-OF-THE-CYCLE FRENZIES

As noted in chapter 2, deal framing—the way executives perceive the value of acquisition opportunities—may cause rivals to overestimate acquisition opportunities in hot deal markets, perhaps when their share prices are at their peak or when they have had recent acquisition successes. Such biased views in the endgame may deliver a negative-sum game for rival consolidators, resulting from excessive acquisition premiums, intense competition for assets, overcommitment, and bidding wars that reduce the size of the economic pie by attracting capital into the industry at excessive levels relative to the potential returns. As noted, overcommitment can arise

- During acquisition frenzies, which can be leading indicators of the approaching top of an economic cycle as bidders appear to display a herd mentality

- When target value is hard to ascertain and is based on relative valuations in exuberant markets

- When CEOs are overconfident, with their egos stroked by a recent spell of success in acquisition battles

---

[13] See Copeland and Tufano (2004).

- In situations when the sunk cost fallacy is applied, which, irrespective of the cost of the bidding process, promotes the possibility of achieving better outcomes by bidding further

In such overheated contests, playing against overconfident and overoptimistic rivals, the optimal strategy is likely to be not to invest.

TAKE INITIATIVE WHEN RIVALS FALL ASLEEP AT LOWER DEMAND LEVELS

Cold deal markets may induce executives to frame deals as being too risky, leading them to hold back for too long. During the decline in financial markets in 2008, volatile demand and limited competition for deals pushed the whole market into a strategic wait-and-see approach to takeovers—and a small number of cash-rich investors were able to increase their M&A activity and snap up significantly undervalued businesses. Similarly, in the early stages of an industry consolidation, rivals may have a conservative strategy and frame acquisitions too narrowly, holding back from making what they perceive as risky consolidating acquisitions.

Recognizing this bias allows a canny consolidator to identify where and when to make an early bid to avoid ending up in a bidding contest later in the game. As a consequence, a behavioral view of the option games analysis shows that the game can be won at low and intermediate demand levels. For instance, a bidder who moves early in an industry on the threshold of a consolidation wave can enjoy significant advantages compared to late movers in acquiring companies and building competitive positions. At intermediate expected demand levels (see Box 4.2), the strategic context may result in a Grab the Dollar game, that is, a situation where preemptive bids are likely. When expected demand is low, a preinvestment—in the form of a minority or blocking stake—can be another way to increase a bidder's ability to gain control. As we will analyze in more detail in the next chapter, Xstrata experienced many of these biases and option games in its quest to become a leading diversified mining major.

CONCLUSIONS

OPPORTUNISM IN ACQUISITIONS STRATEGY

In a buy-and-build strategy the investor aims to consolidate several smaller companies into a more efficient, larger-scale industry network. The most capable acquirers resolve the necessary trade-offs between the need for a clear

BOX 4.2 TECHNIQUES FOR STRATEGIC ACQUISITION TIMING

A simplified structure of an acquisition option under demand uncertainty is given by the combined options and games analyses shown in Panel A. The left-hand part shows how the available acquisition option can be exercised according to the resolution of relevant uncertainties (shown by the branches). The right-hand part illustrates how an acquisition subgame is played at each level of expected demand.

Panel A. An Acquisition Subgame Embedded in a Dynamic Option Analysis

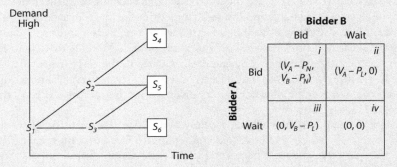

TECHNIQUES: FROM OPTION TIMING ANALYSIS TO AN OPTION GAME

In a traditional real option valuation, an intended future acquisition resembles a call option. When the acquisition value (V_t = standalone + synergistic option value) of the target develops favorably relative to its price (P_t = standalone + acquisition premium), the bidder can make the acquisition and realize the excess value ($C_t = V_t - P_t$). Thus a standard real option valuation is an optimization against uncertainty, with an option value at each node $C = Max[V - P$ (acquire); $(pC^+ + (1 - p)C^-) / (1 + r)$ (wait); 0 (abandon)], with p being the risk-neutral (option) probability and r the risk-free interest rate. Passing a threshold level (e.g., price or demand level) triggers the acquisition, so management acquires procyclically (e.g., if industry demand follows the path S_2, S_4) and waits or abandons otherwise (e.g., if the demand follows the path S_3, S_6).

In an integrated option game analysis, the timing game in the right of Panel A is played at the end of each tree branch. Bidder A chooses from the upper "bid" or the lower "wait" row, while bidder B chooses from the left-hand "bid" or the right-hand "wait" column. So the bidding game has four investment-timing scenarios: (i) when both players bid and enter a contest (N), the winner gets the target for a price which equals (at least) the rival's value $C_{A,B} = V_{A,B} - P_N$ and (ii) and (iii) when one player (A or B) places a bid and the other waits (L). In this case when one bidder preempts the other, the value creation for the first mover equals $C_{A,B} = V_{A,B} - P_L$. Where both firms wait/don't invest (iv), the value (for both) equals 0.

Option games theory predicts that acquisition waves appear rationally procyclical (but the behavioral component warns that managers shoot, not overshoot or fall asleep). In an option game, demand as well as rivals affect the timing of acquisitions:

At high demand levels (e.g., subgames on the $S_1 \Rightarrow S_2 \Rightarrow S_4$ path in Panel A), an acquisition has a positive expected payoff, regardless of the competitor's acquisition strategy—i.e., $V_A - P_N > 0$ and $V_A - P_L > 0$. At high demand, a Nash equilibrium in pure strategies for this "Land Grab" subgame results in the upper-left cell, where both bidders contest for the acquisition, and one just outbids its rival with a value creation equal to $C_A = C_B = V - P_N$ (which = 0 if rivals assign identical values).

At intermediate expected demand levels, the strategic situation between the rivals may result in preemptive bids ($V - P_L > 0$ and $V - P_N < 0$) in a "Grab the Dollar" game. At such demand levels, bidders' prospects will be favorable only if they are the only player. When the rival bids as well at intermediate expected demand levels, both will lose as the final price is likely to be too high.

By contrast for low demand levels, a pure Nash equilibrium for the "Musical Chairs" subgame (e.g., $S_1 \Rightarrow S_3 \Rightarrow S_6$) results in the values in the lower right-hand cell, which shows that both bidders would follow a wait-and-see strategy ($V - P_N < 0$ and $V - P_L < 0$).

Column 1 of Panel B illustrates these strategies when rivals are equal (shared option) and column 2 when competitors' relative market power or asset bases differ ("proprietary" option). At intermediate levels of expected demand, exercising the option to bid is going to be more valuable for a consolidator than for another player, when the consolidating firm is a market leader by virtue of its size and complementary assets. For very high levels of expected demand, the better positioned bidder is likely to capture the target against a price that is equal to the value of the target to a lower bidder. At lower levels of expected demand companies defer, with the dominant firm more likely to appropriate any future option value. Column 3 points to real option exercise biases—that is, invest either prematurely or belatedly based on personal predispositions and risk profile can result in

BOX 4.2 (CONT.)

too early or too late exercise of real options. In hot deal markets exuberant bidders may overbid and pay too much, while in cold deal markets bidders may fall asleep and underinvest.

Panel B. The Competitive Landscape (Subgame Equilibrium) for High, Intermediate, and Low Demand Trajectories

Demand trajectories	Shared option (1)		Proprietary option (2)		Irrational over- and undervaluation of options (3)
	Payoff structure (for both)	Nash equilibrium	Payoff structure (for both)	Nash equilibrium	
High	$V - P_L > 0$ $V - P_N > 0$	*Land Grab* Both bid	$V - P_L > 0$ $V - P_N > 0$ With $V_A > V_B$	Dominant bidder captures the company and option value	Exuberant bidders overinvest and pay too much
Intermediate	$V - P_L > 0$ $V - P_N < 0$	*Grab the Dollar* Either one of the bidders captures the platform company	$V - P_L > 0$ and $V - P_N > 0$ while $V - P_N < 0$ for the other	The advantaged bidder captures the target	Bidders fall asleep and underinvest
Low	$V - P_L < 0$ $V - P_N < 0$	Music stops in *Musical Chairs*, both wait	$V - P_L < 0$ $V - P_N < 0$	Both wait at very low levels of demand	

intended strategy and the instinct to be opportunistic by continuously seeking to reposition their firms within their competitive space to be able to appropriate new options as they arise. The discipline of identifying and, where possible, analyzing the value of newly created options is an integral component of the strategic assessment of potential acquisitions. When an acquisition creates a new path, the consolidator must maximize its ability to take advantage of favorable future investment opportunities quickly, to respond appropriately to threatening competitive moves, and to limit losses from adverse market devel-

$PVGO$ = Value of Future (Shared) Synergistic Opportunities − Price

Step 1.	Step 2.	Step 3.	Step 4.
Identify and Sequence the List of Targets (Figure 4.1)	Organic or Acquisitive Growth (Figure 4.3)	Timing Strategies (Figure 4.4)	Play Poker against Biased Rivals
First, classify investment opportunities based on simple or compound option characteristics and proprietary or shared nature to help focus managerial attention on the embedded strategic and growth option value of targets.	Second, in a build-up, the company must decide if it should expand through organic growth or acquisitions, which could invite a different market response and reaction value (resulting in positive or negative sum option games).	As a third step, use the timing framework to shed light on the value of a first-mover competitive advantage, depending upon the quality and market power of the platform and the generic or proprietary nature of the company's position.	As a final step, predict and rationally respond to rivals' irrational behaviors, depending on the context of the bidding game.

Figure 4.5 Executive Summary: Conceptual Implementation of Bottom-Up Option Games

opments. In an uncertain competitive landscape, exercising such strategic opportunism is essential for the success of a firm's consolidation strategy.

ACQUISITIONS STRATEGY AS CONCEPTUAL OPTION GAMES

A new element of the approach presented in this book, as compared to traditional capital budgeting, is the use of real options and game theory not only to evaluate individual acquisitions but to shape the entire strategic thinking process. By way of a summary, Figure 4.5 describes the steps for the implementation of the option game concept that this chapter has presented, from sequencing the list of targets, to the balance between organic and acquisitive growth, and optimal timing without overshooting in the up-cycle or becoming overly cautious in a down-cycle. Rather than replacing existing NPV methods, this chapter proposes a dynamic strategy valuation process that encompasses NPV analysis and incorporates real options and game theory approaches only when relevant. NPV analysis can capture the value of an expected scenario of cash inflows, while real options techniques are appropriate when the plan has the potential to unfold differently than expected. Furthermore, when competitors affect each other's behavior, an expanded or strategic analysis (often relying on game theory and behavioral principles) is called for. Behavioral theory should help managers recognize situations where they are vulnerable to over- or undervalue growth options and so exercise their real options suboptimally—either prematurely or belatedly.

The advantage that results from combining a conceptual option game approach as presented in this chapter with a PVGO analysis is the simplification of a normally complex analytical task, facilitated by the fact that the market perception of growth options is consistent with and reinforces the intuitive strategic logic underlying much buy-and-build investing.

A strategy's valuation components should also be consistent with its underlying logic and design. In short, methods like real options techniques and game theory complement the strategic thinking process in an interactive way—they do not replace it. The investor first has to determine why a particular strategy leads to value creation. Combining the quantitative options models developed in finance with game theory principles from economics and the qualitative insights from strategic management theory provides a richer framework that helps us understand the restructuring of fragmented markets better, and that perhaps helps to justify the substantial takeover premiums in certain acquisitions.

SUGGESTED READING

Amram, M., and N. Kulatilaka. 1999. *Real Option: Managing Strategic Investment in an Uncertain World*. Boston: Harvard Business School Press.

Ferreira, N., J. Kar, and L. Trigeorgis. 2009. "Option Games: The Key to Competing in Capital-Intensive Industries." *Harvard Business Review* 87, no. 3: 101–7.

Smit, J. T. J. 2001. "Acquisition Strategies as Option Games." *Journal of Applied Corporate Finance* 14, no. 2: 79–89.

SUGGESTED MATERIALS, TOOLS, AND GADGETS

Han Smit's page on valuation tools provides strategy tools and webcasts. Links to the page can be found on this book's Princeton University Press website: http://press.princeton.edu/titles/10333.html.

CHAPTER 5

DUAL REAL OPTIONS VALUATION

THE XSTRATA CASE

It's unwise to pay too much, but it's worse to pay too little. When you pay too much, you lose a little money. You pay too little, it's because the thing you bought was incapable of doing the thing it was bought to do.

—John Ruskin

Until 2001 Xstrata was a nondescript Swiss-listed ferrochrome and zinc business attached to the Glencore metals trading house.[1] The introduction of a new management team under Mick Davis in late 2001 led to a listing on the London Stock Exchange and the subsequent completion of a series of acquisitions, including Glencore's coal assets (2002); the Australian coal, copper, and zinc group MIM (2003); and (in 2006) the Tintaya copper mine in Peru, a one-third share of the Cerrejón coal mine in Colombia, and the Falconbridge Group in Canada. In only five years, this acquisition journey transformed Xstrata from a $500 million minnow into the fifth largest mining group in the world, worth over $80 billion at the peak of the cycle.

It's a story that acquirers like to play out in consolidating industries such as natural resources, telecom, banking, airlines, and various private-equity-backed retail chains. The traditional logic of an acquisition is based on interasset synergies that are expected to arise when the merged organizations can support activities more profitably in combination than they could separately. The real options approach agrees with traditional views that value can be created through consolidation, as scale and the accumulation of high-quality assets and capa-

[1] The views in this chapter are those of the authors and are further developed in their article "Serial Acquisition Options," *Long Range Planning* 43, no. 1 (2010): 85–103. They do not necessarily reflect Xstrata's opinion. The authors would like to thank Charles Baden-Fuller, Hugh Courtney, and two anonymous referees for their comments and suggestions that have benefited this chapter. The link to the article hosted on Science Direct is http://www.sciencedirect.com/science/article/pii/S0024630109000909.

bilities modify the strategic position of the bidder and can even change the industry structure. In fact, the real options approach deals with the uncertainties involved in a strategy better than traditional approaches. Serial acquisition strategies typically have long-term horizons, in which unforeseen economic events or rival moves are likely to change originally envisioned plans. Real options theory encourages the active inclusion of flexibility in an acquisition strategy, where valuable new growth options can arise—or existing ones become obsolete—as uncertainty resolves. Moreover, by analyzing these *potential* acquisitions as options, the method can show how financial markets can inform the direction of an acquisition strategy.

In real option theory, the market value of companies is not just the net present value of its future cash-flows—which is what an NPV analysis provides— but also incorporates the prospective value of its growth and other options.[2] Thus, to an extent, it encompasses the value of the *potential* options that might come the company's way in the future, as well as the company's evolving and future strategic position. In fact, the theory holds that the strategic value of these growth opportunities constitutes a significant part of a company's market value, and thus explains any value differential relative to competitors' apparently comparable collections of assets and future cash flows. Thus,

$$\text{Market Value (MV)} = \text{Assets in Place (PV)} + \text{Present}$$
$$\text{Value of Growth Options (PVGO),} \qquad (5.1)$$

where PV represents the present value of earnings (as an annuity) generated by assets in place, and PVGO represents the value of the growth opportunities—a portfolio of organic and acquisition options.

As noted, PVGO can be estimated either bottom-up (i.e., from the company's assets and options) or top-down (i.e., directly from the financial markets). The bottom-up approach requires the identification of the various types of options (e.g., platform investment, expansion, or divestment options) embedded in the organization and its businesses and company assets, and the use of option valuation methods to establish their value. But identifying these options and performing the valuation analysis are both complicated exercises, and depend on a wide range of assumptions and unforeseen events, which can deter executives and other decision makers from using these quantitative approaches. Some would even say such valuations are just guesswork with numbers attached and, thus, likely to be sensitive to biased intuition.[3] To address such obstacles we combine a conceptual real options approach with top-down valuation. The top-down (or market method) bypasses the modeling challenges by using the consensus market assessment of the firm's set of embedded real op-

---

[2] The value of a firm as consisting of assets in place and growth opportunities is considered by (among others) Miller and Modigliani (1961), Myers (1977), and Pindyck (1988).

[3] For instance, see Smith (2007).

tions as reflected in its current stock price,[4] and is the one commonly used in empirical research for estimating a company's growth option value.

The key contribution of this chapter is the application of the top-down and bottom-up duality of the real option frameworks to valuing serial acquisitions. We develop the market-based PVGO method into a framework that directly connects serial acquisition strategy to value creation on financial markets, and so helps to explain the full market value of companies in consolidating industries. In addition, in a bottom-up approach, we consider acquisitions as portfolios of interrelating acquisition options, each stage being an option on the next, which can develop the firm's asset base dynamically and opportunistically. We call this dual approach to value acquisition programs the market method for acquisitions (MMA).

ILLUSTRATIVE EXAMPLE OF THE DUAL APPROACH: XSTRATA'S JOURNEY

When Xstrata was launched in 2001, Mick Davis and his management team wanted to build a firm that would deliver superior returns and, hence, attract investors. The proposition the team offered Xstrata's shareholders was to create a diversified mining group that had superior growth prospects to those of its larger, more established peers.

Although the conventional industry paradigm predicted that organic growth had the potential to deliver superior returns, Davis was convinced that the "terms of trade would improve, demand would increase and the supply side would not be able to meet demand". His team realized that acquisitions would become increasingly important, since they could deliver important synergies through rapid increases in scope and scale via entries into new geographies, commodities, services, currencies, or customers, and so quickly generate valuable new organic growth as well as increasing the organization's embedded options. This conviction was strengthened by the observation that large diversified mining groups are valued more highly than single commodity companies, generated more stable cash flows, and enjoyed better access to growth options than their smaller, more focused counterparts. In five years, the execution of a series of acquisition options transformed Xstrata into a major diversified miner—worth over $50 billion—with greater access to essential new opportunities and finance to fuel its strategies.

Figure 5.1 shows (with the benefit of some hindsight) the evolution of Xstrata's market value (right axis) over the high-cycle period against the evolu-

---

[4] The extensive work of Tony Tong has shown many novel empirical implications of growth options. See also Kester (1984), Chung and Charoenwong (1991), Tong and Reuer (2006), Tong, Reuer, and Peng (2008), Tong and Reuer (2008), Reuer and Tong (2010), van Bekkum, Smit, and Pennings (2011).

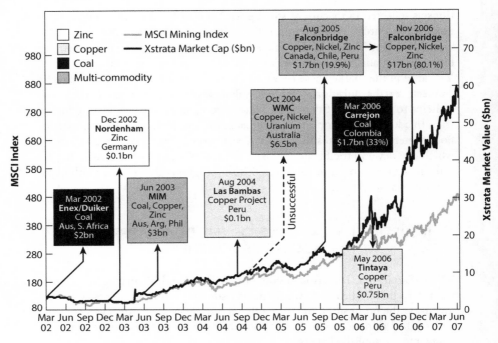

Figure 5.1 Xstrata's Market Value as It Evolved into a Major Mining Company
Source: Xstrata plc., Bloomberg.

tion of the MSCI index of mining companies (left axis) as its acquisition journey proceeded. Although the figure illustrates the relative growth of the company in *market value* (and not *value creation*) terms, it shows how Xstrata's acquisition strategy enabled it to outgrow the average industry player.

Three years of cyclical heights then encouraged most mining companies to adopt the "new paradigm"—the view that Asian demand growth heralded a step change in prices. In this model, high expected commodity prices transformed organic growth options into attractive investments with relatively high perceived NPVs, and highlighted the significant opportunity cost of deferring cash-flows, inducing firms to invest and consolidate to share the high infrastructure investments involved in large-scale mines. Increasing demand—and the inability of the industry to increase supply due to infrastructure bottlenecks—drove further consolidation, as larger entities could more easily carry the enormous infrastructure investments required.

Xstrata's acquisition story in the mining industry can illustrate the use of a dual options framework, first looking from the bottom up, which involves sequencing the target list in a strategy path.

TABLE 5.1 XSTRATA'S RAPID GROWTH TRAJECTORY THROUGH M&As IN EARLY YEARS

Company	Timing	Rationale	Size (billions of US dollars)
IPO, Enex Coal acquisition	March 2002	Cash-generative assets with scale, critical mass, and geographic diversification Cash flow and earnings accretion and stronger balance sheet Growth platform in a liquid market with sector familiarity New commodity: thermal coal New geography: Australia	2.1
MIM	July 2003	Cash-generative assets with critical mass and platform growth optionality Enhanced diversification by geography and commodity Platform entry into two new global businesses: copper and coking coal	2.96
⅓ Cerrejón	March 2006	World-class coal mine with scale and significant growth options Growth potential, margin improvement, geographic diversification of coal business	1.7
Tintaya	May 2006	Further growth and diversification of copper business, with synergy upside Strengthened regional position in Latin America and specifically southern Peru Significant organic growth options	0.75
Falconbridge	August 2006	Creation of a broadly diversified super-major with outstanding prospects Platform entry into nickel; substantial augmentation of South American copper business	18.6
Eland	August 2007	Entry into platinum, leveraging XTA's mining, smelting, and refining abilities in South America	1.0
Anvil Hill/ Australia	October 2007	Further consolidation of the thermal and coking coal industry Increases coking coal production by 25% Regional scale options	0.9
Jubilee	October 2007	Further consolidates nickel sector Gains access to prospective Western Australian nickel province	2.9

Source: Xstrata.plc.

BOTTOM-UP FRAMEWORK:
XSTRATA'S SERIAL ACQUISITIONS

Xstrata designed its strategy using a growth options perspective, where each acquisition was seen as a link in a chain of investments, exercised under expected commodity growing demand, and generating new investment opportunities with embedded (proprietary) organic growth options. Xstrata's CEO Mick Davis describes the optionality of his acquisition strategy:

> We spent the first five to six years making rapid acquisitions, seeing opportunities where other people were behind and not seeing what we could see. We captured these opportunities; we integrated them and ran them well and added value to them. At the same time we nurtured the optionality which we bought with these companies. The projects that they had, we built them up over a period where we can now translate them into reality. In the next two or three years we are going to increase production by 50% and lower our costs by 20%, and beyond that there are the second stage projects that can come through.

Having the momentum to generate new opportunities is a key value driver. The imperatives to first select appropriate targets that meet defined value criteria, and then to execute the relevant transactions successfully are far greater in the context of a serial acquisition strategy, as failure at one step of the process could cause the strategy to stall or to fail later on. Each transaction on Xstrata's acquisition path (as shown in the transaction list in Table 5.1 on the previous page) was in a different commodity and had its own dynamics, but each was designed to fill specific gaps in the company's portfolio, and to deliver, step-by-step, a rerating relative to its competitors that would help it to become a major global diversified company, and thus deliver superior shareholder value. As Xstrata's consolidation strategy matured to the point where it had become a medium-sized global diversified company, *merger options* also became feasible. In fact, in 2013, Xstrata merged with the world's leading commodity trader—Glencore—to form a substantial and uniquely diversified natural resource supermajor.

STEP 1: CLASSIFYING XSTRATA'S ACQUISITION OPTIONS

Let us classify Xstrata's targets using the framework discussed in the previous chapter. Following the typology presented in Table 5.2, Xstrata's acquisition of Glenore's coal assets in 2002 can be categorized as a *proprietary platform (compound) option* under uncertain commodity prices. From an options perspective, Xstrata could then either continue to expand operations if demand remained strong in a commodity—in effect, select one of the newly created *shared asset options*—or decide not to proceed to the next stage of the acquisition strategy. The purchase of MIM was a proprietary *platform acquisition*, and was followed by smaller *shared asset* acquisitions—although in some cases Xstrata ended up being the sole bidder—of the copper mines Las Bambas (2004) and Tintaya (2006) and of a one-third share of the Cerrejón coal mine (2006)—as well as another (hefty) *platform acquisition* of Falconbridge in 2006. Subsequent acquisitions of Jubilee Nickel in Western Australia, Eland Platinum, and 25% of Lonmin—which gained Xstrata a *proprietary asset option* to acquire a major platinum producer—created further diversity and optionality in its platform portfolio. Xstrata had secured the finance necessary to take Lonmin over completely in 2008, but having what was effectively a blocking stake meant it did not need to hurry. In retrospect, not completing the Lonmin acquisition at the time—just as the financial crisis was beginning—proved a wise application of real options thinking, given the subsequent collapse in the platinum industry and, consequently, the valuations of platinum producers. Like Falconbridge, the bidding game involved in Xstrata's offer for the Australian miner WMC can be characterized as a *shared platform option game* and was one it lost, as a dominant rival (BHP Billiton) seized the target at the eleventh hour.[5] Table 5.2 provides an overview of the typical options that are important in a serial acquisition strategy, together with examples from the Xstrata case.

STEP 2: MAP ALTERNATIVE ACQUISITION PATHS IN A TREE

One way to structure the list of target options into a diversified consolidation strategy is to map alternative acquisition paths—that is, to create schematic illustrations of the contingent long-term series of acquisitions and organic investments mapped against key uncertainties, so that the available options change as the uncertainties become resolved. Sequencing the list of targets in a series of acquisition options requires projecting the series *forward* by creating a number of *industry endgame scenarios* so that, by then reasoning *backward*, each potential juncture at which an acquisition could be made can be evaluated. Multiple platform acquisitions allow organizations to develop multiple possible paths: similar paths can also be constructed for major competitors and then solved using game theoretic principles, generating insights into their possible moves and the relative values of each target to each competitor, and thus the likely outcomes of any bidding wars.[6]

To give an example, Figure 5.2 (see page 111) maps Xstrata's journey as a series of options, showing the complexity of a serial acquisition strategy as a series of different types of interacting acquisition options: new platform acqui-

---

[5] Xstrata made an $8.2 billion bid for WMC Resources, the world's third biggest nickel miner, which also owned the Olympic Dam copper and uranium project in South Australia's arid heartland.

[6] The reasoning is equivalent to the backward induction principle of formal option valuation and finding equilibriums in dynamic games. For more detailed treatment of the topic of using game theory in real options analysis, see Smit and Trigeorgis (2004).

TABLE 5.2 COMMON CORPORATE REAL OPTIONS IN ACQUISITIONS

Category	Description	Option Definition	Xstrata Example
Option value characteristics			
Timing of asset acquisitions (simple option to defer)	Timing to acquire a target if demand or (commodity) prices rise and justify making the investment. A firm will continue to consolidate as long as the net synergies of the acquisition at that time are sufficiently valuable. Lambrecht (2004) shows that merger waves occur procyclically when they are motivated by economies of scale.	Each opportunity to bid for a target can be viewed as a call option on the company value for the bidder (underlying asset), with the initial bid as the exercise price and time to maturity being equal to the horizon of the acquisition opportunity. This is similar to a call option on the value of synergistic benefits where the exercise price is the cost of the merger.	Examples include smaller follow-on acquisitions such as Las Bambas in 2003 or Tintaya copper mines in 2006.
Multiple or parallel platform options (series of compound growth option)	An early investment (e.g., new geography) is a prerequisite to or a link in a chain of interrelated acquisitions, opening up future growth opportunities—either organically or through acquisitions (e.g., access to a new market, strengthening of core capabilities, strategic positioning investments). The investor executes a series of platform acquisitions to "opportunistically" position itself for multiple follow-on acquisitions using the buy-and-build principle. Serial acquisitions help firms learn new knowledge or build new competences and to subsequently diversify (economies of scope) in each sector.	This is a compound option—an option on options. The platform can be viewed as a call option on follow-on investment opportunities (underlying call option), with the exercise price the cost of the follow-on target and time to maturity being equal to the horizon. A valuation of a series of parallel compound options is more complex in that it may involve a collection of interacting sequential options. Additional operating value of this network derives from the opportunity to benefit from uncertainty by coordinating the operations of subsidiaries that may be geographically dispersed (e.g., see Kogut and Kulatilaka 1994a).	The acquisition of similar-sized rivals such as MIM and Falconbridge quickly increased Xstrata's scale and diversity. Acquiring Falconbridge (and its inbuilt assets) shaped Xstrata's future acquisition opportunities and merger alternatives by offering Xstrata access to world-class resources, further diversification into nickel and North America, an industry-leading copper organic growth portfolio, further industry consolidation in zinc and copper, and significant scale as the world's fifth largest public mining house.

Category	Description	Option Definition	Xstrata Example
Price characteristics			
Proprietary acquisition options	Proprietary acquisitions provide an exclusive opportunity for the bidder. For instance, a preinvestment in a minority stake may increase the bidder's ability to gain control.	Valuation according to standard option theory.	The minority stake in Lonmin—the specialized platinum miner—in 2008 provided Xstrata with a proprietary option to acquire the balance of the company and can be classified as a proprietary option.
Shared acquisition options	Shared acquisition opportunities are available to more than one rival in an industry. This situation arises, for example, when the target is offered at an auction or when multiple bidders make an offer for a publicly traded firm. The competitive aspect of shared options makes it difficult for strategic and financial buyers to avoid paying for at least part of the synergistic value and strategic optionality they perceive.	Shared options are likely to require a more complex, game-theory-based, analysis. If there are opportunity costs to waiting, such as the threat of preemption, the holder will seek to exercise the option early.	The Falconbridge acquisition was a shared option with rival bidders. It was clear to Xstrata that a number of potential natural suitors existed for Falconbridge: in particular, Inco had significant potential synergies due to its adjacent operations.

sition options, follow-on asset acquisition options, and exit or merger options. By expressing an acquisition path as a series of such options, with clear go/no go intersections, the methodology focuses attention on the relevant uncertainties—in this case commodity prices—and provides a rational way to choose whether to proceed with, alter, or defer decisions, depending on the evolution of the external environment.

Xstrata's strategic position was partly determined by the commodity and geographic diversity of its asset base and of its embedded acquisition options, as well as the company capabilities that allowed it to respond rapidly to changing industry conditions. The platform acquisition of similar sized rivals—such as MIM—quickly increased Xstrata's scale and diversity, and gave it new growth options in various commodities (e.g., coal, copper and zinc). Having multiple platforms on a broad base is especially valuable when major uncertainty—including the outlook for prices—surrounds the consolidation strategy. Creating the potential for growth is a key step in an accumulation strategy, and for responding to parallel actions by competitors. For instance, it was crucial that Xstrata preempted its similar sized rivals by acquiring platform acquisitions from a shortlist of potential targets that could quickly give it increased scale and diversity. Once uncertainty about the success of the first stage of the consolidation was resolved, management could either continue to expand operations if demand remained strong in a commodity, or proceed with the next stage of the acquisition strategy—in effect, select one of the newly created real options over another—as conditions dictated.

STEP 3: TIMING OF ACQUISITION OPTIONS AND INDUSTRY RESPONSE

As noted above, timing of investments is an important factor in a consolidation strategy, and Xstrata started its journey when the commodity cycle was in the doldrums. The timing of Xstrata's serial acquisitions strategy was (then) unconventional, as is was generally considered a cold market. The company's active Grab the Dollar approach was unconventional in the early 2000s compared to the organic growth model more widely followed in the mining industry at the time. As a late entrant into the game, Xstrata was under pressure to preempt potential competitors and so pursued its acquisitions relatively early in the cycle (at the intermediate demand level) to avoid being left out in the cold.

Its acquisition of Glencore's coal assets gave it a platform of sufficient bulk for the company to be listed on the LSE, which then provided it with the equity to fund further growth—both organic and acquisitive. Shortly after its second major acquisition—of the Australian group MIM—the cycle turned upward, so Xstrata found itself in a strong position to continue its growth trajectory. So, as events turned out, Xstrata's unconventionally timed moves

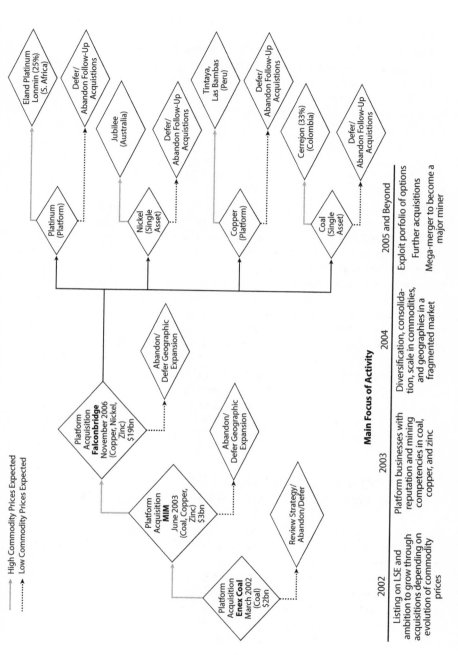

Figure 5.2 Xstrata's Acquisition Paths as a Series of Platform and Asset Options

had put it into a strong position as consolidation gained momentum in the industry.

As a late entrant into the mining consolidation game, Xstrata could not afford to follow conventional organic growth strategy and was forced to go ahead and try to build scale and diversity through acquisitions when most observers considered prices to be at their peak. Xstrata's boldness was facilitated by its larger competitors playing by the conventional industry rules and abstaining from the acquisition fray. Xstrata's strategy was partly founded on its management's view in 2003 that this cycle would be longer than previous ones, which gave it the courage to be more aggressive in pursuing leveraged acquisitions while their competitors awaited the downturn to undertake their (more traditional) countercyclical investment strategies. And, indeed, the 2004–8 high-demand cycle did prove longer and stronger than most industry analysts expected. Increased demand—and the inability of the industry to increase supply due to infrastructure bottlenecks and historic underinvestment—further drove rapid consolidation in the mining and metals sectors, as only larger entities could manage the enormous investments required to expand capacity. But the three years of cyclical highs that followed encouraged most mining companies to adopt the "new acquisition paradigm"—too belatedly to produce positive results in some cases. The new view—that demand growth in the Asian markets would herald a step change in prices—resulted in Xstrata encountering fierce competition for its subsequent acquisitions, such as Falconbridge.

When markets declined and growth expectations reversed (post-2008), the industry entered into a (low demand) Musical Chairs game and industry acquisitions dried up. Xstrata's rivals also deferred acquisitions, options were not preempted, and a more cautious strategy emerged across the industry in general. In the next chapter we analyze a detailed example of the quantification of option games in the case of the Falconbridge acquisition.

TOP-DOWN FRAMEWORK FOR LISTED COMPANIES: HOW FINANCE CAN ENLIGHTEN STRATEGY

The next step in the dual options framework—following a bottom-up analysis—is using an industry analysis to apply a top-down perspective. As a starting point, it is possible to ascribe the differential market value of leading industry players to the superior set of options they possess. Of course, not all mining stocks generate the same earnings stream or have the same growth potential: the global diversified groups with high-quality resources and greater geographic spread are valued more highly than single commodity companies, and typically yield higher price earnings and market-to-book ratios.

Financial markets not only inform but may also drive strategy. To reflect a company's value fully, growth opportunities, strategic position in the industry, and eventually the economic logic of consolidation should all be encapsulated in relative stock prices, so companies' market values—especially of known consolidators and of their targets—incorporate the prospective value of their growth options. As a starting point, the differential market rating of leading industry players can be seen as a reflection of their superior set of options.

As noted, the gap between a company's market value and the present value of the earnings capacity of its assets in place represents the value placed on the firm's strategy to appropriate profitable corporate growth opportunities. The present value of its growth options (PVGO) can therefore be estimated from the value of assets in place and the market value of the firm. The value of assets in place is estimated using standard DCF techniques, and the residual equity value is then taken to reflect the firm's set of growth options (PVGO). So,

$$\text{Implied PVGO} = \text{Market Value (MV)} - \text{Assets in Place (PV)}, \quad (5.2)$$

where MV represents the value of the firm's equity as traded in financial markets and PV is the present value of the earnings capacity generated by its current assets (estimated as an annuity).

As the creation of shareholder value is the key criterion in assessing the advisability of making an acquisition, the value added by a firm's consolidation strategy should ultimately equal the amount by which its future value exceeds the sum of the costs of the individual acquisitions and of any organic growth the firm pursues. A study of the relative financial market appreciation of companies in an industry can help financial analysts and management teams identify markets and companies that are ready for consolidation. The pursuit of growth, scale, and scope, coupled with the superior performance of industry leaders relative to smaller players in certain industries—due to diversification or size premiums in financial markets—creates the momentum for consolidation toward a small number of powerhouse companies dominating their industries.

Indeed empirical studies confirm that the market-based PVGO is related to option characteristics.[7] For consolidation strategies, firm-specific sources of option value are considerably larger than industry effects. So the value of a serial acquisition strategy is likely to be both company and industry specific (depending on the presence of economies of scale and scope and a firm enjoying a favorable starting position for becoming a consolidator or, for example—as in Xstrata's case—an industry trend toward high commodity prices due to demand from emerging economies).

When fragmented markets are ripe for a consolidation strategy, financial markets may exhibit the following characteristics:

---

[7] PVGO is related to R&D, to idiosyncratic risk and the skewness of returns, to past sales growth and cash flow volatility, to firm and industry effects, to country effects, to downside risk of multinational corporations, and to international joint ventures. See Cao, Simin, and Zhao (2006), Tong and Reuer (2006, 2008), and Tong, Reuer, and Peng (2008).

- *Relative appreciation of assets in place and implied growth option value for leading corporations.* For consolidation to make sense, an efficient financial market should assign a higher value to leading companies' growth opportunities and their assets in place than to those of smaller firms. The lower cost of capital of the larger firms results in an appreciation of their assets in place (PV), and their superior growth prospects can also be reflected by them having higher PVGO-to-price (and EV/EBITDA) ratios than smaller industry players. The relative appreciation of leading companies allows them to acquire more cheaply, taking advantage of their highly valued equity to finance their transactions.

- *Potential to improve the overall economics of all firms in the relevant sector through consolidation.* The most strategic consolidators see themselves as operating a positive-sum game, simultaneously pursuing the dual objectives of improving overall industry returns due to a concentrated industry structure, while also positioning themselves to enjoy a disproportionate share of these returns.[8]

Xstrata used the relative PVGO levels observed in financial markets as a reality check of estimated bottom-up values. In this case, unexpectedly high commodity demand from China coupled with the industry's inability to respond due to constrained supply changed industry economics. High commodity prices changed marginal "out of the money" opportunities with little net value into lucrative "in the money" options. The capital-intensive and large-scale growth options available to industry leaders were reflecting in their greater stock prices relative to those of smaller players.

Table 5.3 lists mining's leading players mid-2006, ordered from the least to the most diversified, with estimates of the value of their future growth options at that point. The market value of equity (column 1) is the stock price times the number of shares in issue. Continuing value estimates of assets in place (column 2) are based on current earnings and the average of analysts' earnings forecasts for 2006 and 2007 using the Institutional Brokers Estimate System, adjusted for the phase of the economic cycle.[9] The market's assessment of growth options to equity (column 3) equals the value of equity (column 1) minus the value of assets in place (column 2), expressed as a percentage of equity value. An efficient market has a clear appreciation of a firm's set of corporate real options (PVGO), and financial markets implicitly assign higher value

[8] For instance, see Grossman and Hart (1980), Kamien and Zang (1990, 1993), Stigler (1950), and Perry and Porter (1985)

[9] The cost of equity (Ke) based on the market model is estimated as: risk free rate + β adjusted × (equity premium). The beta (β) of the company's equity is then based on a regression of monthly total returns (including reinvested dividends) of the company's stock returns versus returns on the S&P 500 index over a period of three years (36 months). The estimated beta is adjusted for the recent excess volatility of metals and mining relative to the rest of the economy.

TABLE 5.3 GLOBAL DIVERSIFIEDS HAVE A HIGHER PROPORTION OF GROWTH OPTION VALUE (PVGO) TO EQUITY

Firm	Price	Assets in Place		PVGO/P
	1. Market Value of Equity (millions of US dollars)	2. Various Estimates of Assets in Place		3. Growth Options to Equity (%)
		Current Earnings @ Ke	I/B/E/S Earnings @ Ke	
Inco	11,400	7,700	11,300	1–32
Teck Cominco	14,400	9,300	13,400	7–35
Xstrata	26,600	13,800	20,400	23–48
Rio Tinto	92,600	52,600	66,800	28–43
BHP Billiton	141,500	83,300	107,300	24–41

Source: Thomson as of May 5, 2006 (before announcement of Teck offer for Inco).

to the growth opportunities of global diversifieds (24–41%) than to those of more focused firms (1–35%). At the time, Xstrata was midsized, and the wider range of its PVGO estimates (23–48%) reflects its dynamic position as a developing player and aggressive acquirer.

Consider, for example, the estimate of the proportion of Teck Cominco's market value that was made up of the present value of its future growth options (PVGO/P) as of May 5, 2006 (before the announcement of its bid for Inco in the Falconbridge contest). The present value of its assets in place can be relatively easily estimated, but the continuing value estimates of those assets are sensitive to the phase of the cycle. We developed two scenarios where earnings estimates by different analysts were adjusted for the high commodity prices at the time and discounted at varying rates. Using the perpetuity equation, these resulted in values of $9.3 and $13.4 billion for the capitalized value of such earnings (under a "no further growth" policy). As Teck Cominco's market value of equity on May 5, 2006, was $14.4 billion, the market's assessment of the PVGO embedded in this market value ranged between $1.0 and $5.1 billion, depending on the methodology deployed, and its PVGO/P can be said to have ranged between 7% and 35% of its market value. We found that PVGO estimates for these firms changed over time, according to both their consolidation strategies and general industry conditions, and also that rising commodity prices between 2002 and 2008 increased the value of mining companies' current resources and expansion options.

Thus leading diversified mining corporations established a virtuous circle of value creation, and reaped related levels of support from investors. Successful competitors require increased capabilities and scale if they are to take on the considerable additional risk associated with expanding into new locations or sectors—but such diversification across geographies is essential to mitigate geopolitical, economic, currency, and other localized risks. Diversifying across related sectors that involve different economic cycles, price volatility, and customer segment exposures can, in fact, lead to an overall reduction in risk, and thus produce steadier revenue streams. Benefits such as increased scale, the ability to manage risk across a diversified global portfolio, greater access to essential capabilities, access to new opportunities, regulatory influence, and a more consistent stream of revenues all contribute to improved credit ratings and, subsequently, to global diversifieds such as Rio Tinto and BHP Billiton enjoying a lower weighted average cost of capital (WACC). As a result of this, and of their economies of scope across countries and resources, financial markets implicitly assign a higher value to their growth opportunities than to those of smaller firms such Inco and Teck Cominco. In turn, their lower WACC permits the larger firms to generate higher returns on their existing investments and to compete more aggressively for the most attractive assets, thus further growing their resource bases and continuing the virtuous circle, further enhancing the growth option values embedded in their stock price. The investment community's assessment that large diversified companies are more likely than their smaller competitors to exercise specific options successfully further amplifies the present value of their growth opportunities. These sources of competitive advantage are difficult for smaller firms to imitate without making the kind of significant investments in multiple commodities across multiple geographies, which are generally beyond their capacity.

Consistent with the framework presented in the previous chapter (Figure 4.3), the relative market power and asset bases of the companies listed in Table 5.3 differ—either globally or regionally—which determines their ability to appropriate targets. Global diversifieds (e.g., Rio Tinto, BHP Billiton) have already acquired an advantaged or dominant position, as reflected in their size and lower cost of capital. The natural growth path of such leading players is organic in times of high expected commodity prices, since they have mature positions in regions and commodities and can safely time acquisitions and decide to invest if and when the market continues to develop favorably. Dominant players may outbid weaker competitors who trigger bidding wars (as shown when BHP Billiton, a late entrant, managed to acquire WMC from Xstrata's grasp at the eleventh hour). Medium-sized companies—like Xstrata and Anglo American—had the most to gain from consolidation acquisitions or mergers that increase scale and scope on the path to becoming a global diversified, while smaller "local heroes"—such as Freeport, Lonmin, and Impala—are incentivized to seek to consolidate so as to become the new midcaps or face being acquired or marginalized as niche players.

The mining and metals industry has witnessed a revival of "related diversification" strategies and presents a number of successful examples of related diversified conglomerates, including BHP Billiton, Rio Tinto, Anglo American, Xstrata itself—and, subsequently, the newly formed Glencore, resulting from the merger of Xstrata and Glencore in May 2013. Ambitious companies aim to develop simultaneous presences in multiple regions and across multiple resources to gain access to new operations, to spread geographic risk, leverage capabilities over regions, and to build a wider scope from which to optimize their growth option values. Being able to invest in capital-intensive growth options and having operational flexibility and the ability to switch options between geographies and product/service groups changes such companies' risk profiles. It is the ability and scale to appropriate these embedded operational switching flexibilities, and new external options, that differentiate the value of the portfolios of such related diversified conglomerates from those of smaller firms.

GENERAL IMPLICATIONS AND LIMITATIONS

APPLICATION OF THE TOP-DOWN FRAMEWORK BEYOND MINING

The important contribution of the implied PVGO framework is that opportunities along the acquisition path can—in principle—be quantified and related directly to the value they create for the firm in financial markets. The approach is simple and more generally applicable than complex option valuation models. Many real option bottom-up analyses have focused on the mining industry, where the concept of replicating future cash flows can be utilized.[10] In contrast to the evaluation of organic investment projects, the advantage gained in applying the option approach to acquisitions is that market methodologies can be applied in general, since there are corresponding company values in financial markets. The growth option value can be directly "backed out" from stock prices and adjustments made for intertemporal synergies in accumulation strategies. Targets are appreciated not only for their inherent value—that is, the present value of potential future cash flows—but also for their ability to increase the acquirer's growth options value.

As an efficient market can reflect a firm's set of corporate real options, it can also indicate the value of consolidation (to both bidder and target) when the differentials between the value of assets in place and market value are higher for consolidated firms than for their constituent parts. While this method is mostly

[10] The estimated value of a producing mine can be directly based on its relationship with commodity prices. However, in other industries an insufficient number of observable quotes of related financial instrument is a general implementation problem of the replication argument of real options (e.g., in the valuation of R&D programs) and requires a valuation of the underlying value and an assumption of completeness.

used for empirical studies, we show how financial markets can guide strategy by applying this "dual valuation" approach—a combination of top-down estimation with the bottom-up mind-set of option games. In this approach, simplified option game modeling is combined with MMA—estimations of growth option values. The identified acquisition options are building blocks that must add up to a sound overall strategy, defining the sequence of acquisitions and resulting in an appreciation of the combined entity's assets in place and growth options value. Similarly, using top-down to compare the rerating of consolidating companies that successfully acquire specific targets or pursue alternative strategic paths can help point to those options that offer maximum value, as well as assisting companies to assess trade-offs in and attach price tags to their acquisition decisions.

SIMPLIFIED BUT COMPREHENSIVE ANALYSIS

Even in mining, overcomplicating the real option analysis puts the very strategic perspective being pursued at risk. Much of the desired value can be gleaned from a judiciously simplified application of the implied real option techniques. The bottom-up application shows that an acquisition strategy is not directly analogous to a standard call option, but rather to a *series* of such options and, therefore, requires a more complex analysis of the option portfolio. Considering the variety of acquisition options for a company and its competitors resembles a corporate war-gaming exercise, and can serve as a good tool for generating and testing strategic ideas. The true value of an investment is a combination of the specific asset acquired and the value of other new embedded corporate real options that accrue to the acquirer. Such embedded optionality may include the options to divest a division or abandon an investment altogether, to reduce production in one region while increasing in another, to favor one product group over another, and so on. But more important than such new operational flexibility are the options to undertake further new acquisitions, which are seen as growth options for bidders operating in consolidating markets.

CONCLUSIONS

This chapter argues that strategic approaches to sequencing acquisitions, setting bidding prices, and defining industry strategy should be guided by financial analysis. Our framework for serial acquisitions offers a dynamic view that augments descriptive theories about serial buy-and-build principles in strategic management and advocates the option-based design and quantification of acquisition strategies. By way of an overview, Figure 5.3 provides executives a summary of the metrics and tools developed and implemented in this chapter.

Implied *PVGO* = Market Value (*MV*) – Assets in Place (*PV*)

Step 1. DCF	Step 2. Regression of Relative PVGO/MV to Size	Step 3. Regression
First, back out the value of the firm's growth option set from its equity value by deducting the static present value (PV) component associated with the firm's continuing current operations or assets in place (in a "no-growth" scenario) from its market capitalization.	Second, a study of the relative financial market appreciation of companies in an industry can help financial analysts and management teams identify markets and companies that are ready for consolidation or, by contrast, for restructuring. For consolidation to make sense, an efficient financial market should assign a higher value to leading companies' growth opportunities and their assets in place than to those of smaller firms. By contrast, when the differential in *PVGO* is smaller for the majors (often conglomerates) than smaller companies, this may point to the need for restructuring strategies.	Third, check whether the conventional (market-based) growth options measures are driven by overvaluation of an entire sector and need to be corrected for mispricing. *Market Value = Value of Assets in Place + Fundamental PVGO + Excess Pricing*

Figure 5.3 Summary for Implementing Top Down Valuation

We offer a dual framework for evaluating serial acquisition strategies for executives managing acquisitive companies or their targets, partners of private equity, hedge funds, and financial market analysts. Combining market-based with traditional bottom-up valuation techniques serves as a useful reality check and can encourage opportunism in an acquisition strategy. When executing transactions, sophisticated investors should recognize that pricing the first of an expected series of acquisitions requires a dynamic analysis of the sector consolidation game. When evaluating an acquisition (or any other investment) that is part of an organization's development path, its stand-alone value needs to be augmented with an assessment of the value of the new options the investment brings to the portfolio. Furthermore, real option analysis can promote a better understanding of the acquisition premium that may have to be paid, especially in an environment with multiple bidders.

The application of new academic ideas to acquisition strategies has become increasingly important to consolidation strategy practitioners. Besides providing strategic management and finance practitioners with a greater understanding of consolidation strategies and the acquisition premiums that need to be paid for certain takeover targets, this real options framework for serial acquisitions may also suggest new areas for further theoretical and empirical research. The strength of the top-down PVGO methodology lies in the fact that financial markets, rather than complex real option models, determine growth options value, avoiding the need for specific company information and making it possible to handle large data sets. This approach may benefit from the further development of a more sophisticated estimation of the PVGO measure, when investor overreaction may at times result in stocks being over- or underpriced.

The needs for efficiency or diversification and the chance to take advantage of global investment opportunities have driven many industries—such as banking, airlines, telecom, and mining—to become increasingly consolidated. We believe that the strategic option perspective considered here, when properly applied, can help clarify the relationships between the restructuring of fragmented markets and specific companies' strategies and their market values. A company must be able to understand the value of true long-term growth, the optimal balance between organic growth and acquisitions, and how they are linked with market values. As a response to the dangers of short-termism, this method may help both managers and financial analysts better understand the importance of a company's potential for long-term growth—rather than just for current profits—and so make a direct link with companies' long-term well-being and the creation of shareholder value.

SUGGESTED READING

Bekkum, S. van, J. T. J. Smit, and H. P. G. Pennings. 2011. "Buy Smart, Time Smart: Are Takeovers Driven by Growth Opportunities or Mispricing?" *Financial Management* 40, no. 4: 911–40.

Tong, T. W., T. M. Alessandri, J. J. Reuer, and A. Chintakananda. 2008. "How Much Does Country Matter? An Analysis of Firms' Growth Options." *Journal of International Business Studies* 29, no. 3: 387–405.

Tong, T. W., and J. J. Reuer. 2006. "Firm and Industry Influences on the Value of Growth Options." *Strategic Organization* 4, no. 1: 71–95.

SUGGESTED MATERIALS, TOOLS AND GADGETS

Han Smit's page on valuation tools provides strategy tools to estimate the PVGO from a company's market value. Links to the page can be found on this book's Princeton University Press website: http://press.princeton.edu/titles /10333.html

PART III

LEARNING TO VALUE
UNCERTAINTY

CHAPTER 6

OPTION GAMES VALUATION

In war the will is directed at an animate object that reacts.
—Karl Von Clausewitz

Learning to value uncertainty in strategy requires the development of quantitative models reflecting the conceptual options games view on strategy. It is well recognized that when acquisitions generate follow-on growth options, when the economic environment is uncertain, and when competing bidders exist, both discounted cash flow valuation methods and traditional approaches to strategy development need to be extended, if acquisition strategies are to be successfully analyzed, valued, and designed.[1] While an executive team may envision a serial acquisition strategy, executing a premeditated set of transactions is difficult: forces such as uncertainty and competitor preemption can render intended targets unavailable or unattractive, presenting management teams with dilemmas. On the one hand the "flexibility" argument—which stems from real options theory[2]—suggests that, in uncertain environments, firms should defer making irreversible commitments, and instead phase their investments sequentially so that their investment plans can be revised in the light of changing conditions. On the other hand, the "early commitment" argument—which originates from game theory—holds that acquisition opportunities are limited and the missed chance is a very real threat, so firms should be keen to appropriate options within their selected strategic battlegrounds as and when they arise. Without appropriate valuation tools, navigating this conundrum is a nearby impossible task.

---

[1]   This chapter uses (in part) concepts developed in Smit and Trigeorgis (2004), Dixit and Nalebuff (1991), and Tirole (1990).
[2]   Classic papers on the real options view discuss projects that are the subject of staged investments under conditions of high uncertainty, such as the development stages of new drugs, staging investments in exploring and developing natural resources, and amplifying investments to maximize the growth options of technological innovations and their interactions with financial structures. See Trigeorgis (1996) and Dixit and Pindyck (1994) for a more complete literature overview.

The application of fresh ideas based on two major strands in the existing literature—*real options* and *game theory*—has become of increasing interest, both to academia and to acquisition strategy practitioners.[3] Despite the mathematical elegance of option game models, the key metrics and tools for implementation have not yet been fully developed, especially with regard to providing relevant managerial guidance. Our in-depth examination of Xstrata's Falconbridge acquisition through option and game lenses yields insights into the implementation of these new and effective quantitative real option models in practice, as well as pointing out their limitations.

DESIGNING AND SOLVING AN OPTION BIDDING GAME

To apply game theory to strategic bidding decisions, management needs to know the possible actions and timing strategies available to each rival (e.g., whether one of the players can gain an advantaged position by virtue of investing (or not) in a minority stake, or whether or not to enter a new geographical market), and the payoffs associated with each possible action.[4] Although these concepts may seem difficult to estimate from an outsider's point of view, competitors within an industry often do have the ability to make reliable estimates of the investment costs or intentions of their rival bidders, and the potential synergies available to them.

The context of a target determines the way in which a particular bidding game is shaped. Evaluating an acquisition opportunity in a bidding context, and determining a target's likely price, presupposes a clear description of the structure of the game. Specifically, games are characterized by four dimensions: the players, the actions available to them, the timing of these actions, and the payoff structure associated with the various possible outcomes of those games. In what follows, we discuss the basic rules and dimensions required for structuring and solving games:[5]

STEP 1: DETERMINE THE PLAYERS OF THE ACQUISITION GAME: RIVALS, POTENTIAL ENTRANTS, AND UNCERTAINTIES

In a bidding contest, obviously a rival bidder and the target's management team should be seen as players in the game. But other firms who might enter the

---

[3] New research in finance addresses this embedding of a game of capacity expansion within a dynamic real options–based investment analysis; see, for example, Smit and Ankum (1993), Grenadier (1996, 2000a, 2000b), Lambrecht (2004), Lambrecht and Myers (2007), and Smit and Trigeorgis (2004) for a more complete literature overview of option games. See also Boyer (1997) and Ghemawat and del Sol (1998) on the trade-off between flexibility and commitment.

[4] This section is based on concepts developed in Smit and Trigeorgis (2004) and Dixit and Nalebuff (1991).

[5] See Smit and Trigeorgis (2004) and Dixit and Nalebuff (1991).

bidding—or any other firm that might affect the outcome of the game—must also be considered as players and included in the analysis. For instance, in the case of Inco's and Xstrata's bidding contest for Falconbridge, additional players like Phelps Dodge and Teck Cominco entered the game as time passed and changed the strategies and the payoffs in the bidding game. In such a bidding frenzy, one rival may even change roles and themselves become a target.

In a bidding contest, a player's actions may depend not only on his or her beliefs about his or her rivals' behavior, but also on the uncertain external events that might affect the payoff. For instance, uncertain evolutions of industry prices, industry demand, or the global economy are important factors in determining the payoffs to bidders, and thus their strategies. Uncertainty is considered as *nature*, a player that randomly defines the state of the world.

STEP 2: DETERMINE THE SEQUENCE OF PLAY

Understanding how decisions are interdependent is essential in a realistic game theoretic analysis. Bidders can choose among a set of actions at certain points in time, called decision nodes (e.g., to make an early, preemptive bid or a responsive, late bid). Consequently, the sequence of play and the associated decision interactions can develop in two ways. If players make their decisions one after another, the later player being able to observe the earlier player's action, we speak of a *sequential move* game. An example is a bidding contest that is structured as an English auction, in which each firm has the opportunity to raise their initial bid after having observed the bid(s) of other player(s).

Alternatively, if a bidding situation is instantaneous, we speak of a *simultaneous move* game, for example, in case of sealed bid auctions for a company. In this case, players cannot observe each other's bid before placing their own: but competing bidders will be aware of their opponent(s) and the potential choices each might make. It is not sufficient to merely take notice of the opponent's position in a game—the strategist must also consider that the opponent's strategic thinking process simultaneously has an impact on his or her own position.

We know from the conceptual framework in the previous chapter that the success and payoff of a bidding strategy in a sequential game vis-à-vis potential rivals is partly based on a timing advantage. An acquirer must look ahead to see how a bid (or any other strategic move) would affect its rivals and how they might react—for example, if they will back down or retaliate with a higher bid—and how these future reactions will affect the bidder's current actions. For example, when Xstrata considered investing in a minority stake in Falconbridge, it had to value the different ways it would gain an advantaged position. Xstrata would be partly hedged against the effect of an increased rival bid on the acquisition price of Falconbridge, as the value of its minority stake would rise in line with the acquisition price paid for the company if the contest was won by another player, making such a stake a valuable "put" option. In addition, the initial minority stake ensured that Xstrata's average cost of acquiring Falconbridge would always be lower than that of a rival, thus making it a valuable "call" option. Thus, in a sequential game, executives have to look at the future consequences of the moves they make today.

STEP 3: DETERMINE THE CHOICES AND INFORMATION OF THE RIVAL BIDDERS

The next step involves determining the various possible moves present in a bidding game. Players face different choices (or action sets), and may possess different information sets on which to base their decisions. Examples of their choices include the decision to bid, and the level and timing of the first (and any subsequent) bids. Depending on the information known at each decision point, players assign payoffs to different actions, and choose to pursue those actions that yield the highest payoffs. A *pure strategy* is a conditional path of a player's optimal moves for each information set, and may include potential moves at decision points that might not actually be reached when the game is put into play. For instance, the bidder may have a pure strategy (independent of any action of the rival) to acquire when demand turns out to be high, and a pure strategy to wait when it is low.

In games with *complete* information, the rivals know the complete structure of the game, and can therefore predict their rivals' potential moves and the possible associated payoffs. However, in real-life acquisition games, it may be unclear to all players where their rivals are at each point. Executives may be unsure about such factors as a rival's perception of this target's value, whether a rival will consider the acquisition a threat, and how far the rival is in the negotiation process. In bidding games where information is *incomplete*, rival bidders may not have the same information about the target or the target's value to their opponents in the acquisition game. In private equity auctions, sector-specialized funds may have superior information about the profitability of the investment relative to less experienced funds. A problem that commonly arises in bidding games where information is incomplete—like auctions—is the winner's curse, which involves overestimating the worth of an asset and so winning by overbidding. Naturally, investing heavily in due diligence often pays off.

STEP 4: ESTIMATE THE PAYOFF STRUCTURE FOR EACH PLAYER (RIVAL BIDDERS AND TARGET)

An important question to address in the context of bidding contests and auctions is whether the target has a *common value* or a *private value* to different bidders. In our financial context, we consider private value items to be assets with an idiosyncratic value to each bidder, which may depend on that bidder's idiosyncratic characteristics. For instance, when a strategic player who wants to realize synergies and a financial player aiming at a leveraged buyout are involved in a contest, they are likely to assign different (private) values to the target. Conversely, a target may have a common value to two financial players where both want to execute a similar leveraged buyout. Even when bids do not differ because of bidders' differing characteristics, bidding divergence of a different nature can still be observed when common value objects are auctioned off, stemming from the uncertainty about the true, yet unknown and unobservable value of the asset; that is, bidders place different bids because their estimations of an object's true value differ. Examples of uncertain common value items include the value of unproven oil reserves, of an Internet company—or even of a jar filled with coins.

STEP 5: LOOK FORWARD AND REASON BACKWARD TO FIND THE MOST LIKELY OUTCOME

After the bidding problem is specified in a game, we solve the game by predicting player behavior and determining the optimal decision points along each possible trajectory. The solution in standard game theory assumes that players behave rationally; that is, decision makers choose their actions based on internally considered criteria, and such rationality is accepted as common knowledge: each player expects the others to act rationally, and acts accordingly. This assumption imposes an important limitation, since in most acquisition situations such rationality is bounded and a realistic analysis cannot ignore the likelihood of behavioral biases affecting the actions of some players. Classic game theory applications are based on the assumption that each player adopts a strategy that optimizes its payoff—that each is aiming to maximize value for itself. However, in situations where loss aversion is a significant driver of players' decisions, we can apply a nonlinear utility preference for each player over the possible outcomes of the game.

What game theory does is unify and systematize a strategic situation in which the solution concept may help to predict its likely strategies and outcomes. In classic game theory, the solution of the game should form a Nash equilibrium, named after Nobel Prize winner John Nash. At the start of the game the bidder determines what to do in later stages of the game, given the other players' possible rational actions. A *Nash equilibrium* is a set of strategies such that no player can do better by unilaterally changing his or her position or strategy. In simple games these rational outcomes may seem self-evident. However, a science or theory that takes simple ideas and brings out their full explanatory and predictive power and scope for more complex situations is all the more valuable for that. Solving a simultaneous move game differs from a sequential move game. Dixit and Nalebuff (1991) and Smit and Trigeorgis (2004) catalogue the following rules as a practical guide for solving different sorts of games.

1. *Finding the dominant acquisition strategy in simultaneous move games (e.g., sealed bid auctions).* First consider whether an acquirer's bid strategy will outperform all others regardless of what rivals do. Although a dominant strategy might not be obvious at the outset, successively eliminating strategies that are always going to be worse than any other strategy (i.e., dominated strategies) is a way to simplify the bidding game. By eliminating dominated strategies, a simultaneous move game can be reduced to its simplest form. Eliminating players' dominated strategies at a previous stage may reveal dominated strategies of other players and finally lead to finding each player's best strategy. If a player has no dominant strategy, but there is one for a competitor, the first player should find his or her best response to that competitor's dominant strategy. Even when there are no dominant strategies, cell-by-cell inspection and reasoning can lead to finding a Nash equilibrium of the acquisition game.[6] This is how it works: Since, in a Nash equilibrium, each player's strategy is the best response to his or her rivals' strategies, to choose his or her best strategy a player must form a belief about the strategies other players will adopt. As all players will base their beliefs on the strategies they believe are optimal for the other players, taken together, the strategies adopted by all players should lead to a Nash equilibrium, representing each player's best response to his or her rivals' optimal moves.[7]

2. *Look forward and reason back (backward induction) for solving sequential games (e.g., an opening bid in a contest).* When the game is sequential in nature, players' early moves may change the nature of competition later in the game. For instance, if one acquires a minority stake, a potential rival will observe this move and use this information to decide on whether or not to enter a contest in what is now a disadvantaged position. Thus, the outcome is likely to be different than when rival bidders enter a contest simultaneously, without earlier moves.

Identifying the dominant strategies of players is a useful approach to predicting the outcome of a simultaneous game. In contrast, in sequential games, moving first gives you the opportunity to influence

---

[6] When there is no Nash equilibrium in pure strategies, in a *mixed strategy* players assign probabilities to their actions and in a *mixed equilibrium* they randomize over their actions so that all players are indifferent between these actions. In a practical sense this captures the value of being "unpredictable," or preventing others from exploiting any systematic pattern in one's behavior. For instance, when a geographical serial strategy becomes increasingly clear to rivals, they may identify likely intended future targets. In a parallel strategy the bidder may randomize over geographies.

[7] When more than one pure Nash equilibrium may exist in a game, one must predict which equilibrium is the most likely outcome of the game. In coordination games there might be a *focal point* equilibrium, representing a natural or intuitive preference because of an asymmetry in the game that is common knowledge.

your rival's behavior—if your rival acts first, you still have to choose a dominant strategy, but now must take your rival's action as a given. Thus, in sequential move games, all players should try to anticipate their competitors' responses, and use that information to determine their own best options—which they can do by looking forward to a rival's likely reaction and then reasoning back to their best next move (in a process called *backward induction*). Players must anticipate where their initial positions or choices will ultimately lead them, and use this information to calculate the best current choice by reasoning back given optimal future behavior. Starting at the end-node payoffs, a backward induction process works through the complete tree to determine each firm's optimal set of actions at each nodal point, and then infers their actions from that information. The equilibrium paths take into account the future consequences as the valuation process works backward in time.

3. *The equilibrium set of strategies in a multistage game under uncertainty can also be found by backward induction.* The total multistage supergame may involve subgames in different stages. A subgame is a game within the total game, for instance a competing offer in an acquisition game, or a contest for a follow-on acquisition in a total serial acquisition strategy.[8] Thus, like valuing an option, a multistage game is solved by looking forward to the future consequences (outcome of subgames) and reasoning backward to the optimal current actions required to arrive at the endgame. Smit and Trigeorgis (2004) add another rule to solving multistage games. In finding the equilibrium in an overall multistage game under uncertainty, players can move backward over strategic choice branches using game theory analysis, and move backward over random moves using certainty-equivalent binomial tree option valuation. In other words, in an integrated options and games treatment, the synergistic option value at the end of each branch in the binomial option tree now equals the equilibrium outcome of a simultaneous investment subgame. This new approach makes it possible to value complete strategies in a competitive context in a fashion that it is consistent with both modern economics and finance theory. Box 6.1 illustrates how a (simplified) option game works.

---

[8]   A *subgame perfect equilibrium* is a set of strategies for each player such that any of the strategies is also a Nash equilibrium for every subgame of the game. See Selten (1965). A player may sometimes use a *threat* in an attempt to get another player to believe it will employ a specific strategy. Backward induction should utilize only *credible threats* and ignore *noncredible threats*. For a threat to be credible it must be in the player's interest to carry out the threat and so typically involves a cost or a partially irreversible decision. For instance, while an acquisition of a minority stake is a credible threat of a war of attrition, just an announcement (without likely cost) is less credible.

BOX 6.1. HOW THE OPTION GAME VALUATION OF ACQUISITION OPPORTUNITIES WORKS

Consider the case of two comparable bidders (A and B) each having the opportunity to acquire a target.

An option games valuation works backward based on the following steps:

(A) Calculate the payoff values of the target for bidder A and bidder B in a 2 × 2 matrix (subgame)

(B) Determine dominant bidding strategies and the Nash equilibrium in each 2 × 2 subgame

(C) Use option valuation to work backward along the binomial tree using the equilibrium values from the two subgames in the up- and down-cycle states

Consider a situation in which the current value of the company for bidder A equals $4 billion and for bidder B $3.2 billion. Uncertainty in the cycle and company value is modeled by a lattice approach where the value can either move up (u = 1.25) or down (d = 0.80) depending on industry product demand.

A. PAYOFFS IN THE 2 × 2 MATRIX (BIDDING SUBGAME)

Making a bid corresponds to taking or increasing a stake in a target. Exercising the option early may preempt the rival's acquisition opportunity, but deferring a bid is consistent with a cautious strategy that is less expensive, more flexible, and safer in case of unfavorable economic developments. The figure (see page 132) shows the payoffs in this economic uncertainty dilemma.

Consider first the up-cycle scenario. The left 2 × 2 table summarizes the payoffs (bidder A, bidder B) in four investment-timing scenarios at an upward moving market situation:

(i) When both firms enter into a contest and bid (simultaneously) the total expected synergies are reflected in the price. Suppose that in the up-cycle the target value for bidder A is $5 billion ($V^+ = uV$) and for bidder B $4 billion. The bidding costs are equal at $0.5 billion. The NPV for bidder A equals the target private value for the bidder − price − bidding cost, that is $0.5 = 5 − 4 − 0.5$. Since bidder A assigns a higher value to the target (due to its complementary assets), bidder B will be outbid and its NPV equals the bidding cost—$0.5 billion, resulting in a (0.5, –0.5) payoff for each bidder, with bidder A capturing the target at B's target value.

(ii) / (iii) When one investor bids while the other makes no offer, the bidder preempts the target for $3.5 billion and captures a larger part of the value creation for themselves (5 - 3.5 – 0.5 = 1 for bidder A), resulting in a payoff of (1, 0) if bidder A bids and B does not or (0,0) if B bids and bidder A does not (4 – 3.5 – 0.5 = 0 for bidder B).

(iv) When both firms decide to wait, they share the total additional value created by the timing flexibility equally, cushioning their downward losses, and their respective payoffs equal (0.75, 0.25).

B. DOMINANT STRATEGIES AND NASH EQUILIBRIUM

The next step is to identify dominant strategies in the above subgame and determine the resulting Nash equilibrium. Dominant strategies are those actions that always give a player a higher payoff value than any alternative action, whatever the other player decides to do.

Consider the equilibrium implications of an asymmetric payoff structure as in the bidding game shown on the following page. Suppose that bidder A's payoff for pursuing the acquisition (upper row) exceeds the payoff of letting it go (lower row), no matter which strategy bidder B chooses ($0.5 billion > $0 and $1 billion > $0.75 billion). Thus, bidder A has a dominant strategy to pursue the acquisition. Given this, firm B will not pursue the acquisition (since $0 billion > –0.5 billion). The Nash equilibrium (marked *) outcome of this game is given by the upper-right cell (1, 0), where bidder A acquires the company against firm B's target value.

In a down-cycle we can make a similar analysis. Here we assume the payoff in the right-hand 2 × 2 matrix below represents the Nash equilibrium where neither firm can generate net synergies from the consolidation—so neither will make an offer, resulting in a (0, 0) payoff.

C. BACKWARD OPTION VALUATION OF GROWTH OPPORTUNITIES (PVGO) ALONG THE BINOMIAL TREE

For the up- and down-cycle situations, the subgames have (different) Nash equilibriums in pure strategies. As we see on the following page (see also left 2 × 2 matrix), in the up-cycle the advantaged bidder captures the opportunity with Nash equilibrium values being $1 billion in box (ii). But in the down-cycle, the Nash equilibrium is for both bidders to wait instead

BOX 6.1. (CONT.)

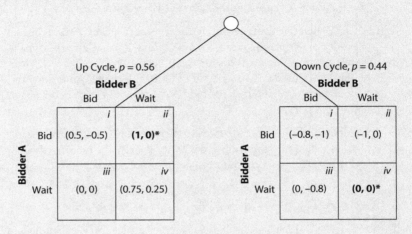

Note: Payoff in each cell is for (Bidder A, Bidder B);
Strategies of bidder A: Bid (upper row) or wait (lower row);
Strategies of bidder B: Bid (left column) or wait (right column).

The risk neutral probability equals $\quad p = \dfrac{(l+r)-d}{u-d} = \dfrac{(1+0.05)-0.80}{1.25-0.80} = 0.56$

(thus receiving $0 in box (iv) in the right-hand 2 × 2 matrix). The present value of the growth opportunity for bidder A to acquire the target (PVGO) is the discounted weighted average of the Nash equilibrium outcomes across the up- and down-cycle states.

Backward induction using the subgames represented by the above two 2 × 2 matrixes (under up- vs. down-cycles) results in a (subgame perfect) equilibrium trajectory. The process moves backward over random demand moves using the associated risk-adjusted probabilities to calculate values at the beginning of the binomial tree. To determine the growth option value, the average is computed as the risk-adjusted expectation of the two equilibrium outcomes (1 for high cycle, 0 for low cycle) using the risk-adjusted probabilities ($p = 0.56$ for an up-cycle trend and 0.44 for a down-cycle trend), discounting at the "riskless" interest rate of r = 0.05.

$$\text{PVGO}_A^* = \frac{0.56(1) + 0.44(0)}{1.05} = 0.53\text{bn}$$

QUANTIFYING THE OPTIONALITY OF
THE FALCONBRIDGE EPISODE

We can take a specific real-life option game valuation example to demonstrate its effective application.[9] Consider first the classification in value and price terms of Xstrata's 2006 acquisition of the Canadian miner, Falconbridge. The investment was a *platform acquisition* insofar as it was viewed by most bidders as a first step on a path toward future synergistic deals—so it was an option whose value depended on uncertain market developments, consolidation strategies, and synergistic opportunities with other players. Acquiring Falconbridge and its embedded assets gave Xstrata access to world-class resources, further diversification into nickel and North America, an industry-leading copper organic growth portfolio, further industry consolidation in zinc and copper, and significant scale as the world's fifth largest public mining house—a newfound scale and positioning that opened up new acquisition and merger options that had previously been beyond Xstrata's reach. The path Xstrata chose (including the Falconbridge bid) not only determined the reputation and investment alternatives open to the firm from that point on, but also constrained its firm's future choices (i.e., its set of corporate real options).

Acquisitions by aggressive companies such as Xstrata may trigger a series of mergers and acquisitions, changing the probability of success at the time and in the future. Unlike the MIM acquisition (which was a proprietary acquisition, where Xstrata had less competition for the target compared to later acquisitions) the acquisition of Falconbridge was an option that was shared with rival bidders. It was clear to Xstrata that a number of potential natural suitors existed for Falconbridge—in particular, Inco had significant potential synergies in that it had adjacent operations and Falconbridge would have provided it with diversification into copper. As a first step, Xstrata acquired 20% of Falconbridge from a single shareholder in an attempt to simulate a proprietary option. As expected, Inco entered the bidding contest, but when the price for Falconbridge reached a level that would have stretched its financial capacity, Inco's executives introduced a new player into the game—Phelps Dodge, a US copper producer seeking to diversify its portfolio into nickel—which launched a bid for both Inco and Falconbridge. But while Phelps Dodge's bid was to be funded by its shares, Xstrata's was in cash, so it ultimately gained control of Falconbridge. The fact that its initial 20% stake (its real option) had been acquired at

---

[9] The views in this section are those of the authors: they do not necessarily reflect Xstrata's opinion. The case is simplified and aimed to illustrate the model, not to document reality. The numbers in this case are consistent with financial market values and acquisition premiums at the time of the Falconbridge acquisition, but do not necessary correspond with the valuation that Xstrata used at the time. Xstrata's real figures are unavailable.

a significantly lower price than the ultimate high bids for the whole company proved decisive, as it made Xstrata's overall bid cheaper than those of other potential suitors. The Falconbridge transaction can thus be classified as a *shared platform acquisition* for Xstrata (as it would have been for its rival, the Inco/Phelps Dodge consortium). Such contests force bidders to take competitors into account and the winner invariably pays a premium (i.e., the amount by which the eventual price paid exceeds the prelaunch market value) that inevitably accounts for at least a portion of the target's potential synergy profits and thus of its strategic value.

When companies face this type of strategic uncertainty, it is possible to estimate the value and the likelihood of different outcomes, including failure. If Phelps Dodge had succeeded in acquiring Falconbridge, Xstrata would have been left out in the cold in the overall industry consolidation. Xstrata executives thought that the (largely negative) effects of failure for Xstrata would have included a loss of its reputation as an industry consolidator, a reduction in the number of its future options, as well as, potentially, the stalling of its consolidation strategy—all of which could have significantly affected its PVGO and market value.

THE VALUE OF THE FALCONBRIDGE PLATFORM

Analysts agreed that Falconbridge represented a *platform acquisition* for Xstrata, insofar as it could lead to a possible follow-on merger, depending on the later-stage evolution of the business cycle. Falconbridge's value to Xstrata expressed as an equation:

$$\text{Expanded PV}_{\text{Xstrata}} = \text{Present value of the cash flows} + \text{growth options value}$$

$$= [\text{stand-alone value Falconbridge} + \text{option to realize synergies at stage 1}] + [\text{present value of future merger options at stage 2}]$$

STAGE 1: STAND-ALONE VALUE AND INTERASSET SYNERGIES

Falconbridge's stand-alone equity value as at October 2005 was about C\$10 billion (based on C\$27 per share) but could increase or decline in line with commodity price changes. If it succeeded in this acquisition, Xstrata's plan was to encourage the Inco mining group to do something that Falconbridge had failed to do: combine their respective operations in the valuable Sudbury Basin via a joint venture to realize cost savings. For the particular set of input variables we use here, this led to a total valuation of Falconbridge (including its Inco joint venture synergies) of C\$12 billion.

STAGE 2: PRESENT VALUE OF THE FUTURE ACQUISITION (AND MERGER) OPTIONS (PVAO)

Acquiring Falconbridge and its inbuilt assets gave Xstrata access to world-class resources and newfound scale, and its new position opened up new merger options that had previously been beyond its reach. Although the growth option value of a follow-on merger is hard to estimate, Box 6.2 shows the simplified structure of the two-stage Falconbridge platform acquisition game. After the first bidding game for Falconbridge itself in 2005, uncertainty about demand was resolved (as reflected by the branches), and Xstrata faced a second-stage merger game.[10]

If Xstrata completed the Falconbridge acquisition, the estimated value of the envisaged *incremental* merger activities (as at 2005) would equal C$1.5 billion. Falconbridge, therefore, offered Xstrata access to the high-quality assets and organic growth options of Falconbridge itself (valued at C$10 billion), the potential for a joint venture with Inco to realize significant synergies (C$2 billion), and future merger or acquisition opportunities (C$1.5 billion). Valued as a platform, the value Xstrata stood to gain totaled [10 billion + 2 billion] + 1.5 billion = C$13.5 billion, a value that can be termed as a private value in that it applied only to Xstrata—and then only when Falconbridge (and its assets) were fully in its hands.

BIDDING GAMES ACQUIRERS PLAY

When it was considering acquiring Falconbridge, it was clear to Xstrata that a number of potential natural suitors existed, among whom Inco had significant potential to realize synergies with Falconbridge's Sudbury operations. In addition to the conceptual framework discussed in chapter 4, quantifying different bidding game scenarios in stage 1 of the overall (super)game (in Box 6.2) can help executives better understand the competitive forces that operate in consolidating industries, making the likely outcomes of any bidding wars clearer and so indicating which strategic moves would be more effective for appropriating options under uncertainty conditions. Table 6.1 (see page 140) illustrates an overview of four potential bidding game scenarios that we discuss in the next sections, in which Xstrata or Inco can modify their positions to appropriate Falconbridge by virtue of (1) its size or complementary assets, (2) early-mover advantages, (3) minority stake, or (4) consortium membership.

---

[10] We later subdivide the first stage in a first bidding game for a 20% stake in Falconbridge in 2005 and a subsequent game for the balance of the company it did not own.

BOX 6.2 THE CASE OF A PLATFORM ACQUISITION

We start with the real options value of this deal as a platform acquisition for Xstrata—i.e., one that opens up new merger growth options. Consider the case of two rival bidders (Xstrata and Inco) each having the opportunity to acquire Falconbridge (stage 1), potentially leading to follow-on merger options (stage 2), allowing an options game tree to be constructed (as illustrated in the figure below). In the subperiod (2 years) of demand uncertainty, the option value of the merger can be estimated and modeled by a lattice approach, where the value can move up (u) or down (d) with (average) binomial parameters. An option games valuation of the two-staged supergame works backward in three steps:

(1) Calculate the payoff values for players Xstrata and rival R at the end game

(2) Determine dominant strategies and the Nash equilibrium in each 2 × 2 subgame

(3) Use option valuation to work backward in the binomial tree using these subgame equilibrium values in high and low demand states.

STEP 1. PAYOFFS IN THE 2 × 2 MATRIX (SUBGAME)

Consider first the 2 × 2 matrix for a follow-on merger in the high demand scenario after Xstrata acquires Falconbridge (shown in the left-hand column, 1). This bidding game has four investment-timing scenarios:

(i) when both players bid: The winner gets the target for a price which equals (at least) the value of the target to the rival, the value creation = bidder value – price – cost = 44 billion – 40 billion – 0.5 billion = 3.5 billion

(ii) and (iii) when either player bids and the other waits: In this case, when the first mover (Xstrata) preempts the other, the value creation for Xstrata equals 44 billion – 40 billion – 0.5 billion = 3.5 billion and for the rival –0.5 billion

(iv) when both decide to wait and not invest, the value equals 0 (for both)

The payoffs of the different subgames in high and low demand states, and when the follow-on merger option is either proprietary or shared, are given on the facing page.

STAGE 2 END NODE PAYOFF PROPRIETARY AND SHARED MERGER OPTION GAMES

	Proprietary follow-on merger options		Shared follow-on merger options	
Value for Xstrata Value for rival (R)	High demand (u) $suV_0 = 44$ billion $uV = 40$ billion (1)	Low demand (d) $sdV = 11$ billion $dV = 10$ billion (2)	High demand (u) $uV = 40$ billion (3)	Low demand (d) $dV = 10$ billion (4)
(i) Bid Bid	$NPV_X = 44 - 40 - 0.5 = 3.5$ $NPV_R = -0.5$	$NPV_X = 11 - 10 - 0.5 = 0.5$ $NPV_R = -0.5$	$NPV_X = 40 - 40 - 0.5 = -0.5$ $NPV_R = -0.5$	$NPV_X = 10 - 10 - 0.5 = -0.5$ $NPV_R = -0.5$
(ii) Bid Wait	$NPV_X = 44 - 40 - 0.5 = 3.5$ $NPV_R = 0$	$NPV_X = 11 - 10 - 0.5 = 0.5$ $NPV_R = 0$	$NPV_X = 40 - 40 - 0.5 = -0.5$ $NPV_R = 0$	$NPV_X = -10 - 10 - 0.5 = -0.5$ $NPV_R = 0$
(iii) Wait Bid	$NPV_X = 0$ $NPV_R = -0.5$	$NPV_X = 0$ $NPV_R = -0.5$	$NPV_X = 0$ $NPV_R = -0.5$	$NPV_X = 0$ $NPV_R = -0.5$
(iv) Wait Wait	$NPV_X = 0$ $NPV_R = 0$	$NPV_X = 0$ $NPV_R = 0$	$NPV_X = 0$ $NPV_R = 0$	$NPV_X = 0$ $NPV_R = 0$

BOX 6.2 (CONT.)

STEP 2. DOMINANT STRATEGIES AND NASH EQUILIBRIUM

The next step is to identify dominant subgame strategies and determine the resulting Nash equilibriums. Dominant strategies are those actions that always give a player a higher payoff value than any alternative, whatever the rival player decides to do. Considering the high demand scenario in the end node first, our simplified example shows an asymmetric payoff. Xstrata's payoff from pursuing the follow-on merger exceeds the payoff of letting it go, no matter which strategy the rival (R) chooses (3.5 billion > 0 billion). Appreciating this dominant strategy, its rival will not pursue the acquisition (since 0 billion > –0.5 billion). The Nash equilibrium outcome of this subgame is the upper-right cell (3.5 billion, 0), where the advantaged bidder (Xstrata) acquires a follow-on merger (minimally for a price equal to the rival's value, to deter them). A similar analysis can determine the Nash equilibriums for all the subgames in the second stage, at low and high demand, whether or not Xstrata invested in the platform.

STEP 3. BACKWARD OPTION VALUATION OF ACQUISITION GAMES

The present value of the acquisition opportunity is the discounted weighted average of the Nash equilibrium outcomes across the high and low demand states. In determining the growth option value, the average is computed as the expectation of the two equilibrium outcomes (3.5 billion for high demand and 0.5 billion for low demand) using the risk-adjusted probabilities (p = 0.39 for high demand move and 0.61 for a low demand move), discounted at the riskless interest rate, r = 0.082, over the 2 years. Backward induction using the two subgames above (represented by the 2 × 2 matrixes, under high vs. low demand) results in a (subgame perfect) equilibrium trajectory:

$$PVAO^* = \frac{0.39(3.5) + 0.61(0.5)}{1.082} = 1.5bn,$$

Incorporating both the standalone value as well as the strategic acquisition option potential, the expanded value of Falconbridge as a platform acquisition in a competitive bidding environment for Xstrata can be given by:

$$Expanded\ PV_{Xstrata} = [\text{stand-alone value Falconbridge} + PV$$
$$\text{of the synergies at stage 1}]$$

$$+ \text{present value of stage 2 (equilibrium) acquisition opportunity (PVAO)}$$

$$= [10 + 2] + 1.5 = 13.5$$

We use this value in the different first-stage bidding games for Falconbridge, where the NPV_X = expanded $PV_{Xstrata}$ – price – bidding cost = 13.5 –12.5 – 0.5 = 0.5 billion.

Simplified Example of the Platform Valuation of the Falconbridge Acquisition Game

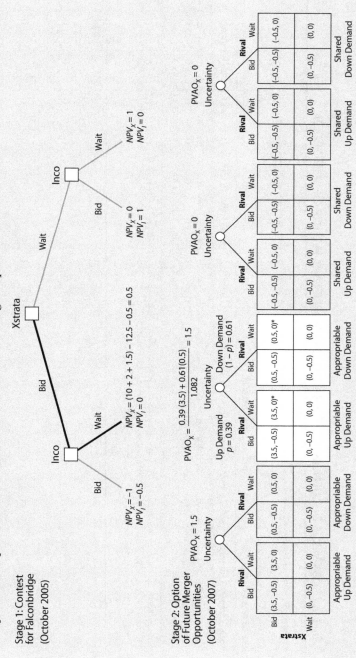

Parameter values: The standalone value V^I for Falconbridge equals 10 billion at $t = 0$ for both bidders, the total synergies for Inco equals 4 billion, and joint venture for Xstrata equals 2 billion. The value of the follow-on merger equals $V^{II} = 20$ billion at $t = 0$ and $s^{II} = 1.1$ (asymmetry in value after platform acquisition). Demand over the period can either move up ($u = 2$) or down ($d = 0.5$), the interest rate (over the subperiod) $r = 1.082$; the option probability $p = 0.39$; the bidding cost = 0.5.

TABLE 6.1 SCENARIOS INFLUENCING THE SHARED OR PROPRIETARY NATURE OF THE OPTION

Scenario 1 Firms use their position due to synergies, platform, or relative size to win a contest	Scenario 2 Use timing of a preemptive bid to appropriate the option	Scenario 3 Acquire a minority stake	Scenario 4 Introduce new players: Bidding consortium
• The company's dominant position allows it to wait to fully appropriate option value and bid as soon as a weaker rival makes an offer or the demand cycle changes. • Disadvantaged bidders should bid immediately, but must be aware that a stronger competitor may appropriate the acquisition in a contest.	• A preemptive bid may deter rivals when a first mover changes a "grab the dollar" game to an acquisition game known as "Burning Bridges," where the first mover makes a pre-commitment. • But, at high demand levels, a first preemptive bid may not be enough to deter a rival from entering an acquisition frenzy.	• A small but decisive stake in the target can enable even a smaller disadvantaged bidder to appropriate a target. • A minority stake may lead to a lower average price if the contest is won, or represent a hedge if it is lost.	• At medium and high expected demand levels, the largest alliance may preempt growth options against smaller rival bidders whose synergies are at a smaller scale.

A. *Simultaneous* Asymmetric "Grab the Dollar" Game

B. *Sequential* Bidding Can Burn Bridges

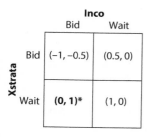

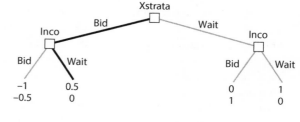

Payoff in Each Cell Is for (Xstrata, Inco)

Company Strategy	Xstrata NPV = (Standalone Value + Joint Venture Synergies + PVAO) – Price – Bidding Cost	Inco NPV = (Standalone Value + Synergies) – Price – Bidding Cost
Bid, Bid	$NPV_X = (10 + 2 + 1.5) - 14 - 0.5 = -1$	$NPV_I = (10 + 4) - 14 - 0.5 = -0.5$
Bid, Wait	$NPV_X = (10 + 2 + 1.5) - 12.5 - 0.5 = 0.5$	$NPV_I = 0$
Wait, Bid	$NPV_X = 0$	$NPV_I = (10 + 4) - 12.5 - 0.5 = 1$
Wait, Wait	$NPV_X = 1$	$NPV_I = 0$

The standalone value platform company (October 2005) equals $V^I = 10$ billion for both bidders, the synergies for Inco equal 4 billion and joint venture synergies for Xstrata 2 billion, the acquisition option for Xstrata equals 1.5 billion

Figure 6.1 Simultaneous versus Sequential Bidding

SCENARIO 1: BIDDERS CONSIDER THE ACQUISITION OPTION SIMULTANEOUSLY

We start the analysis with a potential scenario as at 2005, describing the strategic game *before* the acquisition of Falconbridge. Before any moves are made, the options available to the potential bidders (Xstrata and Inco) are matched. Looking first at simultaneous bidding strategies for Falconbridge—represented in panel A of Figure 6.1 in a normal matrix format—we can see the top-left cell of this payoff table shows a battle as the worst scenario for both sides.[11] Having lost an earlier battle with BHP Billiton for the Australian miner WMC, Xstrata was concerned that losing another battle would affect its reputation as a serial acquirer. If the battle was bitter, the respective payoffs could be expected to be (–1, –0.5) for Xstrata and Inco, respectively.[12] The next worst scenario for each bidder would be to follow a passive strategy and allow its rival

---

[11] For Xstrata, the estimated 2005 value of Falconbridge as a platform equaled C\$13.5 billion (as noted above); calculating its "private" value to Inco, based on the commodity prices prevailing at that time, gave a stand-alone value plus a synergistic value of C\$14 billion.

[12] If the price rose in a bidding contest to C\$14 billion, the negative value for Xstrata (including costs) would equal –C\$1 billion: for Inco, a bidding battle would also have an expected negative

to acquire Falconbridge—this would have resulted in a zero payoff for both sides (bottom-left and top-right cells). Even if the nonacquirer focused on other merger opportunities instead, this choice would represent an erosion of their investment opportunities in a rapidly consolidating industry. Inco's best strategy would be to acquire the target at once by making a bid of C$13 billion, which (if successful) would appropriate C$14 billion – C$13 billion = C$1 billion worth of the total available synergies (bottom-left cell). The best scenario for Xstrata would be for both firms to avoid an intense battle and wait until commodity prices stabilize at a higher level.[13]

In this Grab the Dollar payoff structure, bidders evaluate the shared option, but want to avoid a head-on contest. Simultaneous games can be solved by dominant strategies: Xstrata's payoff for the waiting strategy (lower row) exceeds the payoff of a bidding strategy (upper row), no matter whether Inco chooses to bid or not (0 > C$–1 billion and C$1b > C$0.5 billion). Consider the implications of a Grab the Dollar game. In 2005 (before Xstrata acquired its minority stake) Inco could have taken advantage of Xstrata's unwillingness to engage in another fight on disadvantageous terms to try to win the battle for the target: the outcome of this rivalry would be given by the Nash equilibrium (*) in the bottom-left cell (0, C$1 billion). If Inco had bid earlier—when expected demand levels were low to intermediate—it might have preempted Xstrata and won the game. So in this first scenario where both simultaneous evaluate a shared option Xstrata's hands are tied—to avoid a head-on bidding contest it has no other option but adopt a wait-and-see strategy.

SCENARIO 2: PREEMPTIVE COMMITMENT USING FIRST-MOVER ADVANTAGE

We next quantify another potential scenario as of 2005: the commitment value of a preemptive bid by Xstrata. The idea is that—in a situation where a CEO has a strong reputation as a successful deal maker—the threat of a battle could actually work in Xstrata's favor, if it were the first to make an offer for Falconbridge. Burning Bridges is a strategy where Xstrata could preempt its rival by cutting off its option to wait and perhaps deter them from entering the contest at all (as when an army burns the bridge behind it, making retreat impossible). The question then becomes, which bid strategy (wait and see or preemptive bid) should Xstrata follow, given that it could influence the strategy of a potential future rival?

Panel B in Figure 6.1 presents the game in an extended (decision tree) form, but with the same payoffs as before. In a *sequential* version of the game (scenario 2), Xstrata must now consider all possible future scenarios and then rea-

---

payoff of –C$0.5 billion. (As noted, this potential scenario is an academic illustration, and differs from the actual evolution of the bidding game.)

[13]   When Xstrata would be more likely to win due to its acquisitions experience and lower financing costs (which we can suppose are worth C$1 billion to Xstrata and 0 to Inco).

son backward to consider its value as a first mover. Considering the right-hand branches of panel B first, if Xstrata waits (right branch) to see if commodity prices stabilize, Inco might respond by acquiring Falconbridge, so that Xstrata's payoff would be $0. However, if Xstrata makes the first bid (left-hand side), Inco could only respond by not entering the contest at all, or by entering at a disadvantage, in which case Xstrata's payoff will be C$0.5 billion. By bidding first, Xstrata would signal a credible early commitment to acquire the company, which (at intermediate demand levels) would be likely to deter Inco. Such a strategically timed move would cause equilibrium forces to lead to a more desirable payoff for Xstrata (of C$0.5 billion) than in the earlier (simultaneous) game (with $0 payoff).[14]

SCENARIO 3: A MINORITY STAKE GIVES FLEXIBILITY AND COMMITMENT VALUE

However, full acquisition of a similar sized company, which scenario 2 would likely lead to, could have exposed Xstrata to the high risk of economic uncertainties, while deferring the offer (as in scenario 1) would represent a cautious (option) strategy that was less expensive and more flexible, and would be safer if economic developments turned out unfavorably, but would likely have resulted in a missed chance. In August 2005 the opportunity arose for Xstrata to purchase a stake in Falconbridge (of about 20% of its common shares) from Brascan for C$2 billion, which would effectively give Xstrata an advantaged position to exercise the shared real option in Falconbridge, while at the same time retaining the flexibility to guard against reversals in the economic climate.[15]

A simplified valuation of the minority stake option game is depicted in Figure 6.2. In this modified first stage subgame, Xstrata can invest upfront in an minority stake that also gives it a shared option to buy the rest of Falconbridge's shares, which has a maturity period of nine months (given the break fee in the Brascan deal to recognize commodity price uncertainty).[16] If commodity prices decline, Xstrata will still hold a minority stake in Falconbridge— if they rise further, Xstrata will have an advantaged position in the bidding game (against Inco) for the remaining 80% of Falconbridge, as its total price to appropriate the whole company would always be lower than Inco's. But if Inco bids a higher price than Xstrata's maximum—and thus acquires Falconbridge— Xstrata has the option to sell its 20% stake to Inco at a profit.

[14] Following the highlighted (bold) branches in the figure in Box 6.2 also corresponds with the sequential, early move bidding game.

[15] See also, for instance, Eckbo (2009), Bulow, Huang, and Klemperer (1999), and Singh (1998) on bidding strategies and takeover premiums.

[16] The basic price was C$28 per share, but the deal also involved a "top-up." If within nine months of this acquisition Xstrata made an offer for Falconbridge at a greater price per share, Xstrata would pay Brascan that excess for the minority stake (20% of the common shares) it had originally purchased.

Consider the payoffs in 2006 if commodity demand (and prices) were very high or very low,[17] and consequently when the acquisition subgame would have different Nash equilibriums in dominant strategies.[18] If demand and commodity prices were very high, the outcome would be a contest in which Inco would be outbid and Xstrata would capture the target, resulting in a (C$2 billion, C$0) payoff for Xstrata and Inco respectively. But if demand and prices were low, both firms would defer their acquisition plans, with equal payoffs of (C$0.2 billion, C$0.2 billion). The shared option to acquire the remaining 80% of the company is the discounted weighted average of the Nash equilibrium outcomes across the high and low demand states. The stand-alone value of Falconbridge in August 2005 was C$9 billion (based on the average stock price of C$23), so the value of the minority stake is given by:

Value Minority Stake Xstrata = [20% of stand-alone value Falconbridge] + [shared option to acquire remaining 80%]

= 20% (9 bn) + 1 bn = 1.8 bn + 1 bn = C$2.8 bn

This option valuation of C$2.8 billion justified Xstrata's actual August 2005 bid (of C$2 billion) for the 20% stake.[19] During 2005 and the first half of 2006 the values of all miners rose due to increasing commodity prices and on October 11, 2005, Inco and Falconbridge (who were aiming to avoid a takeover by Xstrata) announced an agreed proposal for Inco to acquire Falconbridge for C$12 billion. Inco increased this offer in May 2006 to C$19 billion, again on the basis that prices for base metals were rising (including for nickel, Falconbridge's primary commodity). Xstrata reacted by making a C$52.50 per share

---

[17] The payoff in the two by two matrixes are as follows: (i) If Inco and Xstrata enter into a bid contest, the total expected synergies will be partly reflected in the cost to whichever of them wins the contest. If we assume that the up-cycle increases the stand-alone value of the target to C$15 billion by June 2006 and synergies in Inco's case equal C$5 billion, Inco's offer would be C$20 billion. But increased value of the follow-on merger opportunity—derived from a similar procedure as in the Box 6.2—would increase the platform's value to Xstrata to C$22 billion and the payoff for Xstrata to C$2 billion (at a price of C$20 billion), resulting in a comparative payoff between the two bidders of (C$2 billion, 0). (ii)/(iii) If one rival bids but the other doesn't, the bidder will preemptively acquire the target for a lower price (C$19 billion). Investment opportunities in a rapidly consolidating industry are limited, the worst scenario for each bidder (resulting in a –C$0.1 billion payoff for both sides) is to allow its rival to acquire Falconbridge without a fight, resulting in payoffs of (C$2.8 billion, –C$0.1 billion) or (–C$0.1 billion, C$1 billion) for Xstrata or Inco respectively. (iv) When both firms decide not to bid (to cushion any downward losses), we can assume the option payoffs are (C$2 billion, C$0).

[18] For simplicity we assume from here on that bidding costs are included in the price. When the option value for follow-on opportunities for Xstrata increases to C$6 billion in the up-cycle in June 2006 (and assuming they can be achieved only after control of the company is secured), the payoff for the remaining 80% shares of Falconbridge equals 0.8 (C$15 billion – C$20 billion) + C$6 billion = C$2 billion.

[19] The valuation is simplified in various ways. For consistency of the numerical example, we here assume that the shared option value of the minority stake as of August 2005 was also C$1 billion.

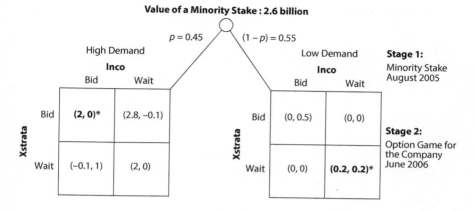

Value of a Minority Stake : 2.6 billion

$p = 0.45$ $(1 - p) = 0.55$

High Demand   Low Demand   **Stage 1:**

Inco   **Inco**   Minority Stake

Bid   Wait   Bid   Wait   August 2005

Stage 1 grid (Xstrata / Inco High Demand):
- Bid, Bid: **(2, 0)***
- Bid, Wait: (2.8, −0.1)
- Wait, Bid: (−0.1, 1)
- Wait, Wait: (2, 0)

Stage 1 grid (Xstrata / Inco Low Demand):
- Bid, Bid: (0, 0.5)
- Bid, Wait: (0, 0)
- Wait, Bid: (0, 0)
- Wait, Wait: **(0.2, 0.2)***

Stage 2:
Option Game for the Company
June 2006

Stage 1: Bidding Game for the Remaining Shares (2006)		Stage 0: Monthly Stake in Platform 2005
High Demand ($uV = 15$)	**Low Demand ($dV = 6.7$)**	
Bid $NPV_X = 0.8(15 − 20) + 6 = 2$	$NPV_X = 0.8(6.7 − 6.7) = 0$	Value of the minority stake =
Bid $NPV_I = 15 + 5 − 20 = 0$	$NPV_I = 6.7 + 0.5 − 6.7 = 0.5$	20% of standalone value
Bid $NPV_X = 0.8(15 − 19) + 6 = 2.8$	$NPV_X = 0.8(6.7 − 6.7) = 0$	Falconbridge + shared option to acquire 80% of the company
Wait $NPV_I = −0.1$	$NPV_I = 0$	
Wait $NPV_X = −0.1$	$NPV_X = 0$	$= 20\% (9) + \dfrac{0.45(2) + 0.55(0.2)}{1.04}$
Bid $NPV_I = 15 + 5 − 19 = 1$	$NPV_I = 6.7 − 6.7 = 0$	$= 1.8 + 1$
Wait $NPV_X = 2$	$NPV_X = 0.2$	
Wait $NPV_I = 0$	$NPV_I = 0.2$	

The value creation for Xstrata equals NPV = stake (bidder value − price) + ($PVAO$ and JV synergies), option value or 0 (no bid).

The value creation for Inco equals NPV = bidder value + synergies − price, option value, or 0 (no bid).

Parameter values: minority stake is 20% and the remaining shares 80%; standalone value 9 billion (August 2005); $r = 4\%$, $u = 3/2$, $d = 2/3$, $p = 0.45$ (over period Oct 2005–June 2006).

Upward business cycle (June 2006), $PVAO$ and joint venture synergies Xstrata = 6 billion, synergies for Inco = 5 billion; $P = 20$ in contest; $P = 19$ without contest.

Downward business cycle (June 2006); $PVAO$ Xstrata = 0, synergies for Inco = 0; $P = 6.7$ billion.

Figure 6.2   Strategic Option Value of a Minority Stake

bid (worth C\$20 billion in total) for the 80% of Falconbridge shares it did not already own.

SCENARIO 4: NEW PLAYERS RAISE THE STAKES

Early in 2006 Inco sought a white knight to strengthen its position in bidding for Falconbridge, and found one in the form of US copper producer Phelps Dodge. Showing considerable nerve, Phelps Dodge upped the ante to produce

Phelps Dodge Inco

	Bid	Wait
Bid	**(0.4, 0)***	(2, –0.1)
Wait	(–0.1, 2)	(0, 0)

(left axis label: Xstrata)

	Xstrata	Phelps Dodge-Inco
Bid, Bid	$NPV_X = 0.8(15 - 22) + 6 = 0.4$	$NPV_I = 15 + 7 - 22 = 0$
Bid, Wait	$NPV_X = 0.8(15 - 20) + 6 = 2$	$NPV_I = -0.1$
Wait, Bid	$NPV_X = -0.1$	$NPV_I = 15 + 7 - 20 = 2$
Wait, Wait	$NPV_X = 0$	$NPV_I = 0$

Stage 1: Bidding game for the remaining shares (2006) with new players entering the game. Payoff in each cell is for (Xstrata, Phelps Dodge Inco).

Xstrata's strategies: Bid (upper row) or wait (lower row).

Phelps Dodge Inco's strategies: Bid (left column) or wait (right column)

Figure 6.3 New Players Scramble for Global Mining Assets

a new, more complex bidding situation. Effectively, Xstrata was pursuing Falconbridge, as was Inco (which was simultaneously under threat from Canada's Teck Cominco). Phelps Dodge waded straight into the Canadian battle by bidding for both Inco and Falconbridge simultaneously, raising the price stakes significantly. Effectively, Phelps' bid for Inco increased the latter's market value, which automatically increased Inco's partial share-based offer for Falconbridge. Phelps Dodge bid US$40 billion to take over both Inco and Falconbridge, aiming to create the Phelps Dodge Inco Corp., which would have been the world's fifth largest mining company, its largest nickel producer, and second largest copper producer.

Figure 6.3 updates the payoffs in the bidding game for the remaining Falconbridge shares for this hot deal market. Steeply rising commodity prices pushed the stand-alone value of Falconbridge up from C$9 billion in early 2005 to C$15 billion by June 2006, while the new synergies and lower cost of capital for the combined entity further increased its incremental value to Phelps Dodge-Inco from C$5 billion to C$7 billion, valuing the Falconbridge part of the deal at about C$15 billion + C$7 billion = C$22 billion. This meant that Xstrata would have had to increase its bid for the remaining 80% shares if it wanted to outbid Phelps Dodge-Inco.[20] As Figure 6.3 shows, this results in a (C$0.4, 0) payoff if both rivals bid, while the payoff of a preemptive acquisition

---

[20] Rising commodity prices also meant that the growth option value to Xstrata of the Falconbridge platform had increased to C$6 billion in 2006, so the payoff for Xstrata at the new valuation paradigm would equal C$0.4 billion (0.8[C$15 billion – C$22 billion] + C$6 billion). As noted, this is an academic illustration of the use of option games. Xstrata's actual numbers are unavailable.

would be (C\$2, –C\$0.1) or (–C\$0.1, C\$2), respectively, if either Xstrata or Phelps Dodge Inco acquired Falconbridge. When both companies perceive these (high) payoffs, the Nash equilibrium for this bidding subgame results in the outcome given in the upper left-hand cell, suggesting that the bidder with the lowest average price would acquire the target. Phelps' intervention was bold but insufficient: Xstrata's original 20% stake meant that its average price would always be lower than Inco's—and Xstrata's bid was in cash (which was more attractive to its investors) so, ultimately, it won control of Falconbridge.

CONCLUSIONS: HOW OPTION GAMES CAN DELIVER THEIR POTENTIAL

The quantitative models presented here apply leading-edge academic theory in ways that can be meaningful in a boardroom context, and may help change how executives and private equity partners view serial buy-and-build acquisitions. Looking at the Falconbridge episode through an option games lens reveals various insights as to how a company might apply such a valuation tool in practice, and how such valuations might change its strategy.

HOW TO APPLY AN OPTION GAME VALUATION EFFECTIVELY

While real option proponents argue it represents a superior approach to valuing businesses and acquisition targets—especially within a serial acquisition strategy—most executives are too daunted by its technical complexity to apply quantitative real options models in real-life situations. Applying a quantitative option game analysis to Xstrata we find it useful to perform several procedures and adjustments to set the game up: subdividing the strategy into "building blocks," employing some "art" to simplify the game, and applying it in ways that can help a firm influence situations to its advantage.[21]

  1. *Subdivide a complex strategy into simpler building blocks.* A serial growth strategy consists of a complex combination of shared options. The strength of an option game approach lies in its ability to analyze very complex strategic problems (such as in buy-and-build strategies), subdividing them into various types of options (shared vs. proprietary and asset vs. platform) and so provide deeper understanding of the complex dynamics of how competitive acquisition strategies can create value. A real options method analyzes the potential sequencing of a serial strategy and, within this, reveals the power and optionality embedded within platform acquisitions.

---

[21] See, for instance, Mylonadis (2010) for an excellent guide for how to define and structure problems in decision making.

2. *Lay out the game realistically.* A quantification of each option game requires some skill in simplifying the game while still including all the possible combinations, sequencing of targets and estimates of the likely number of players. By expressing an acquisition path as an option tree, with clear go/no go intersections and strategic moves, our methodology focuses attention on key uncertainties (such as commodity prices in the case of the mining industry), key internal uncertainties, and the company's strategic position—thus providing a rational way to choose whether to pursue, alter, or defer decisions according to the evolution of those uncertainties.

A basic premise for developing these deeper insights for buy-and-build strategies is that the various strategic options can be specified over certain periods. Endogenous uncertainty in identifying targets is limited, in that they are known at the inception of the strategy, so (compared to many other situations involving explorative investments, e.g., R&D) a company can specify its intended option acquisition strategy and the associated horizon period a priori. For this purpose, the analysis encompasses two phases: the consolidation game phase where possible bidder-target combinations are identified as feasible over a game horizon of (typically) three to five years, and the second phase, where the model assumes that the hand has been played.[22]

3. *Experiment with the game's assumptions and specifications.* Option game models are part of a framework for sensible guidance, but don't cover all the angles for a successful acquisition strategy, which in reality is richer, with many more complexities than the stylized option games presented here. For instance (as our Falconbridge example shows) market demand uncertainties, the intensity of competition or the appearance of entirely new bidders can significantly modify the game. Moreover, the standard analysis prescribes what players will do, assuming they behave rationally—but while a rational player may perceive the state of game clearly and make consistent decisions, an overconfident rival may still outbid them in auctions. Using insights from behavioral economics to play with the assumptions behind a game may help bidders to respond *rationally* to their rivals' *bounded rational* behavior (which might, for example, unrealistically increase their perception of a target's value).[23] In the same way as war games provide

---

[22] The number of nodes in demand projections should be limited to preserve the intuition of scenario analysis, but can be converted to a shorter subperiod for greater valuation accuracy. See Cox, Ross, and Rubinstein (1979).

[23] See also Brandenburger and Nalebuff (1995), Camerer (1991, 2003), and Smit and Trigeorgis (2009) for the use of game theory in strategy.

insights into possible strategy outcomes, or learning the opening moves in chess gambits improves appreciation of a game's possible early phases, different variants of an acquisition game's first phase can be worked through, helping to guide an intended acquirer's strategic and tactical moves—such as preemptive execution timing, sequencing, acquiring stakes, or joining bidding consortia—that can alter the rules of the bidding game. Working backward from an industry end game allows decision makers to trace the values at each phase of an acquisition strategy, and intuit the value of different strategies from the relative magnitudes of their outcomes. The learning and insights the model is designed to provide can, in fact, be more important than achieving accurate valuation.

4. *Limitations of the option game approach:* The empirical literature on the failures of corporate M&A and the premiums involved in acquisitions strengthen the arguments for new types of valuation methods. Improved valuation models can mitigate bidding mistakes based on stock market mispricing and should help discipline hubris, overconfidence and empire building. As with all analyses, there is always a danger that real options can be used for self-justification or rationalization, and the high degree of subjectivity inherent in designing acquisition paths and the variables used in real options analysis mean the techniques involved can also be inappropriately used to justify preferred courses of action or bidding more than a target is worth. To suppress overconfidence and avoid committing to acquisitions too early, targets should be selected from a comprehensive list and care should be taken not to overestimate the levels of added value associated with each opportunity—in terms of either synergies or future options. Integrating game theory into executives' thinking generally lowers option value. As discussed in chapter 2 further adjustments should be made to the payoffs depending on whether bidders find themselves in hot or cold deal markets. Despite its comprehensiveness, the approach of combining real options with game theory cannot cover all the angles for successful strategic behavior in acquisitions, but can complement and also discipline the intuitive strategic thinking process in dynamic ways.

SUGGESTED READING

Camerer, C. F. 2003. "Behavioral Studies of Strategic Thinking in Games." *Trends in Cognitive Sciences* 7, no. 5: 225–31.

Eckbo, B. E. 2009. "Bidding Strategies and Takeover Premiums: A Review." *Journal of Corporate Finance* 15, no. 1: 149–78.

Smit, J. T. J. 2003. "Infrastructure Investment as a Real Options Game: The Case of European Airport Expansion." *Financial Management* 32, no. 4: 27–58.

SUGGESTED MATERIALS, TOOLS AND GADGETS

For links to webcast, tools and presentations of this book see http://press .princeton.edu/titles/10333.html

For game theory resources for educators and students: lecture notes, text books, interactive game theory applets and online games, see http://game theory.net

CHAPTER 7

CONCLUSION AND IMPLICATIONS

Turn him to any cause of policy,
The Gordian Knot of it he will unloose,
Familiar as his garter

—William Shakespeare

In 333 BC, while wintering at Gordium, Alexander the Great attempted to untie the Gordian Knot. When he could not find the end of the knot to loosen it he simply sliced it in half with a stroke of his sword, producing the required outcome—an action that has since been referred to as the Alexandrian solution. In this book we seek ways for managers to cut the Gordian Knot to resolve a set of dilemmas—in the broadest sense—facing senior executives when developing their company's strategy and specifically illustrated here in the context of deciding on and executing acquisition strategies.

The Gordian Knot when it comes to developing business strategy at all organizational levels is to find a resolution between seemingly opposing philosophies. In the one corner is the "strategist" or "designer"—the executive who creates a clear picture of the organization's direction toward a predefined goal, making clear choices about the opportunities they do or don't want to pursue, the organization's systems and structure, and so on. Vulnerable to overconfidence, ignoring uncertainty and blinded by the illusion of control, such executives bring their subjective static long-term views to every kind of decision making, inevitably resulting in them risking making suboptimal decisions and thus suffering their unintended consequences. In the other corner we have the "opportunist"—the executive who sees opportunities everywhere, but may be reluctant to make choices, which they perceive might limit their options in the future. Eager to capture opportunities as they arise, their rationales can also be bounded and overoptimistic when markets are hot. Or, by contrast in cold markets, when keeping their options open becomes entrepreneurs' dominant approach to strategy, they become highly reluctant to make decisions that reduce their chances of doing so. While the designer may justify his or her view by misusing a static DCF analysis, the opportunist can do so by abusing real options analysis. In a world in which new competitive frontiers unfold at an ever increasing pace, and desired opportunities are captured by unexpected competitors, often changing the competitive landscape of entire industries, neither approach on its own can ensure that an executive team will consistently be able to navigate its organization toward its goals. Those who are stewards of today's corporations must demonstrate the mental agility required to conceive and implement strategy successfully, avoiding the pitfalls of either the opportunist or the designer.

Today's strategic financial valuation tools are inadequate to address the challenges presented by these real-life dilemmas. Like trying to untie a knot with no ends, it is very difficult for anyone—least of all successful executives—to de-bias their decision making and ensure their long-term strategy is rational, without first recognizing and correcting their *own* perspectives. However, it is much easier for them to identify acquisition *situations* that are vulnerable to biases, and apply self-correcting tools and procedures that can (for instance) help them recognize overheated or cold deal markets and acquisition frenzies or adjust growth option valuations in light of the economic cycle phases. So executives need to be retooled for success. A new approach to thinking about the conception and execution of strategy and strategic choice, by employing self-correcting mechanisms to mitigate executive bias, can offer them the swords to slice through the knots they face.

This book makes a key contribution to resolving the quandaries highlighted here by unifying arguments from behavioral economics with DCF, real option valuation, and game theory literature to provide much-needed extensions to current valuation techniques. Organizations need a clear sense of where they compete and how value is created in their chosen battlefield, and how to respond appropriately to the positive and negative implications of the uncertainty that inevitably affects all markets and all sectors. Balancing the strategies of the *opportunist* and the *designer* can lead to a stance we term *strategic opportunism*. Our tools connect decision making under uncertainty more *directly* to fundamental company value and mispricing than today's strategic frameworks. This is more important than ever today, when executives have great difficulty in assessing—at the corporate or business unit level—how their, largely qualitative, strategic choices lead to value in practice and in the eyes of investors, whether public or private.

BIASES AND OPTIONS ARE EVERYWHERE

The pitfalls and solutions in acquisition decision making under uncertainty described in this book are quite general. Biases tend to appear in human decision making in many strategic investments, for example, public policy makers deciding on infrastructure investment, or property developers on land development, or a pharmaceutical company developing a new product, a venture capitalist financing the stages of a new venture, or even important individual financial decisions, such as buying a house. Indeed, just as expenditures on military and transportation infrastructure projects are prone to exceed their budgeted costs, due to such (designer) decision biases as overconfidence, excessive optimism, and the planning fallacy—so are many corporate infrastructure projects, such as software installations, not completed within budget and on time. While the complex nature of infrastructure projects and the long-term construction periods involved seem to make it difficult to estimate investment outlays accurately, estimating the elusive growth option values involved can be even harder. As a strategic opportunist, it is preferable to improve policy makers' and their advisors' analyses by improving their ability to recognize and guard against their own psychological biases when seeking to objectively estimate both costs and the elusive real growth options of infrastructure projects, rather than to succumb to the temptation to inappropriately modify quantitative valuations, for example, by unconsciously underestimating costs or uncertainty to justify the intention to proceed with projects. In such a real options analysis, infrastructure development including investments in land, distribution, communication, human capital, or technology, is considered a platform for a firm's potential future real growth options.

We hope this book may even help readers apply an options perspective to significant nonfinancial decisions, including such vital life decisions such as the design of one's education strategy or career plan, or more common problems such how to plan holiday journeys. We believe valuable lessons can be learned as the reader applies the insights in this book to a broader set of uncertainty problems, although they are impossible to quantify.

As in many corporate strategies, the decisions one takes in *planning an education strategy* involve multiple dependent stages. With a designer's view students tend to overcommit to a fixed plan, are often also too optimistic about the success of their studies, and so can become disappointed if they fail to reach their designed milestones. But with a purely opportunist view, students can easily be distracted by short-term opportunities that may detract from reaching such long-term goals as an MBA or PhD. However, a strategic opportunist's perspective considers the strategy in terms of behavioral real options and uncertainty and avoids an overly optimistic expectation of performance relative to the other students. Instead of following the herd, it may help in better choosing the courses and electives that have good future prospects. In a sense, the high school one goes to and the grades one achieves increase one's future chances of getting accepted by a good college, which in turn shapes one's options and increases one's chances of receiving an MBA at a top business school, where selection and competition are more intense. From a strategic opportunist's perspective, each stage in an education can be considered an option, accumulating capabilities, skills, experiences, and even a network of contacts, improving one's strategic position and generating future options under uncertainty. Just like strategic acquisitions, there are intertemporal synergistic opportunities: each stage can function as a platform that generates future options—but depending on choices made and only if conditions and performance turn out favorably.

Similarly, in *planning a career*, biases can affect perceptions of path-dependent growth opportunities. A designer can be confronted with unexpected realities, when job markets change or rival candidates are strong, while a pure opportunist will take any job that gives him or her a higher short-term payoff and might end up not having achieved his or her long-term ambitions. A strategic opportunist will consider the growth options and uncertainties associated with each new position, objectively estimating capabilities and performance relative to his or her reference group. Some affiliations are platforms that generate network connections or knowledge, or give valuable experience or other growth options. In this way a position early in a career (e.g., at a private equity fund, investment bank, or consultancy) may not give the highest direct payoff, but might serve as a valuable springboard and provide a large network.

You can apply this kind of thinking not only to long-term strategic decisions (education, career, building your professional network); it can be a useful type of thinking in less important choices in life, such as *planning a journey*. As a strategic opportunist, you combine the best of the designer's approach to plan your trip meticulously—the sites to visit, and all the connections and hotels—whereas in between, adopting an opportunist approach allows you to see where the wind will take you. From a strategic opportunist perspective, visiting, for instance, Paris, you might plan to visit the important sites, museums, and shops in each arrondissement (e.g., 4: Île de la Cité and Le Marais), so you have several options open to revise the trip or timing depending on your experiences, or the weather. Biases and options are everywhere—from product development or infrastructure development to personal choices in life. If you wish, real options could apply even to decisions about marriage, divorce, and social networking.

THE PROBLEM: SELECTED PITFALLS IN ACQUISITION DECISION MAKING

If you have not yet have experienced the excitement and anxieties involved in a corporate takeover, the acquisition pitfalls described in this book are very similar to those you may encounter in major personal transactions, such as buying a house. For instance, in selecting your property, you may remember that your enthusiasm may make you prone to overoptimism or overconfidence when estimating maintenance or renovation costs, and also get too easily used to real estate prices that are—with hindsight—excessive. This hot market attitude is

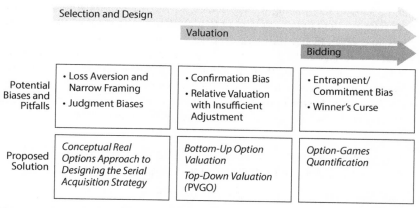

Figure 7.1 Potential Biases, Pitfalls, and Solutions at Each Phase of the Acquisition Process

particularly likely when eager bankers support the real estate market by providing easily available high-rate mortgages. Even experienced brokers' valuations can be anchored on too high prices when similar local properties are also overvalued. So, before it comes to bidding, you need to conduct careful research into the building and land concerned, to make sure you are well informed and not fall prey to the winner's curse. And of course (after reading this book) you will regard selling brokers' stories of "rival buyers" with some skepticism, and if you do enter a bidding contest, avoid escalation and forget the sunk cost of the time and money you have spent.

In analogy with this real estate metaphor, the problems and solutions discussed in detail in this book for corporate acquisitions are quite similar and general for strategic decisions under uncertainty. Figure 7.1 presents an overview of the biases and solutions relevant to various stages of the corporate acquisition process: the design of acquisition strategies, the analysis of target valuations, and the bidding processes, all of which are vulnerable to cognitive biases.

PITFALLS IN STRATEGY DESIGN

WARNING 1: THE MANNER IN WHICH EXECUTIVES PERCEIVE UNCERTAINTY VERSUS GROWTH LEADS THEM TO OVERINVEST IN HOT DEAL MARKETS AND/OR TO BE OVERCONSERVATIVE IN COLD DEAL MARKETS

The focus on growth and underestimation of uncertainty in hot deal markets results in some acquirers tending to overshoot in price, further reinforcing hot markets. In contrast, it seems the way managers perceive risk in cold markets often results in them being too cautious. *Loss aversion* by investors, and executives framing the target's role and potential value to the organization too narrowly, may result in an overly conservative acquisition strategy in such markets, which fails to take full advantage of their potential for upward movement and results in suboptimal growth in shareholder wealth. This often results in missed opportunities, especially in the many industries that are consolidating and/or globalizing, trends which are gaining increased impetus as firms seek to build scale and diversity and to reposition themselves to compete globally.

WARNING 2: JUDGMENT BIASES CAN RESULT IN UNDERESTIMATION OF RISK AND OVERINVESTMENT IN ACQUISITION STRATEGIES

While loss aversion (warning 1) results from the way executives *perceive* risk, other biases result from the way decision makers *estimate* risk, cash flows and investment. Executives wishing to mitigate estimation biases should be aware that biased perceptions of deals may be reinforced by their boards and advisors, the aggressive acquisition behavior of their rivals, or the exuberance of the investor community. One of the key biases executives need to overcome in estimating risk is *overconfidence*, overestimating the potential for success, postacquisition synergies and a target company's value to their organization, while neglecting important—and potentially damaging—uncertainties. Another key bias *is overoptimism* in estimating cash flows or costs. Overconfident executives are frequently surprised, while overoptimistic executives are often disappointed. *Judgment* and *confirmation biases*, reinforced by *groupthink* and the disregard of warning signals, can mean envisioned strategies are based on overly optimistic expectations of synergies and the *illusion of control* over the acquisition and bidding process.

POTENTIAL PITFALLS IN VALUATION ANALYSIS

After a strategy has been designed and targets selected, the acquisition process is often vulnerable to *valuation biases*.

WARNING 3: WHEN VALUATIONS SUIT BIASED MIND-SETS

The improper use (conscious or otherwise) of any valuation model to justify and implement a predetermined strategy can bolster an executive's false sense of confidence, can justify or confirm incorrectly held expectations about the realization of synergies, or can create unjustified illusions about potential growth. When overcommitted to a static strategy, valuation teams are prone to anchor on comparable valuations based on the value of earlier deals. Ambiguous and/or overoptimistic estimates of input variables are particularly likely to lead to the irrational infection of model estimation, that is, adjusting model inputs to give the higher output values executives expect. On the other hand, undervaluation may also occur, perhaps due to executives, analysts, or investors applying too short a time horizon or too narrow a view of the target's potential to create new options for the combined entity when environments are uncertain, so underappreciating the potential added value of long-term contingencies or failing to identify and assess the future gains that could flow from follow-on investments.

WARNING 4: RELATIVE VALUATION WITH INSUFFICIENT ADJUSTMENT

While relative valuation using transaction multiples may serve as a reality check on fundamental valuations, these relative valuations are themselves sensitive to inconsistencies or overexuberance in financial markets, which behaviorists claim is caused by investors' bounded rationality. When the value of an asset is hard to assess using traditional DCF models—as in the case of high-tech startups, for example—executives will tend to base their estimates and decisions on familiar positions or *anchor* on multiples. As a consequence, when comparable valuation methods are used, assets acquired by one industry player—for their own unique strategic reasons—can contribute to the misperception of the value of opportunities across an entire sector, so that prices deviate from fundamental values across the board, as happened in tulip mania in 1636, the Internet bubble that shook financial markets in the early 2000s, and the excessive prices of leveraged private equity transactions in 2006.

POTENTIAL PITFALLS IN THE BIDDING PROCESS

WARNING 5: GETTING TRAPPED IN ESCALATING BIDDING CONTESTS

Behavioral economists have demonstrated that participants in company auctions are vulnerable to getting trapped in escalating bidding contests. Auctions structured over several rounds (common in private equity and privatizations) can increase the chances that bidders will become overcommitted, a dynamic that is mimicked in situations of competitive bidding for public companies. The costs—financial, emotional, and reputational—escalate as the process unfolds. Moreover, herd behavior and corporate mimicry on the part of competing acquirers in consolidating industries can induce them to go on making acquisitions long after the optimal economic point in a business cycle,[1] or the relevant level of industry consolidation, has passed,[2] and may promote frenzied waves of consolidation mergers, with bidding wars involving multiple bidders, potentially leading to many financially unsound mergers.

---

[1] See Brewster-Stearns and Allan (1996).
[2] See Scharfstein and Stein (1990).

WARNING 6: THE WINNER'S CURSE—THE COSTS OF SUCCESSFUL
BIDDING BASED ON INACCURATE INFORMATION

In addition to irrationally escalated bidding, underestimating the degree of uncertainty involved in an asset's value can also result in the winning bid exceeding the target's value. Because auction rules specify that the company is sold to the highest bidder, the winner's curse is likely to deliver a target—of uncertain value—*to the bidder that most overestimates its value*; a risk that is more significant where that value is elusive. This is likely to occur when the target has growth options with indefinable value, that is commonly apprized by all bidders, with high uncertainty over its value resulting in a wide distribution of bids, since they are all based (more or less entirely) on estimates.

The 2000–2001 auction of 62 UMTS (3G) licenses in the European telecom market, which realized a total of €109 billion, offers an object lesson in the winner's curse. Market misperceptions of the value of these licenses were amplified by operators' overconfidence in their abilities to increase scale, and this cumulative overvaluation—which caused even the average bid to be higher than the true value—further increasing the winning bid and thus the extent of the winner's curse.

THE SOLUTION: HOW EXECUTIVES CAN DE-BIAS THEIR ACQUISITION DECISIONS

The current methodologies for analyzing transaction strategies have not kept pace with the new developments in economics. Ignoring managerial biases and uncertainty may influence strategy timing and commitments, valuation, deal execution and the ultimate price paid. These biases make objective decision making increasingly complicated and subjective, obliging us to seek to augment our current toolset with more sophisticated approaches.

This book provides strong arguments for implementing valuation methods to account for the notion of optionality and the reality of uncertainty, and checklists that can help correct for managers' inherent uncertainty biases, providing a framework to account for seemingly irrational rivals, or to reconcile underlying asset valuations with irrational prices on financial markets.

The modified valuation approach advocated here is an attempt to support objective decision making by applying the discipline of a more rigorous analytical and rational process to counter biases, and even to avoid the inappropriate use of the new valuation tools—such as real options—to justify overpayment. Figure 7.2 presents a summary of the methodology of this more sophisticated analysis, which comprises the following:

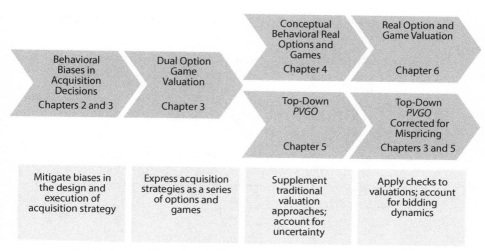

Figure 7.2 Summary Scheme of Behavioral Option Games

1. A set of real options extended valuation tools and checklists for hot and cold deal markets that executives and decision makers pursuing transactions can use to increase their awareness of the potential for inherent biases to influence the key decisions about the selection and valuation of targets and the execution of acquisition strategies.

2. A valuation method that takes advantage of the dual approach in which executives seek better valuation methods and complement strategic intuition by using financial market data to give their analysis an external view or investor perspective of growth option value. In this dual approach, growth option value can be estimated either bottom-up (i.e., from the company's assets and opportunities) or top-down (i.e., directly from the financial markets).

3. A bottom-up approach that analyzes acquisition considerations and requires

   • The consideration of a firm's *entire* acquisitions strategy through a real options lens, which can help integrate valuation and strategy under uncertainty by identifying and valuing sequential optionality—either in the design of the acquisition strategy or in the target company

   • The analysis of prices (or investment outlays) and rivals' likely actions by using a game theory extension to reflect on the dynamics of a multibidder context and their likely impact on timing and price

4. A complement to the bottom-up approach in the form of a top-down PVGO quantification that uses direct information from financial markets to

- Offer a reality check by backing out the value of the firm's growth option set from its equity value

- While at the same time checking whether the conventional (market-based) growth options measures are driven by overvaluation of an entire sector, and need to be corrected for that mispricing

BOTTOM-UP APPROACH

The new and general proposition presented here is that acquisitions are not isolated events, but are the result of—and create—*intertemporal* synergies and path dependencies. Acquisitions open up new options and therefore have long-term implications. The bottom-up approach requires an organization to identify the various types of options (e.g., platform investment, expansion option, or divestment option) facing it, and to use option valuation methods to value the set of real options. For the practical implementation of the bottom-up process, we consider a step-by-step approach with increasing technical complexity as one moves from the application of conceptual real option reasoning (complemented with game theory) to full quantification of an option game. We suggest the following steps for the conceptual real options approach:

Step 1: Create and sequence a list of targets and organic growth options. Our framework classifies investment opportunities based on their characteristics as simple or compound options, and whether they are proprietary or shared, which helps focus managerial attention on growth options in which they have appropriation advantages.

Step 2: Balance organic and acquisitive growth. When considering the options for growth, executives must take into account the expected investment environment in defining the appropriate balance between organic or acquisitive growth, which could invite different market responses. Extending the framework to incorporate rivals' behavioral pitfalls allows investors to take acquisitive initiatives when rivals become conservative, or avoid irrational herding when consolidation frenzies lead to excessive acquisition activity.

Step 3: Determine timing strategies. This can be done by utilizing a conceptual timing framework, which differentiates the generic or proprietary natures of the company's position and its rivals' expected behaviors, even when their rationality is likely to be bounded.

Value and price are rarely equal. The value of a target differs for each acquirer, while the price is what is ultimately paid, may be influenced by bidding dynamics, and is often unrelated to the ultimate acquirer's objectives or view of value. Future growth only generates value for the bidder if the gross growth option value exceeds the price:

$$\text{PVGO} = \text{gross value of future (shared) synergistic opportunities} - \text{price paid} \qquad (7.1)$$

This book demonstrates the various ways in which bottom-up option analyses can and need to be extended with game theory to avoid the pitfalls in setting prices in bidding situations. As strategic bidding dynamics and behavioral valuation pitfalls are interrelated, we argue that price analysis forms an integral component of valuation analysis. For a quantification of option games, we continue with:

Step 4: Quantify the bidding context using an option game analysis. In addition to identifying the players and determining the sequence of play, the analysis should also include predictable choices and the payoff structure for each player.

Step 5: Work through variations of an acquisition game. Do this to learn which opening moves can improve the strategic position later in the game. This discipline helps to guide strategic and tactical moves—such as preemptive timing, sequencing, acquiring stakes, or joining bidding consortia—that can change the rules of the bidding game.

Step 6: Apply insights from behavioral economics to enrich acquisition games. Do this to predict and thus *rationally* respond to rivals' apparently *irrational* behaviors.[3]

TOP-DOWN APPROACH

Analyzing these investment opportunities from an option games perspective is complicated, and depends on a wide range of assumptions and unforeseen events, which could deter executives and other decision makers from using

---

[3] For instance, see Camerer (2003).

these approaches. While real option proponents argue that option games represent a superior approach to valuing businesses and acquisition targets, most executives are too daunted by the technical complexity involved to apply quantitative real options models to real-life situations. In contrast, a conceptual application of option games combined with the top-down (or market method) bypasses many modeling challenges by using the consensus market assessment of the firm's set of embedded real options as reflected in its current stock price. The dual (bottom-up and top-down) decision frameworks presented here together offer a toolkit to aid understanding of value creation in the increasingly turbulent modern world, potentially unlocking opportunities to act selectively without betting the farm at times when others have become paralyzed by fear of the uncertain. The top-down approach involves a three-step procedure:

Step 1. Back out the value of the firm's growth option set from its equity value by deducting the static present value (PV) component associated with the firm's continuing current operations or assets in place (in a no-growth scenario) from its market capitalization—a procedure that can be expressed as:

Implied PVGO = Market Value (MV) – Assets in Place (PV)   (7.2)

Step 2. Study the relative financial market appreciation of companies in an industry. This can help financial analysts and management teams identify markets and companies that are ready for consolidation or, alternatively, for diversified companies for restructuring. Consolidation makes sense when an efficient financial market assigns a higher value to leading companies' growth opportunities and their assets in place than to those of smaller firms. By contrast, when the differential in PVGO-to-price is lower for the majors (often conglomerates) than for smaller companies, this may point to the need for restructuring strategies.

Step 3. Consider other components of company value—such as the decomposition of growth option value, which can account for possible sector mispricing—with the potential to offering novel insights into the makeup of company value. Check whether the conventional (market-based) growth options measures are driven by overvaluation, and need to be corrected for mispricing, as in equation 7.3.

Market Value = Net Value of Assets in Place +
Fundamental PVGO + Excess Pricing   (7.3)

SELECTED IMPLICATIONS TO DEAL RATIONALLY WITH ONE'S OWN BIASES, FINANCIAL MARKETS, AND "IRRATIONAL" RIVALS

IMPLICATIONS FOR STRATEGY

MITIGATING PITFALL 1 (SUBOPTIMAL TIMING OVER THE BUSINESS CYCLE): DOES A REAL OPTIONS FRAME MITIGATE OR REINFORCE OVERINVESTMENT AND UNDERINVESTMENT PROBLEMS?

Since real options theory provides arguments for both caution and for expediting deals, one clearly needs to know the circumstances in which each course of action is most appropriate: indeed, real options analysis can be improperly used to reinforce inappropriate behavior. Introducing a behavioral dimension to real options thinking helps decision makers learn to see uncertainty, amend decisions depending on its resolution, and value uncertainty in a way that tempers their natural tendencies to go for growth in hot deal markets and become risk averse in cold deal markets.

MITIGATING PITFALL 2 (OVERCOMMITTING TO A SUBOPTIMAL STRATEGY): HOW CAN REAL OPTIONS BE USED TO LIMIT THE RISKS OF OVERCOMMITMENT TO A STRATEGY?

A real options model may help prevent the "illusion of control" and the resulting overcommitment to a predefined scenario, and encourage executives to consider conditionality and contingencies. Considering acquisitions as options can add significant insight to adaptive and opportunistic strategies, as the currently envisioned acquisition trajectory is not regarded as static, but allows for the dynamic revision of targets and periodic adjustments in the number and pattern of investments depending on market growth or unexpected adverse external developments. Setting clear thresholds or trigger levels on which decisions should be based, or which would be signs to consider alternative actions—such as deferring or pursuing alternative targets—can help executives adjust their decisions and avoid overcommitment due to their aversion to taking a loss on their sunk capital. Similarly, estimating objective exit thresholds ex ante can provide a valuable discipline that should lead to unprofitable businesses being divested at the right time, while also making it easier for executives to relinquish intended targets without such decision changes implying personal defeats.

IMPLICATIONS FOR VALUATION: RATIONALLY DEAL WITH IRRATIONAL FINANCIAL MARKETS

MITIGATING PITFALL 3 (VALUATION INFLUENCED BY A BIASED MIND-SET): CAN FINANCIAL MARKETS PROVIDE AN EXTERNAL VIEW ON A FULL VALUATION?

We propose a dual—bottom-up and top-down—approach to real option valuation, with various adjustments and hot and cold market checklists to prevent subjective distortion of the rational analysis of valuation. Any top-down market approach to valuing growth option value should be estimated *after* the bottom-up valuation because it is likely to be influenced by it. The direct top-down approach based on the *relative* appreciation of growth option value (of large versus small firms) implicitly avoids the risk of *comparative mispricing* within a specific industry. However, unless the acquisition is to be financed purely by equity, the risk remains that an entire industry may be overvalued. Investors who utilize a combination of loans or cash and equity are advised to correct explicitly for the potential mispricing of the entire industry by applying the dual valuation methodology (with its mispricing correction components).

MITIGATING PITFALL 4 (COMPARABLE VALUATIONS DISTORTED BY MISPRICED INDUSTRIES AND MARKETS): CAN DUAL VALUATION HELP TO PREVENT INFECTION BY FINANCIAL MARKETS?

From time to time, extraneous factors will influence the value of an entire sector or even of the market as a whole—causing firms to be over- or undervalued. Depending primarily on comparative valuations in such environments increases the potential to overpay or, on the other hand, to underbid. For instance, when financial markets were at the peak of their irrational exuberance at the turn of the millennium, Vodafone probably greatly overvalued the entire telecom industry's growth opportunities. The excess pricing of its own shares—as a result of the general overrating of the telecom industry at the time—effectively gave it the ability to pay for its fully priced targets with an inflated currency. "New Economy" firms were in hot demand into 2001, so it would be going too far to hold Vodafone responsible for the general overvaluation of the telecom industry. However, the cost of its serial acquisition strategy—and of building the company to be the world leader it is today—was borne by those investors who bought Vodafone shares at the top of the cycle in 2001.

Combining market-based (top-down) with fundamental (bottom-up) valuation techniques serves as a useful reality check and can encourage caution or opportunism in an acquisition strategy as appropriate, while preventing over-reliance on relative values and heuristics. The strength of the top-down PVGO methodology is that financial markets—rather than complex real option models—ultimately determine growth option value, obviating the need to apply complex real options designs and handle large data sets. When it is corrected for investors' over- or underpricing of stocks, the top-down approach (as further developed here) offers a more sophisticated PVGO estimation measure than a traditional implied PVGO estimation.

IMPLICATIONS FOR BIDDING: RATIONALLY DEAL WITH BOUNDED RATIONALITY OF RIVALS

MITIGATING PITFALL 5 (IRRATIONAL PRICE ESCALATION IN MULTIBIDDER CONTEXTS): IS IT POSSIBLE TO AVOID OVERPAYMENT AND DETERMINE EACH PLAYER'S PRICE BY ASSESSING THEIR BIASES AND OBJECTIVES?

The rational bidder should take an opportunistic (real option) view and try to avoid battles that lead to escalating commitment to bidding. Bidders can recognize situations that might lead to overcommitment by themselves or rivals.[4] As already noted, such overcommitment arises in situations in which the bidding process is costly but there still seems to be the possibility of achieving better outcomes by going on bidding. This is particularly so when acquisition value is hard to ascertain, where there is interest from multiple bidders, or where bidders have experienced a recent period of successes in acquisition battles, making them overconfident. While an overconfident and overoptimistic rival is hard to beat in a bidding contest without paying an excessive premium, real options analysis helps executives to remember that exiting the bidding game can also be a valuable option.

Rational bidders who are alive to the possible biases affecting their rivals, and have an assessment of the perceived value of the target to their competitors, can design their bidding strategies to account for these influences. For instance, bidders from different stances—for example, a private equity bidder versus a strategic player or consolidator versus a nonconsolidating bidder—are likely to assign different values to the same target. Similarly, in the early stages of industry consolidation, rivals may have a conservative strategy and frame acquisitions too narrowly, holding them back from making what they perceive to be risky acquisitions. Recognizing such biases allows a canny consolidator to identify where and when to make an early winning bid to avoid ending up in a bidding contest later in the game. Vodafone's aggressive buildup strategy allowed it to seize the initiative in a growing but still fragmented telecom market by moving into an aggressive acquisition growth program earlier than its rivals, which would enable the enlarged firm to gain increasing market share and become an industry leader in a growing sector.

---

[4] See, for instance, Schwenk (1986).

MITIGATING PITFALL 6 (WINNER'S CURSE): CAN REAL OPTION
VALUATION HELP AVOID THE WINNER'S CURSE?

The winner's curse underscores the importance of relying on fundamental methods for valuing targets in competitive settings. In particular, when a target's value is illusive and there are multiple bidders, some may overvalue and others undervalue the assets being sold. Thus, in the Vodafone case, the general market environment made telecom assets (such as mobile licenses) difficult to value, often making auction bidders overly dependent on their relative valuation of the target's peers or of rival bids, and so more vulnerable to the winner's curse. A fundamental (e.g., real option) valuation could have delivered a clearer view of the worth of targets' optionality, while at the same time incorporating uncertainty into the value estimation model, thereby potentially avoiding the winner's curse. Savvy bidders for an asset with uncertain value will avoid the winner's curse by decreasing their bid, setting it below their (ex ante) estimation of the uncertain value of the target. The less accurate their valuation (e.g., the higher growth option value it includes), the lower the bid should be.

EMPIRICAL EVIDENCE

Despite the frequency with which executives rely on traditional arguments—such as efficiency gains—to justify acquisitions to their shareholders, empirical evidence suggests that (in most instances) the bulk of the value flows to the target's shareholders and that acquisitions are at least partly driven by the behavioral biases of executives, investors, and financial markets.

ACQUISITIONS ARE DRIVEN BY GROWTH
OPTIONS AND MISPRICING

One of the messages offered here is that[5]—apart from new growth options or apparent executive biases—acquisitions can be driven by stock prices when financial markets fail to price firms correctly.[6] The components of fundamental growth option value and excess pricing embedded in total company value in financial markets can even be interrelated: the scope for valuation errors, exuberance, and mispricing is greater when elusive growth options value is a major source of overall market capitalization than when value arises from established products and established markets.

---

[5] The views in this section are further developed by Sjoerd van Bekkum, Han Smit, and Enrico Pennings (2011) in the article "Buy Smart, Time Smart: Are Takeovers Driven by Growth Opportunities or Mispricing." See also Jensen (2005) on the agency cost of overvalued equity.
[6] See Shiller (2000).

TABLE 7.1 INDUSTRY AVERAGE OF THE MARKET VALUE OF GROWTH OPPORTUNITIES, MODIFIED GROWTH OPPORTUNITIES, AND MISPRICING

Sector	PVGO	$\overline{PVGO}$	XSP
Business equipment	0.96	0.84	0.35
Mining	0.92	0.74	0.49
Telecom	0.89	0.75	0.54
Health care	0.87	0.73	0.39
Durables	0.82	0.71	0.54
Chemicals	0.82	0.67	0.53
Manufacturing	0.82	0.72	0.52
Other	0.82	0.72	0.50
Energy	0.81	0.66	0.54
Shops	0.79	0.70	0.49
Nondurables	0.78	0.65	0.50
Finance	0.74	0.76	0.39
Utilities	0.71	0.64	0.60
Total	0.83	0.72	0.48

Source: van Bekkum, Smit, and Pennings (2011).

For each sector, the first column reports the values for market-based growth options values (PVGO), the second fundamental growth options value ($\overline{PVGO}$), and the third excess pricing (XSP): each is normalized to firm value. Summary statistics are reported per sector from 1996 to 2006. Sector definitions are based on the classification as provided by Kenneth French on his website. Business equipment includes computers, software, and electronic equipment; health care includes medical equipment and drugs; mining includes mining and minerals; telecom includes telephone and television transmission; other includes construction, transportation, recreation, business services, and entertainment; chemicals include chemicals and allied products; manufacturing includes machinery, trucks, airplanes, office furniture, paper, and commercial printing; shops includes wholesale, retail, and some services such as laundries and repair shops; nondurables include consumer nondurables; durables include cars, TVs, furniture, and household appliances; energy includes oil, gas, and coal extraction (products); finance includes banks, insurance companies, and other financials; and utilities includes utilities.

As an illustration, Table 7.1 reports excess pricing and mean growth options value by industry using our adjusted (top-down) PVGO approach.[7] In terms of market-based growth options values, important differences exist between sectors. The highest average market-based growth options value is found in the business equipment (PVGO = 0.96), mining (PVGO = 0.92), telecom (PVGO = 0.89), and health care sectors (PVGO = 0.87). In the period analyzed, these industries had more volatile demand and earnings, which increased their option value: some were also characterized by relatively large numbers of

[7] The growth option value in this table is scaled by total fundamental company value to provide an intuitive illustration of the differing growth options components between industries. For this reason, the proportion of PVGO values is somewhat higher than in previous studies (Kester 1984; Tong et al. 2008). Values further increase if growth options value and excess pricing are scaled by equity value.

small and young firms whose value was largely intangible. This is consistent with real options theory, because firms in such industries experience more unexpected technological changes and moves by competitors. In contrast, utilities (PVGO = 0.71) and financial services (PVGO = 0.74) exhibit the lowest growth options value—in these more stable, low-growth income sectors, earnings are more predictable and scale economies are important for all sector firms, increasing the value of assets in place and proportionally decreasing growth values.

Empirical studies of the PVGO approach show that (on average) serial bidders are overvalued, but also have high PVGOs relative to targets and to inactive firms.[8] Thus, merger waves coincide with valuation waves, in part because the overall valuation error of share prices leads to the overestimation of expected synergies,[9] and in part because managers attempt to use their relative overpricing to acquire fundamental growth options. Furthermore, bidders buy growth option value that does not depend on takeover activity (i.e., organic growth) allowing them to retain growth opportunities after takeover activity has abated.

SERIAL ACQUIRERS DO BETTER EVEN THOUGH THEY PAY A PREMIUM

Overall, empirical evidence indicates that gains to serial acquirers are positive on average.[10] Serial acquirers do better than single acquirers in financial markets, in particular if their acquisitions are private, even though they pay a premium for their first deal in a series. Based on US acquisitions from 1986 to 2009, empirical studies have shown that, on average, serial acquirers pay a 17% higher premium for their first public acquisition than do single acquirers, reflecting the value of their intended future growth options, and the premiums tend to decline in follow-on deals.[11] Despite the higher average premiums, the market reacts more favorably to serial acquirers than to single acquirers, showing the serial acquisition intention mitigates the negative market reaction found in public acquisitions.

---

[8] Van Bekkum, Smit, and Pennings (2011).

[9] Rhodes-Kropf and Viswanathan (2004).

[10] Schipper and Thompson (1983) find that firms that announce intentions to undertake entire acquisition programs on average earn significantly positive abnormal stock returns. Song and Walkling (2000) also present evidence that partial anticipation of takeover activity attenuates bidder announcement returns. See also Laamanen and Keil (2008) for returns to serial acquirers.

[11] These results are based on Kil, Smit, and Verwijmeren (2013). Serial acquirers also tend to learn (Barkema and Schijven 2008; Aktas, de Bodt, and Roll 2009, 2011, and 2012) in bidding, especially under CEO continuity and when successive deals are similar.

PROMISING FUTURE RESEARCH DIRECTIONS

Integrating real options, game theory, and behavioral economics to value—or even explain—takeover activity, offers interesting directions for future research. We identify the following research agendas as potentially promising novel insights and results:

RESEARCH DIRECTION 1: A DESCRIPTIVE THEORY OF BEHAVIORAL REAL OPTIONS

We are attracted by the possibility of integrating real option theory and behavioral theory in the strategic management literature. Since real option theory derives from financial economic reasoning, it's not surprising that so far, it has largely followed economic assumptions of rationality. As such, a more descriptive theory of real options—one that explicitly assumes only bounded rationality (and, by extension, allows for cognitive biases as described here)—has not been given much attention, though we feel it may hold considerable promise for both the strategy and finance fields. Furthermore, we think that behavioral theorizing offers an elegant and potentially interesting explanation for various observations: for example, why acquisitions of minority stakes (relative to full acquisitions) are comparatively rare,[12] why serial acquisitions provide higher returns to bidders despite their higher premiums, why acquisitions tend to follow waves and then dry up, and so on. Further theoretical development in real options theory may explore the behavioral pitfalls in the various real options themselves—for instance the derivation of an exercise threshold under prospect theory.

RESEARCH DIRECTION 2: BEHAVIORAL OPTION GAMES PROVIDE WAYS TO OPERATIONALIZE STRATEGIC MANAGEMENT THEORY

Another promising direction of option games—the direction followed here—lies in their normative angle to help individuals make better decisions. Although extant management theories—such as the five forces analysis, the resource-based view, core competences, and the knowledge-based view—deal with relative company positioning and, notionally, with value, they do not provide the tools to make explicit links between the various strategic courses of action and the creation of fundamental shareholder value[13]—nor do they explicitly address uncertainty. In the specific case of acquisition decision making, these perspectives are not explicit about which valuation approach they would

---

[12]   See, for instance, Betton and Eckbo (2000) and Betton, Eckbo, and Thorburn (2009).
[13]   See Smit and Trigeorgis (2013) for a detailed analysis how to operationalize the expanded NPV method.

rely on when actually implementing these management theories. To operationalize management theory and execute acquisition decisions, there must be some underlying valuation approach that ultimately integrates with the reality of executing strategy under uncertainty. An extended real options and game theory approach is as necessary as NPV to portray a management theory such as the resource-based view accurately, and thus enable scholars and decision makers to move from concepts and propositions to strategy valuation and implementation. This book opens up options for the further integration of the methodologies we examine and these extant management theories into an academic framework supporting the principles of strategic opportunism we define here.

RESEARCH DIRECTION 3: EMPIRICAL RESEARCH USING THE TOP-DOWN DECOMPOSITION

The decomposition of firm value offers new insights into each of the three value components (assets in place, PVGO, and excess pricing).[14] Our key contribution, however, lies in unifying arguments from different streams of literature and adding nuance to the rationality-irrationality dichotomy. Thus, by considering the behavioral and growth option components simultaneously, our method indicates that strategic arguments and behavioral finance are interrelated. While mispricing is a well-known factor in M&As, distinguishing between growth opportunities and mispricing may add further insight to previous studies into the growth options value of international joint ventures and firm, industry, or country effects.[15]

RESEARCH DIRECTION 4: EMBEDDING BEHAVIORAL THEORY IN NEW VALUATION TOOLS IN PRACTICE

We close this section with a call to use behavioral theory in valuation in practice. From a practical perspective, growth options are an important concept for professionals who need to select profitable investment opportunities and decide when to execute them. The bursting of the US real estate bubble and the subsequent impact on global financial markets amply illustrate the need to adjust for irrational pricing behavior. By incorporating an awareness of irrationality into a rational decision framework, our methods and metrics offer a tool to aid understanding value creation in today's uncertain global environment. A better understanding of their options under uncertainty should increase managers' willingness to venture forward. By estimating the option value of investment opportunities more accurately, or exercising the option to abandon sooner

---

[14] See, for instance, van Bekkum, Smit, and Pennings (2011)
[15] The work of Tony Tong provided many new insights in this literature.

when key uncertainties have rendered their strategy ineffective, or being more cautious and waiting when their strategy appears to have potential but still requires uncertainties to be resolved, firms may be better able to see their strategies as more than all-or-nothing affairs. Deferring or staging acquisitions allows allowing them to take the first steps and, subsequently, to respond more appropriately to desirable or undesirable developments.

BROADEN YOUR VIEW WITH OPTION GAMES

This book focuses on the value of option games to acquisition strategies.[16] However, a general treatise on option games is broadly applicable to organic growth, ranging from capacity expansion, R&D, new entry decisions, and development, across several industries, such as consumer electronics, airplane manufacturing, pharmaceuticals, steel, and mining, particularly when investments in production facilities are capital-intensive and lumpy, and their ability to yield value is uncertain.

For instance, applying option game logic can explain prolonged cycles and boom-bust behavior in *urban land development*. From a real options perspective, owners preserve their development options until they are clearly going to be lucrative. However, in the face of declining demand and property values, developers may still proceed, and cause prolonged cycles in which accelerated development occurs during market downturns.[17] We believe the additional insights of anchoring and mispricing may also apply to *real estate* markets. The competitive interaction in rivals' growth options values can also be found in capacity expansion in various industries, such as *consumer electronics/manufacturing*.[18] Philips and Sony's strategies to commercialize the CD and DVD were affected by the competitive decisions of Toshiba and Time Warner, and vice versa. By building a larger plant for manufacturing compact disks, Philips was able to preempt Sony and other potential competitors, and thus discourage them from building their own CD plants.

The competitive effect is particularly important for investments with high growth option value such as innovation in pharmaceuticals, the valuation of biotech ventures, exploration in mining, and other platform investments with uncertain long-term strategic implications. Because biotechnology represents a set of skills removed from traditional research in pharmaceuticals, agriculture, and chemicals, a key objective of investors in such sectors is the internalization of R&D capabilities. When considering investments in resources and knowl-

---

[16] See also Smit and Trigeorgis (2004) and Smit and Trigeorgis (2013).

[17] Most notable is Steve Grenadier's rigorous work on option games—see, for instance, Grenadier (1996).

[18] See McGahan (1994).

edge—such as the acquisition of biotech ventures, valuable growth options result from the leveraging effects these unique resources, capabilities, and competences have on other assets.[19] Investment flexibility under uncertainty enables firms to adapt their future decisions in response to changing environments, so optimizing their growth option values. Various innovative technology platform investments in *energy and mining* enable miners to make new investments: for example, huge floating gas platforms help reduce operating costs and enhance the strategic position of the company that owns or operates them to bid for fields in the future. This step will allow Shell to pursue new offshore gas fields that would otherwise be too costly to exploit with older technologies. Besides extracting more from current fields, this will provide it with a preemptive advantage when bidding for new ones.

Thus, although, the methodology presented here has been tailored to the case of corporate acquisitions or investments—due to the long-term strategic implications for the companies and the competitive bidding environments involved—these examples show that the practical application of the option game approach can be used in all kinds of decisions under uncertainty. The insights may even help in daily life when making big decisions—where and what to study, which job to choose, when to buy a house. For instance, you may very easily underestimate the importance path dependencies when deciding on your field study—perhaps even on who you date. You may experience anchoring (or the lack of it) when negotiating for your first job without the external reference points of any other offers, or haggling over a secondhand car against an experienced salesman. Narrow framing in the "penny wise, pound foolish" sense may occur subsequently when you buy a house—negotiating in thousands—and then the next day select your groceries or choose a restaurant. And the overconfidence trap can easily occur when you decide on the number of children you will have, and may be further changing into overoptimism on where they are going to study. History has shown, time and again, how people are influenced by groupthink and common misperceptions, and come to more rational insights only decades later. Remember that your opinions are always likely to be influenced by framing, heuristics, or groupthink—go back to the fundamental analysis and think for yourself. Now you are armed with knowledge—so use it to your advantage.

---

[19] See also Folta and Miller (2002) and Grenadier and Weiss (1997).

BIBLIOGRAPHY

Adner, R., and D. A. Levinthal. 2004a. "Reply: Real Options and Real Tradeoffs." *Academy of Management Review* 29, no. 1: 120–26.
———. 2004b. "What Is Not Real Option: Identifying Boundaries for the Application of Real Options to Business Strategy." *Academy of Management Review* 29, no. 1: 74–85.
Aktas, N., E. de Bodt, and R. Roll. 2009. "Learning, Hubris and Corporate Serial Acquisitions." *Journal of Corporate Finance* 15, no. 5: 543–61.
———. 2011. "Serial Acquirer Bidding: An Empirical Test of the Learning Hypothesis." *Journal of Corporate Finance* 17, no. 1: 18–32.
———. 2012. "Learning from Repetitive Acquisitions: Evidence from the Time between Deals." *Journal of Financial Economics* 108, no. 1: 99–117.
Amram, M., and N. Kulatilaka. 1999a. "Disciplined Decisions: Aligning Strategy with the Financial Markets." *Harvard Business Review* 77, no. 1: 95–104.
———. 1999b. *Real Option: Managing Strategic Investment in an Uncertain World*. Boston: Harvard Business School Press.
Andrade, G., M. Mitchell, and E. Stafford. 2001. "New Evidence and Perspectives on Mergers?" *Journal of Economic Perspectives* 15, no. 2: 103–20.
Asquith, P., R. F. Bruner, and D. W. Mullins. 1983. "The Gains to Bidding Firms from Merger." *Journal of Financial Economics* 11, nos. 1–4: 121–39.
Baker, M., R. Ruback, and J. Wurgler. 2004. "Behavioral Corporate Finance: A Survey." In *The Handbook of Corporate Finance: Empirical Corporate Finance*, ed. E. Eckbo et al. New York: Elsevier: 351–417.
Baldwin, C. Y. 1982. "Optimal Sequential Investment When Capital Is Not Readily Reversible." *Journal of Finance* 37, no. 3: 763–82.
Barberis, N., and M. Hang. 2008. "The Loss Aversion/Narrow Framing Approach to Stock Market Pricing and Participation Puzzles." In: *Handbook of the Equity Risk Premium*, ed. R. Mehra. Amsterdam: Elsevier: 201–28.
Barberis, N., and R. Thaler. 2003. "A Survey of Behavioral Finance." In *Handbook of the Economics of Finance*, ed. George M. Constantinides, Milton Harris, and Rene M. Stulz. Amsterdam: Elsevier: 1052–1114.
Barkema, H. G., and M. Schijven. 2008. "How Do Firms Learn to Make Acquisitions? A Review of Past Research and an Agenda for the Future." *Journal of Management* 34, no. 3: 594–634.
Barnes, J. H. 1984. "Cognitive Biases and Their Impact on Strategic Planning." *Strategic Management Journal* 5, no. 2: 129–38.
Barney, J. 1986. "Strategic Factor Markets: Expectations, Luck, and Business Strategy." *Management Science* 32, no. 10: 1231–41.
———. 1988. "Returns to Bidding Firms in Mergers and Acquisitions: Reconsidering the Relatedness Hypothesis." *Strategic Management Journal* 9, Summer Special Issue: 71–78.

———. 1995. "Looking Inside for Competitive Advantage." *Academy of Management Executive* 9, no. 4: 49–61.

Barth, M. E., W. H. Beaver, and W. R. Landsman. 2001. "The Relevance of the Value Relevance Literature for Financial Accounting Standard Setting: Another View." *Journal of Accounting Economics* 31, nos. 1–3: 77–104.

Beinhocker, E. D. 1999. "Robust Adaptive Strategies." *Sloan Management Review* 40, no. 3: 95–106.

Bekkum, S. van, J. T. J. Smit, and H. P. G. Pennings. 2011. "Buy Smart, Time Smart: Are Takeovers Driven by Growth Opportunities or Mispricing?" *Financial Management* 40, no. 4: 911–40.

Bertrand, M., and A. Schoar. 2003. "Managing with Style: The Effect of Managers on Firm Policies." *Quarterly Journal of Economics* 118, no. 4: 1169–1208.

Bettis, R. A., and M. A. Hitt. 1995. "The New Competitive Landscape." *Strategic Management Journal* 16, no. S1: 7–19.

Betton, S., and B. E. Eckbo. 2000. "Toeholds, Bid Jumps, and Expected Payoff in Takeovers." *Review of Financial Studies* 13, no. 4: 841–82.

Betton, S., B. E. Eckbo, and K. S. Thorburn. 2009. "Merger Negotiations and the Toehold Puzzle." *Journal of Financial Economics* 91, no. 2: 158–78.

Billett, M. T., and Y. Qian. 2008. "Are Overconfident CEOs Born or Made? Evidence of Self-Attribution Bias from Frequent Acquirers." *Management Science* 54, no. 6: 1037–51.

Black, B. 1989. "Bidder Overpayment in Takeovers." *Stanford Law Review* 41, no. 3: 597–660.

Black, F., and M. Scholes. 1973. "The Pricing of Options and Corporate Liabilities." *Journal of Political Economy* 81, no. 3: 637–54.

Bowman, E. H., and D. Hurry. 1993. "Strategy through the Option Lens: An Integrated View of Resource Investments and Incremental-Choice Process." *Academy of Management Review* 18, no. 4: 760–82.

Bowman, E. H., and G. T. Moskowitz. 2001. "A Heuristics Approach to the Use of Options Analysis in Strategic Decision Making." *Organization Science* 12, no. 6: 772–77.

Boyer, M. 1997. "Capacity Commitment versus Flexibility." *Journal of Economics and Management Strategy* 6, no. 2: 347–76.

Brandenburger, A. M., and B. J. Nalebuff. 1995. "The Right Game: Use Game Theory to Shape Strategy." *Harvard Business Review* 73, no. 4: 57–71.

Brewster-Stearns, L., and K. D. Allan. 1996. "Economic Behavior in Institutional Environments: The Corporate Merger Wave of the 1980s." *American Social Review* 61, no. 4: 699–718.

Brouthers, K. D., P. van Hastenburg, and J. van den Ven. 1998. "If Most Mergers Fail Why are They so Popular?" *Long Range Planning* 31, no. 3: 347–53.

Bruner, R. 2002. "Does MA Pay? A Survey of Evidence for the Decision-Maker." *Journal of Applied Finance* 12, no. 1: 48–68.

Bulow, J., M. Huang, and P. Klemperer. 1999. "Toeholds and Takeovers." *Journal of Political Economy* 107, no. 3: 427–54.

Burch, T. R., V. K. Nanda, and W. G. Christie. 2004. "Do Firms Time Equity Offerings? Evidence from the 1930s and 1940s." *Financial Management* 33, no. 1: 4–23.

Camerer, C. F. 1991. "Does Strategy Research Need Game Theory?" *Strategic Management Journal* 12, no. S2: 137–52.

———. 2003. "Behavioral Studies of Strategic Thinking in Games." *Trends in Cognitive Sciences* 7, no. 5: 225–31.

Camerer, C. F., and D. Lovallo. 1999. "Overconfidence and Excess Entry: An Experimental Approach." *American Economic Review* 89, no. 1: 306–18.

Cao, C., T. Simin, and J. Zhao. 2006. "Can Growth Options Explain the Trend in Idiosyncratic Risk?" *Review of Financial Studies* 21, no. 6: 2599–2633.

Chatterjee, S. 1986. "Types of Synergy and Economic Value: The Impact of Acquisitions on Merging and Rival Firms." *Strategic Management Journal* 7, no. 2: 119–39.

———. 1992. "Source of Value in Takeovers: Synergy or Restructuring—Implications for Target and Bidder Firms." *Strategic Management Journal* 13, no. 4: 267–86.

Chi, T. 1996. "Performance Verifiability and Output Sharing in Collaborative Ventures." *Management Science* 42, no. 1: 93–109.

———. 2000. "Option to Acquire or Divest a Joint Venture." *Strategic Management Journal* 21, no. 6: 665–88.

Chi, T., and D. J. McGuire. 1996. "Collaborative Ventures and the Value of Learning: Integrating Transactions Cost and Strategic Option Perspectives on the Choice of Market Entry Modes." *Journal of International Business Studies* 27, no. 2: 285–307.

Chung, K. H., and C. Charoenwong. 1991. "Investment Options, Assets in Place and the Risk of Stocks." *Financial Management* 20, no. 3: 21–33.

Chung, K. H., L. Minsheng, and L. Yu. 2005. "Assets in Place, Growth Opportunities and IPO Returns." *Financial Management* 34, no. 3: 65–88.

Cooper, A. C., C. Y. Woo, and W. C. Dunkelberg. 1988. "Entrepreneurs' Perceived Chances for Success." *Journal of Business Venturing* 3, no. 2: 97–108.

Copeland, T., and V. Antikarov. 2001. *Real Options: A Practitioner's Guide.* New York: Texere.

———. 2003. *Real Options: A Practitioner's Guide.* 3rd ed. New York: Texere.

Copeland, T. E., and P. Tufano. 2004. "A Real-World Way to Manage Real Options." *Harvard Business Review* 82, no. 3: 90–99.

Coval, S., and T. Shumway. 2005. "Do Behavioral Biases Affect Prices?" *Journal of Finance* 60, no. 1: 267–406.

Cox, J. C., S. A. Ross, and M. Rubinstein. 1979. "Option Pricing: A Simplified Approach." *Journal of Financial Economics* 7, no. 3: 229–63.

Cyert, R., and J. March. 1963. "Behavioral Theory of the Firm." In *Organizational Behavior 2: Essential Theories of Process and Structure,* ed. J. B. Miner. New York: M.E. Sharpe: 60–76.

Dierickx, I., and K. Cool. 1989. "Asset Stock Accumulation and Sustainability of Competitive Advantage." *Management Science* 35, no. 12: 1504–11.

Dixit, A. 1989. "Entry and Exit Decisions under Uncertainty." *Journal of Political Economy* 97, no. 3: 620–38.

Dixit, A. K., and B. J. Nalebuff. 1991. *Thinking Strategically: The Competitive Edge in Business, Politics, and Everyday Life.* New York: Norton.

Dixit, A. K., and R. S. Pindyck. 1994. *Investment under Uncertainty.* Princeton: Princeton University Press.

————. 1995. "The Options Approach to Capital Investment." *Harvard Business Review* 73, no. 3: 105–15.

Dong, M., D. Hirshleifer, S. H. Teoh, and S. Richardson. 2006. "Does Investor Misvaluation Drive the Takeover Market?" *Journal of Finance* 61, no. 2: 725–62.

Doukas, J. A., and D. Petmezas. 2007. "Acquisitions, Overconfident Managers and Self-Attribution Bias." *European Financial Management* 13, no. 3: 531–77.

Duhaime, I. M., and C. R. Schwenk. 1985. "Conjectures on Cognitive Simplification in Acquisition and Divestment Decision Making." *Academy of Management Review* 10, no. 2: 287–95.

Eckbo, B. E. 2009. "Bidding Strategies and Takeover Premiums: A Review." *Journal of Corporate Finance* 15, no. 1: 149–78.

Fama, E. F., and J. D. MacBeth. 1973. "Risk, Return, and Equilibrium: Empirical Tests." *Journal of Political Economy* 81, no. 3: 607–36.

Farrell, J., and C. Shapiro. 1990. "Horizontal Mergers: An Equilibrium Analysis." *American Economic Review* 80, no. 1: 107–26.

Ferreira, N., J. Kar, and L. Trigeorgis. 2009. "Option Games: The Key to Competing in Capital-Intensive Industries." *Harvard Business Review* 87, no. 3: 101–7.

Fichman, R. G., M. Keil, and A. Tiwana. 2005. "Beyond Valuation: 'Options Thinking' in IT Project Management." *California Management Review* 47, no. 2: 74–96.

Folta, T. B. 1998. "Governance and Uncertainty: The Trade-Off between Administrative Control and Commitment." *Strategic Management Journal* 19, no. 11: 1007–28.

Folta, T. B., and K. D. Miller. 2002. "Real Options in Equity Partnerships." *Strategic Management Journal* 23, no. 1: 77–88.

Francis, J., and K. Schipper. 1999. "Have Financial Statements Lost Their Relevance." *Journal of Accounting Research* 37, no. 2: 319–52.

Fuller, K., J. Netter, and M. A. Stegemoller. 2002. "What Do Returns of Acquiring Firms Tell Us? Evidence from Firms That Make Many Acquisitions." *Journal of Finance* 57, no. 4: 1763–93.

Garbuio, M., A. Wilcox, and D. Lovallo. 2011. "Looking Inside: Psychological Influences on Structuring Firm's Portfolio of Resources." *Journal of Management* 37, no. 5: 1299–1315.

Ghemawat, P., and P. del Sol. 1998. "Commitment versus Flexibility?" *California Management Review* 40, no. 4: 26–41.

Golbe, D. L., and L. J. White. 1988. "Mergers and Acquisitions in the US Economy: An Aggregate and Historical Overview." In *Mergers and Acquisitions*, ed. A. J. Auerbach. Chicago: University of Chicago Press: 25–47.

Gort, M. 1962. *Diversification and Integration in American Industry.* Princeton: Princeton University Press.

Grant, R. M. 1991. "The Resource-Based Theory of Competitive Advantage: Implications for Strategy Formulation." *California Management Review* 33, no. 3: 114–35.

Grenadier, S. R. 1996. "The Strategic Exercise of Options: Development Cascades and Overbuilding in Real Estate Markets." *Journal of Finance* 51, no. 5: 1653–79.

————, ed. 2000a. *Game Choices: The Intersection of Real Options and Game Theory.* London: Risk Books.

————. 2000b. "Option Exercise Games: The Intersection of Real Options and Game Theory." *Journal of Applied Corporate Finance* 13, no. 2: 99–106.

Grenadier, S. R., and A. M. Weiss. 1997. "Investment in Technological Innovations: An Option Pricing Approach." *Journal of Financial Economics* 44, no. 3: 397–416.

Grossman, S. J., and O. D. Hart. 1980. "Takeover Bids, the Free-rider Problem, and the Theory of the Corporation." *Bell Journal of Economics* 11, no. 1: 42–64.

Gryglewicz, S., K. J. M. Huisman, and P. M. Kort. 2008. "Finite Project Life and Uncertainty Effects on Investment." *Journal of Economic Dynamics and Control* 32, no.7: 2191–2213.

Haleblian, J., C. E. Devers, G. McNamara, M. A. Carpenter, and R. B. Davison. 2009. "Taking Stock of What We Know about Mergers and Acquisitions: A Review and Research Agenda." *Journal of Management* 35, no. 3: 469–502.

Haunschild, P. R., A. D. Blake, and M. Fichman. 1994. "Managerial Over-commitment in Corporate Acquisition Processes." *Organization Science* 5, no. 4: 528–40.

Hayward, M. L., and D. C. Hambrick. 1997. "Explaining the Premiums Paid for Large Acquisitions: Evidence of CEO Hubris." *Administrative Science Quarterly* 42, no. 1: 103–27.

Hietala, P., S. N. Kaplan, and D. Robinson. 2003. "What Is the Price of Hubris? Using Takeover Battles to Infer Overpayments and Synergies." *Financial Management* 32, no. 3: 1–32.

Holmstrom, B., and S. N. Kaplan. 2001. "Corporate Governance and Merger Activity in the US: Making Sense of the 1980s and the 1990s." *Journal of Economic Perspectives* 15, no. 2: 121–44.

Horn, J. T., D. P. Lovallo, and S. P. Viguerie. 2006. "Learning to Let Go: Making Better Exit Decisions." *McKinsey Quarterly*, no. 2: 64–75.

Jarrell, G. A., and A. B. Poulsen. 1989. "The Returns to Acquiring Firms in Tender Offers: Evidence from Three Decades." *Financial Management* 18, no. 3: 12–19.

Jensen, M. C. 2005. "Agency Costs of Overvalued Equity." *Financial Management* 34, no. 1: 5–19.

Jones, M., and R. Sugden. 2001. "Positive Confirmation Bias in the Acquisition of Information." *Theory and Decision* 50, no. 1: 59–99.

Kahneman, D., and D. Lovallo. 1993. "Timid Choices and Bold Forecasts: A Cognitive Perspective on Risk Taking." *Management Science* 39, no. 1: 17–31.

Kahneman, D., and A. Tversky. 1979. "Prospect Theory: An Analysis of Decision under Risk." *Econometrica* 47, no. 2: 263–91.

Kamien, M. I., and I. Zang. 1990. "The Limits of Monopolisation through Acquisition." *Quarterly Journal of Economics* 105, no. 2: 465–99.

———. 1993. "Monopolization by Sequential Acquisition." *Journal of Law, Economics and Organization* 9, no. 2: 205–29.

Kester, W. C. 1984. "Today's Options for Tomorrow's Growth." *Harvard Business Review* 62, no. 2: 153–60.

Kil, J. C. M., and J. T. J. Smit. 2012. "Behavioral Real Options: Uncertainty Neglect in Acquisition Decisions." Working paper, Erasmus University Rotterdam.

Kil, J. C. M., J. T. J. Smit, and P. Verwijmeren. 2013. "Value Perception in Serial Acquisitions: Premiums Paid and the Market's Reaction." Working paper, Erasmus University Rotterdam.

Kogut, B. 1991. "Joint Ventures and the Option to Expand and Acquire." *Management Science* 37, no. 1: 19–33.

Kogut, B., and N. Kulatilaka. 1994a. "Operating Flexibility, Global Manufacturing, and the Option Value of a Multinational Network." *Management Science* 40, no. 1: 123–39.
———. 1994b. "Options Thinking and Platform Investments: Investing in Opportunity." *California Management Review* 36, no. 2: 52–71.
———. 2001. "Capabilities as Real Options." *Organization Science* 12, no. 6: 744–58.
———. 2004. "Real Option Pricing and Organizations: The Contingent Risks of Extended Theoretical Domains." *Academy of Management Review* 29, no. 1: 102–10.
Koller, T., M. Goedhart, and D. Wessels. 2010. *Valuation: Measuring and Managing the Value of Companies.* Hoboken, NJ: John Wiley.
Koller, T., D. Lovallo, and Z. Williams. 2011. "A Bias Against Investment?" *McKinsey Quarterly*, September. http://www.mckinsey.com/insights/corporate_finance/a_bias _against_investment.
Kulatilaka, N., and E. C. Perotti. 1998. "Strategic Growth Options." *Management Science* 44, no. 8: 1021–31.
Laamanen, T., and T. Keil. 2008. "Performance of Serial Acquirers: Toward and Acquisition Program Perspective." *Strategic Management Journal* 29, no. 6: 663–72.
Lafley, A. G., and R. L. Martin. 2013. *Playing to Win: How Strategy Really Works.* Cambridge, MA: Harvard Business Review Press.
Lambrecht, B. M. 2001. "The Impact of Debt Financing on Entry and Exit in a Duopoly." *Review of Financial Studies* 14, no. 3: 765–804.
———. 2004. "The Timing and Terms of Mergers Motivated by Economies of Scale." *Journal of Financial Economics* 72, no. 1: 41–62.
Lambrecht, B. M., and S. C. Myers. 2007. "A Theory of Takeovers and Disinvestment." *Journal of Finance* 62, no. 2: 809–45.
Larwood, L., and W. Whittaker. 1977. "Managerial Myopia: Self-Serving Biases in Organizational Planning." *Journal of Applied Psychology* 62, no. 2: 194–98.
Lieberman, M. B., and D. B. Montgomery. 1988. "First-Mover Advantages." *Strategic Management Journal* 9, Summer Special Issue: 41–58.
Loewenstein, G. F. 1988. "Frames of Mind in Intertemporal Choice." *Management Science* 34, no. 2: 200–214.
Lovallo, D., and D. Kahneman. 2003. "Delusions of Success: How Optimism Undermines Executives' Decisions." *Harvard Business Review* 81, no. 7: 56–63.
Lowry, M., and G. W. Schwert. 2002. "IPO Market Cycles: Bubbles or Sequential Learning?" *Journal of Finance* 57, no. 3: 1171–1200.
Maklan, S., S. Knox, and L. Ryals. 2005. "Using Real Options to Help Build the Business Case for CRM Investment." *Long Range Planning* 38, no. 4: 393–410.
Malmendier, U., and G. Tate. 2005. "CEO Overconfidence and Corporate Investment." *Journal of Finance* 60, no. 6: 2661–2700.
———. 2008. "Who Makes Acquisitions? CEO Overconfidence and the Market's Reaction." *Journal of Financial Economics* 89, no. 1: 20–43.
———. 2009. "Superstar CEOs." *Quarterly Journal of Economics* 124, no. 4: 1593–1638.
March, J. G., and Z. Shapira. 1987. "Managerial Perspectives on Risk and Risk Taking." *Management Science* 33, no. 11: 1404–18.
Margrabe, W. 1978. "The Value of an Option to Exchange One Asset for Another." *Journal of Finance* 33, no. 1: 177–86.

Martin, R. L. 2009. *The Design of Business*. Cambridge, MA: Harvard Business Review Press.

———. 2013. "Rethinking the Decision Factory." *Harvard Business Review* 91, no. 10: 96–104.

Mason, S. P., and R. C. Merton. 1985. "The Role of Contingent Claims Analysis in Corporate Finance." In *Recent Advances in Corporate Finance*, ed. E. Altman and M. Subrahmanyam. Homewood, IL: R.D. Irwing: 7–54.

McCarter, M. W., J. T. Mahoney, and G. B. Northcraft. 2011. "Testing the Waters: Using Collective Real Options to Manage the Social Dilemma of Strategic Alliances." *Academy of Management Review* 36, no. 4: 621–40.

McDonald, R., and D. Siegel. 1985. "Investment and the Valuation of Firms When There Is an Option to Shut Down." *International Economic Review* 26, no. 2: 331–49.

———. 1986. "The Value of Waiting to Invest." *Quarterly Journal of Economics* 101, no. 4: 707–27.

McGahan, A. M. 1994. "The Incentive Not to Invest: Capacity Commitment in Compact Disk Introduction." In *Research and Technology Innovation, Management and Policy* 5, ed. R. S. Rosenbloom and R. A. Burgelman. Greenwich, CT: JAI Press, 177–97.

McGrath, R. G. 1997. "A Real Options Logic for Initiating Technology Positioning Investments." *Academy of Management Review* 22, no. 4: 974–96.

———. 1999. "Falling Forward: Real Options Reasoning and Entrepreneurial Failure." *Academy of Management Review* 24, no. 1: 13–30.

McGrath, R. G., W. J. Ferrier, and A. L. Mendelow. 2004. "Response: Real Options as Engines of Choice and Heterogeneity." *Academy of Management Review* 29, no. 1: 86–101.

McGrath, R. G., and I. C. Macmillan. 2000. "Assessing Technology Projects Using Real Options Reasoning." *Research-Technology Management* 43, no. 4: 35–49.

McNamara, G. M., J. J. Haleblian, and B. J. Dykes. 2008. "The Performance Implications of Participating in an Acquisition Wave: Early Mover Advantages, Bandwagon Effects, and the Moderating Influence of Industry Characteristics and Acquirer Tactics." *Academy of Management* 51, no. 1: 113–30.

Melicher, R. W., J. Ledolter, and L. J. D'Antonio. 1983. "A Time Series Analysis of Aggregate Merger Activity." *Review of Economics and Statistics* 65, no. 3: 423–30.

Merton, R. C. 1998. "Applications of Option-Pricing Theory: Twenty-Five Years Later." *American Economic Review* 88, no. 3: 323–49.

Miller, K. D. 1992. "A Framework for Integrated Risk Management in International Business." *Journal of International Business Studies* 23, no. 3: 311–31.

Miller, K. D., and T. B. Folta. 2002. "Option Value and Entry Timing." *Strategic Management Journal* 23, no. 7: 655–65.

Miller, K. D., and Z. Shapira. 2004. "An Empirical Test of Heuristics and Biases Affecting Real Option Valuation." *Strategic Management Journal* 25, no. 3: 269–84.

Miller, K. D., and H. G. Waller. 2003. "Scenarios, Real Options and Integrated Risk Management." *Long Range Planning* 36, no. 1: 93–107.

Miller, M. H., and F. Modigliani. 1961. "Dividend Policy, Growth, and the Valuation of Shares." *Journal of Business* 34, no. 4: 235–64.

Mitchell, M., and J. H. Mulherrin. 1996. "The Impact of Industry Shocks on Takeover and Restructuring Activity." *Journal of Financial Economics* 41, no. 2: 93–229.

Morellec, E., and A. Zhdanov. 2005. "The Dynamics of Mergers and Acquisitions." *Journal of Financial Economics* 77, no. 3: 649–72.

Myers, S. 1977. "Determinants of Corporate Borrowing." *Journal of Financial Economics* 5, no. 2: 147–75.

Mylonadis, Y. 2010. "Thinking Aloud." *Business Strategy Review* 21, no. 2: 47–48.

Nelson, R. L. 1959. *Merger Movements in American Industry, 1895–1956.* Princeton: Princeton University Press.

Nichols, N. A. 1994, "Scientific Management at Merck." *Harvard Business Review* 72, no. 1: 88–99.

O'Brien, J., and T. Folta. 2009. "Sunk Costs, Uncertainty and Market Exit: A Real Options Perspective." *Industrial and Corporate Change* 18, no. 5: 807–33.

Penman, S. H. 1998. "A Synthesis of Equity Valuation Techniques and the Terminal Value Calculations for the Dividend Discount Model." *Review of Accounting Studies* 2, no. 4: 303–23.

Penrose, E. 1959. *The Theory of the Growth of the Firm.* London: Basil Blackwell.

Perry, M. K., and R. H. Porter. 1985. "Oligopoly and the Incentive for Horizontal Merger." *American Economic Review* 75, no. 1: 219–27.

Petersen, B., D. E. Welch, and L. S. Welch. 2000. "Creating Meaningful Switching Options in International Operations." *Long Range Planning* 33, no. 5: 688–705.

Pindyck, R. S. 1988. "Irreversible Investment, Capacity Choice, and the Value of the Firm." *American Economic Review* 78, no. 5: 969–85.

Porter, M. E. 1980. *Competitive Strategy: Techniques for Analyzing Industries and Competitors.* New York: Free Press.

Prahalad, C. K., and G. Hamel. 1990. "The Core Competence of the Corporation." *Harvard Business Review* 68, no. 3: 79–91.

Putten A. B. van, and I. C. Macmillan. 2004. "Making Real Options Really Work." *Harvard Business Review* 82, no. 12: 134–41.

Reuer, J. J., and T. W. Tong. 2005. "Real Options in International Joint Ventures." *Journal of Management* 31, no. 3: 403–23.

———. 2010. "Discovering Valuable Growth Opportunities: An Analysis of Equity Alliances with IPO firms." *Organization Science* 21, no. 1: 202–15.

Reuters. 2002. "Who Will Blink First in German Telecoms Poker?" *Business World* 3, January.

Rhodes-Kropf, M., and S. Viswanathan. 2004. "Market Valuation and Merger Wave." *Journal of Finance* 59, no. 6: 2685–2718.

Rhodes-Kropf, M., D. T. Robinson, and S. Viswanathan. 2005. "Valuation Waves and Merger Activity: The Empirical Evidence." *Journal of Financial Economics* 77, no. 3: 561–603.

Roll, R. 1986. "The Hubris Hypothesis of Corporate Takeovers." *Journal of Business* 59, no. 2: 197–216.

———. 1993. "The Hubris Hypothesis of Corporate Takeovers." In *Advances in Behavioral Finance,* ed. R. H. Thaler. New York: Russell Sage Foundation: 437–58.

Rumelt, R. P. 1984. "Towards a Strategic Theory of the Firm." In *Competitive Strategic Management,* ed. R. B. Lambrecht. Englewood Cliffs, NJ: Prentice Hall: 556–70.

Scharfstein, D. S., and J. C. Stein. 1990. "Herd Behavior and Investment." *American Economic Review* 80, no. 3: 465–79.

Schelling, T. C. 1980. *The Strategy of Conflict*. Boston: Harvard University Press.

Schiller, R. J. 1981. "Do Stock Prices Move Too Much to Be Justified by Subsequent Changes in Dividends?" *American Economic Review* 71, no. 3: 421–35.

Schipper, K., and R. Thompson. 1983. "Evidence on the Capitalized Value of Merger Activity for Acquiring Firms." *Journal of Financial Economics* 11, nos. 1–4: 85–120.

Schwenk, C. R. 1986. "Information, Cognitive Biases, and Commitment to a Course of Action." *Academy of Management Review* 11, no. 2: 298–310.

Selten, R. 1965. "Spieltheoretische Behandlung Eines Oligopolimodells mit Nachfragetragheit: Teil I: Bestimmung des dynamischen Preisgleichgewitchs." *Journal of Institutional Theoretical Economics* 121, no. 2: 301–24.

Seth, A., K. Song, and R. Pettit. 2000. "Synergy, Managerialism or Hubris? An Empirical Examination of Motives for Foreign Acquisitions of US firms." *Journal of International Business Studies* 31, no. 3: 387–406.

Shapiro, A. C. 1989. "The Theory of Business Strategy." *RAND Journal of Economics* 20, no. 1: 125–37.

Shefrin, H. 2007. *Behavioral Corporate Finance: Decisions That Create Value*. New York: McGraw-Hill.

Shefrin, H., and M. Statman. 1985. "The Disposition to Sell Winners Too Early and Ride Losers Too Long: Theory and Evidence." *Journal of Finance* 40, no. 3: 777–90.

Shiller, R. J. 2000. *Irrational Exuberance*. Princeton: Princeton University Press.

Shleifer, A. 2000. *Inefficient Markets: An Introduction to Behavioral Finance*. Oxford: Oxford University Press.

Shleifer, A., and R. W. Vishny. 2003. "Stock Market Driven Acquisitions." *Journal of Financial Economics* 70, no. 3: 295–311.

Singh, H., and C. Montgomery. 1987. "Corporate Acquisition Strategies and Economic Performance." *Strategic Management Journal* 8, no. 4: 377–86.

Singh, R. 1998. "Takeover Bidding with Toeholds: The Case of the Owner's Curse." *Review of Financial Studies* 11, no. 4: 679–704.

Smit, J. T. J. 2001. "Acquisition Strategies as Option Games." *Journal of Applied Corporate Finance* 14, no. 2: 79–89.

———. 2003. "Infrastructure Investment as a Real Options Game: The Case of European Airport Expansion." *Financial Management* 32, no. 4: 27–58.

Smit, J. T. J., and L. A. Ankum. 1993. "A Real Options and Game-Theoretic Approach to Corporate Investment Strategy under Competition." *Financial Management* 22, no. 3: 241–50.

Smit, J. T. J., and D. Lovallo. 2014. "Adjusting for biases in hot and cold markets." *MIT Sloan Management Review* (forthcoming).

Smit, J. T. J., and T. Moraitis. 2010a. "Playing at Serial Acquisitions." *California Management Review* 53, no. 1: 56–89.

———. 2010b. "Serial Acquisition Options." *Long Range Planning* 43, no. 1: 85–103.

Smit, J. T. J., and L. Trigeorgis. 2004. *Strategic Investment: Real Options and Games*. Princeton: Princeton University Press.

———. 2009. "Valuing Infrastructure Investment: An Options Game Approach." *California Management Review* 51, no. 2: 21–39.

————. 2013. "Strategic Investment Value under Different Information Structures: Learning, Technical Uncertainty and Asymmetric Information." Working paper, Erasmus University Rotterdam.

Smith, C. 2007. "M&A as an Illusion." In *Mergers and Acquisitions*, ed. Duncan Angwin. Malden, MA: Blackwell: 63–86.

Song, M. H., and R. A. Walkling. 2000. "Abnormal Returns to Rivals of Acquisition Targets: A Test of the 'Acquisition Probability Hypothesis.'" *Journal of Financial Economics* 55, no. 2: 143–71.

Stigler, G. J. 1950. "Monopoly and Oligopoly by Merger." *American Economic Review* 40, no. 2: 23–34.

Strack, F., and T. Mussweiler. 1997. "Explaining the Enigmatic Anchoring Effect: Mechanisms of Selective Accessibility." *Journal of Personality and Social Psychology* 73, no. 3: 437–46.

Svenson, O. 1981. "Are We All Less Risky and More Skillful Than Our Fellow Drivers?" *Acta Psychologica* 47, no. 2: 143–48.

Teece, D. J. 1980. "Economics of Scope and the Scope of the Enterprise." *Journal of Economic Behavior and Organization* 1, no. 3: 223–47.

————. 1982. "Towards an Economic Theory of the Multiproduct Firm." *Journal of Economic Behavior and Organization* 3, no. 1: 39–63.

————. 1984. "Economic Analysis and Strategic Management." *California Management Review* 26, no. 3: 87–110.

Teece, D. J., G. Pisano, and A. Shuen. 1997. "Dynamic Capabilities and Strategic Management." *Strategic Management Journal* 18, no. 7: 509–34.

Thaler, R. H. 1988. "Anomalies: The Winner's Curse." *Journal of Economic Perspectives* 2, no. 1: 191–202.

————. 1997. "Giving Markets a Human Dimension." *Financial Times*, June 16, 1997, Mastering Finance 6 sec.

Thijssen, J. J. J., K. J. M Huisman, and P. M. Kort. 2012. "Symmetric Equilibrium Strategies in Game Theoretic Real Option Models." *Journal of Mathematical Economics* 48, no. 4: 219–25.

Tirole, J. 1990. *The Theory of Industrial Organization*. Cambridge, MA: MIT Press.

Tiwana, A., M. Keil, and R. G. Fichman. 2006. "Information Systems Project Continuation in Escalation Situations: A Real Options Model." *Decision Sciences* 37, no. 3: 357–86.

Tiwana, A., J. Wang, M. Keil, and P. Ahluwalia. 2007. "The Bounded Rationality Bias in Managerial Valuation of Real Options: Theory and Evidence from IT Projects." *Decision Sciences* 38, no. 1: 157–81.

Tong, T. W., T. M. Alessandri, J. J. Reuer, and A. Chintakananda. 2008. "How Much Does Country Matter? An Analysis of Firms' Growth Options." *Journal of International Business Studies* 29, no. 3: 387–405.

Tong, T. W., and J. J. Reuer. 2006. "Firm and Industry Influences on the Value of Growth Options." *Strategic Organization* 4, no. 1: 71–95.

————. 2007. "Real Options in Strategic Management." In *Advances in Strategic Management*, ed. J. J. Reuer. Bingley: Emerald: 3–28.

————. 2008. "Real Options in Multinational Corporations: Organizational Challenges and Risk Implications." *Journal of International Business Studies* 38, no. 2: 215–30.

Tong, T. W., J. J. Reuer, and M. Peng. 2008. "International Joint Ventures and the Value of Growth Options." *Academy of Management Journal* 51, no. 5: 1014–29.

Toxvaerd, F. 2008. "Strategic Merger Waves: A Theory of Musical Chairs." *Journal of Economic Theory* 140, no. 1: 1–26.

Trigeorgis, L. 1991. "A Log-Transformed Binomial Method for Valuing Complex Multi-Option Investments." *Journal of Financial and Quantitative Analysis* 26, no. 3: 309–26.

———. 1993. "Real Options and Interactions with Financial Flexibility." *Financial Management* 22, no. 3: 202–24.

———. 1996. *Real Options: Managerial Flexibility and Strategy in Resource Allocation.* Cambridge, MA: MIT Press.

Tversky, A., and D. Kahneman. 1974. "Judgment under Uncertainty: Heuristics and Biases." *Science* 185, no. 4157: 1124–31.

———. 1981. "The Framing of Decisions and the Psychology of Choice." *Science* 211, no. 4481: 453–58.

Varaiya, N. P., and K. R. Ferris. 1987. "Overpaying in Corporate Takeovers: The Winner's Curse." *Financial Analysts Journal* 43, no. 3: 64–70.

Warner, A. G., J. F. Fairbank, and K. H. Steensma. 2006. "Managing Uncertainty in a Formal Standards-Based Industry: A Real Options Perspective on Acquisition Timing." *Journal of Management* 32, no. 2: 279–98.

Wason, P. C. 1968. "Reasoning about a Rule." *Quarterly Journal of Experimental Psychology* 20, no. 3: 273–81.

Wernerfelt, B. 1984. "A Resource-Based View of the Firm." *Strategic Management Journal* 5, no. 2: 171–80.

Wernerfelt, B., and A. A. Karnani. 1987. "Competitive Strategy under Uncertainty." *Strategic Management Journal* 8, no. 2: 187–94.

Williamson, P. J. 1999. "Strategy as Options on the Future." *Sloan Management Review* 40, no. 3: 117–26.

Winter, S. G. 1987. "Knowledge and Competence as Strategic Assets." In *The Competitive Challenge: Strategies for Industrial Innovation and Renewal*, ed. D. J. Teece. Cambridge, MA: Ballinger: 159–84.

Zack, M. H. 1999. "Developing a Knowledge Strategy." *California Management Review* 41, no. 3: 125–45.

Zahra, S., and G. George. 2002. "Absorptive Capacity: A Review, Reconceptualization, and Extension." *Academy of Management Review* 27, no. 2: 185–203.

Zajac, E. J., and M. H. Bazerman. 1991. "Blind Spots in Industry and Competitor Analysis: Implications for Strategic Decisions." *Academy of Management Review* 16, no. 1: 37–58.

Zardkoohi, A. 2004. "Response: Do Real Options Lead to Escalation of Commitment?" *Academy of Management Review* 29, no. 1: 111–19.

INDEX

acquisition decision making, pitfalls of, 154–55; pitfalls of strategy design, 155–56; pitfalls in valuation analysis, 156–57

acquisition decisions, de-biasing of, 158–59; bottom-up approach, 159–61; top-down approach, 161–62

acquisition options, classification of under competition, 78–81; asset acquisition options, 79–80; exit option, 86; merger option, 86; as an option on the buyer's future value, 84; parallel platform acquisitions, 85–86; platform acquisition option, 80, 106, 133, 134; proprietary platform (compound) option, 106; shared asset option, 79, 81, 106–7. *See also* platform acquisition option, example case of

acquisition strategy, 75, 148, 155; as conceptual option games, 99–100; and financial markets, 112–13; opportunism in, 95, 98–99; option-like and competitive characteristics of, 76–77; serial acquisition strategy, 75; techniques for strategic acquisition timing, 96–98 (box); traditional strategy approaches, 76. *See also* buy-and-build strategy

acquisitions, 19–20, 22n11, 76n2; abandoning an acquired company for salvage, 86n9; acquisition frenzies, 94–95; acquisition paths, 58, 79, 87–88, 148; acquisition value, 79; as driven by growth options and mispricing, 166–68; equity financing of, 164; long-term strategic importance of, 22; mapping alternative acquisition paths, 107, 110; multiple acquisitions, 85; parallel platform acquisitions, 46, 85–86; role of bias in, 3, 3n3; staging of an acquisition in a hot market, 34. *See also* procyclical acquisition waves; serial acquisitions (the case of Vodafone)

AirTouch, 43, 44, 45, 45n4; PVGO-to-price ratio of, 63, 63n28

Alexander the Great, 151

Alltel Corporation, 45

"Anchor and Adjustment" experiment, 51, 52

anchoring, 22, 51, 157, 171, 172

Anglo American, 117

ArcelorMittal, 75

auctions, 56n22, 66, 126, 148; bidding auctions, 53, 55–56; company auctions, 7, 19, 157; private equity auctions, 53, 57, 126; sealed-bid auctions, 125, 128

Austria, 75

backward induction, 84, 107n6, 128–29, 129n8

behavioral theory, 3, 5, 11n12, 99–100, 169; embedding of in new valuation tools, 170–71

Belgium, 75

Bell Atlantic, 44, 45, 45n4

Benelux region, examples of exit and divestment options in, 39–40 (box); option to divest various business formats, 39; option to exit real estate, 39

Berg Electronics, 76

BHP Billiton, 116, 117, 141

"Biased Beauty Contest" experiment, 51, 51n19, 52

biases, 41, 95, 165; attribution bias, 26; awareness of, 57; biases that affect career planning, 154; biases that affect company strategy, 49–50 (box); biases that affect company valuation, 52 (box); cognitive bias, 2, 5; commitment bias, 54; confirmation bias, 6, 21, 48, 61, 156; in decision making, 9, 20, 20n5, 45, 152; executive valuation biases, 13–15; exercise bias, 94; investment bias, 78; joint confirmation bias, 48; judgment bias, 46–48, 61, 156; mitigation of through real options, 60; overconfidence bias, 6; personal-level executive bias, 22; psychological bias, 7, 153; recognition of, 20; representativeness bias, 51; and self-attribution, 5, 48; self-serving bias, 47n8, 48; ubiquitous nature of, 152–54; uncertainty-related bias, 5

bidders/bidding, 64nn31–32, 81, 92, 165; irrational bidders, 7; multiple bidders, 67, 157; potential interlopers in the bidding process, 68; potential pitfalls in the bidding process, 157–58; rational bidders, 66–67, 165; "shading" of bids, 67. *See also* bidding game, competition in; option bidding game, designing and solving of

bidding game, competition in, 87–88; bidding games that acquirers play, 135; and changing industry competition (organic growth versus acquisitive growth), 88–91; competitive growth strategies, 89. *See also* option bidding game, designing and solving of
binomial option pricing, 86–87
biotechnology, 171–72
Black-Scholes formula, 86
bounded rational behavior, 148
Brascan, Ltd., 143, 143n16
Bristol-Myers Squibb, 77
Buffet, Warren, 75
buy-and-build strategy, 43, 79; and consolidation strategy, 83; and the financial leverage effect, 82; as an option portfolio, 81–83; strategic value of, 90; synergistic benefits of, 82, 83–87, 84n6

call options, 8, 9; on the value of synergistic benefits, 34n17, 82, 84n7
Candover Investments, 88
capital, cost of, 24
Capoten, 77
career planning, and bias, 154
cash flows, 15, 21, 26, 27, 30, 58, 82, 85, 99, 104, 156; ascertainable cash flows, 56; cash flow variability, 92; cash flow volatility, 113n7; extrapolation of cash-flow growth, 24; free cash flows (FCFs), 23; future cash flows, 102, 117; net free cash flows, 23, 83; net present value (NPV) analysis of forecasted cash flows from a single transaction, 76; operational cash flows, 30, 79, 87. *See also* discounted cash flow (DCF) analysis
CEOs (chief executive officers), 3, 48; acquisition conundrum of, 2; designer CEOs, 1–2, 152, 153; "empire-building" executives, 34n16; opportunist CEOs, 1–2, 151; overconfidence of, 6
Cerrejón coal mine, 101, 107
China, 46, 114
China Mobile, 43; investment made in by Vodafone, 45
cold markets, 20, 151–52. *See also* cold markets, checking DCF undervaluation in; cold markets, and why managers freeze deals
cold markets, checking DCF undervaluation in, 24–25; bottom-of-the-cycle correction of horizon value, 25; entry-exit multiple checks, 25

cold markets, and why managers freeze deals, 21–22; because of anchoring on market valuations, 22; because of passive rivals, 22; because of personal-level executive biases, 22
competition, 90, 112, 128; aggressive approach to, 88; competitive interaction and growth option value, 81n5; extreme forms of, 88; intense competition, 65, 67, 89, 94, 148, 153; limited competition, 22, 95; price competition, 89; principles of, 79. *See also* bidding game, competition in
conditionality, 9, 163
Confirmed experiment, 49–50
conglomerate discount, 14
consolidation/consolidation strategy, 57, 58, 62, 83, 85–86, 99, 106, 107, 110, 119, 133, 134; and consolidation frenzies, 160; and fragmented markets, 113–14; speed of consolidation, 81
control, illusion of, 47, 48, 61, 151, 156, 163

Davis, Mick, 101, 103; acquisition strategy of, 106
decision making, 3, 11, 83, 152; acquisition decision making, 152, 169; biases in, 9, 20, 20n5, 45, 152; objective decision making, 41, 45, 148; rational decision making, 57; strategic decision making, 76; under uncertainty, 26, 34, 152
demand values: high demand levels, 97 (box); intermediate demand levels, 97 (box); low demand levels, 97 (box)
discounted cash flow (DCF) analysis, 12, 22–23, 35, 113; of a buyout, 51n20; checks on DCF overvaluation in hot deal markets, 23–24; checks on DCF undervaluation in cold market deals, 24–25; modification of, 32; static DCF analysis, 152
dot-com bubble, the, 7, 19, 53
Du Pont Merck Pharmaceutical Company, 77
dual real options valuation (the case of Xstrata), 101–3, 118; and the bottom-up framework, 106–7, 110, 112, 164–65; conclusions concerning, 118–20; illustrative example of, 103–4; and the mapping of alternative acquisition paths in a tree, 107, 110; and the timing of acquisition options, 110, 112; and the top-down framework, 112–17, 164–65
Dutch Continental Shelf, developing the reserves of, 34–35, 36–38 (box); insights real-

ized from, 37–38; options available for, 36–37; uncertainty or risk involved, 37

EBITDA (earnings before interest, taxes, depreciation, and amortization) multiples, 51, 51n17, 51n20, 114
equilibrium: finding equilibrium in a multi-stage game, 129; focal point equilibrium, 128n7; mixed equilibrium, 128n6; subgame perfect equilibrium, 129n8. *See also* Nash equilibrium
equity, 7, 24; cost of, 114n9; equity value, 64, 65–66n33, 113, 114, 160, 162, 167n7; minority equity stakes, 34. *See also* auctions, private equity auctions; private equity fund(s); private equity investments/investors
Europolitan Vodafone AB (Sweden), 58
executives. *See* CEOs (chief executive officers)

Falconbridge Group, 101, 125–26; platform acquisition of, 107, 136 (box), 138 (box). *See also* Falconbridge episode, quantifying the optionality of
Falconbridge episode, quantifying the optionality of, 133–34; value of the Falconbridge platform (including present value), 134–35, 141
"Feeling Confident" experiment, 47–48, 49 (box)
financial markets, 112–13, 117, 119–20, 158; characteristics of a fragmented market, 113–14
first-mover advantage, 79, 90, 91; preemptive commitment using first-mover advantage, 142–43
France, 56
Franklin, Benjamin, 43

game theory, 3, 8, 11, 63, 69, 70, 79, 91, 99–100, 123, 149, 152, 161, 169, 170; assumptions regarding classic game theory applications, 127; classic game theory, 127; game theory analysis, 77 (box), 107n6, 129; game theory extension, 159; integration of with options analysis, 58, 61; principles of, 83, 88, 100; real option reasoning and, 160; and strategic bidding decisions, 124
Gent, Chris, 43, 44, 46
Germany, 57, 65, 66, 70, 75
Glencore, acquisition of by Xstrata, 101, 106, 110, 117

Golder Thoma Cressey Rauner, 76
Gordian Knot, 151–52
"Grab the Dollar" game, 91, 95, 97, 110, 142
groupthink, 21, 47, 48, 61, 156
growth: balancing of organic and acquisitive growth, 160; growth expectation, 24. *See also* growth options
growth options, 10–11, 12, 56; appropriate growth options beyond the horizon, 29; competitive interaction and growth option value, 81n5; decomposition of growth option value, 162; as a driver of acquisitions, 166–68; dual valuation of growth option to avoid irrational infection, 61–63; enhancing growth option value, 28; growth option-to-price ratio, 14; growth options value, 117, 118, 134, 152, 159, 161, 166, 167–68, 167n7, 170; growth options value and mispricing, 64, 64n32; growth options value and systemic risk, 62n27; organic growth options, 160

HAL Investments, 75
herding/herding behavior, 21, 160
Hicks Muse Tate & Furst, 76; acquisition of Berg Electronics by, 76; acquisition of Hillsdown by, 82, 88
horizon value(s), 24–25, 26, 28, 29; bottom-of-the-cycle correction of, 25; opportunism in, 32
hot markets, 20; clustering of public offerings in, 40n22; and overconfidence, 154–55. *See also* hot markets, checking DCF overvaluation in; hot markets, and why managers value deals too highly
hot markets, checking DCF overvaluation in, 23–24; consistency checks, 24; extrapolation of cash-flow growth during the estimating period, 24; top-of-the-cycle profitability estimates, 24
hot markets, and why managers value deals too highly, 20–21; because of aggressive rivals, 21; because of exuberant investors, 21; because of groupthink, 21

Inco, 115, 116, 135, 141–42n12, 144, 146
incremental merger activities, 135
information asymmetry, 56
investors, 12, 15, 39n22, 76, 103, 115, 152, 157, 160, 165, 166; buy-and-build investors, 87; cash-rich investors, 95; exuberant inves-

investors (*cont.*)
  tors, 20, 21; and the internalization of R&D
  capabilities, 171; irrational investors, 7; and
  loss aversion, 156; opportunistic investors,
  14, 35, 39 (box); sophisticated investors,
  119. *See also* private equity investment/
  investors
irrational infection, 20, 156
irrationality, 69, 170; rationality-irrationality
  dichotomy, 170
Italy, 56, 66, 70, 75

Japan, 46
Japan Telecom, 45
Johnson & Johnson Merck Consumer Phar-
  maceuticals Co., 77
J-Phone Vodafone, 45
Jubilee Nickel, 107

Kahneman, Daniel, 3n3, 20n5, 22n9; prospect
  theory of, 45–46
Kierkegaard, Søren, 1

Las Bambas copper mine, 107
Lewent, Judy, 76, 77
loss aversion, 22, 22n9, 46, 86, 127, 156
Lovallo, Dan, 3n3, 20n5

Mannesmann AG, 43, 45, 62, 63; Vodafone's
  acquisition price for, 65–66
market capitalization (MV), 64, 64–65n33,
  162, 166
market method for acquisitions (MMA), 13,
  103, 118
market value to book value ratio (MV/B),
  64n31
market values, of targets and bidders, 13–14
Martin, Roger, 1n1
Medco, 77
Merck and Co., Inc., option analysis at, 30, 31
  (box); annual standard deviation of returns,
  31; exercise price, 31; risk-free rate of interest, 31; stock price, 31; time to expiration,
  31
Merck and Co., Inc., options and games at,
  77–78 (box)
mergers, 14, 21, 67, 116, 133; consolidation
  mergers, 157
MIM Group, 101, 106–7, 110, 133
mining/metals industry, 14, 30, 32–33, 114–
  16, 172; estimated value of a producing

mine, 117n10; and the revival of "related diversification" strategies, 116–17. *See also*
  Xstrata, specific acquisitions of in the mining industry
mispricing: comparative mispricing, 164; as a
  driver of acquisitions, 166–68; growth options value and mispricing, 64, 64n32
Monte Carlo simulation, 30
multiple arbitrage, 24
multiples, 157; EBITDA (earnings before interest, taxes, depreciation, and amortization)
  multiples, 51, 51n17, 51n20; price-earnings
  multiples, 51

Nalebuff, B. J., 127
narrow framing, 46
Nash, John, 127
Nash equilibrium, 127, 128, 128nn6–7, 129n8;
  dominant strategies and Nash equilibrium,
  131 (box), 138 (box)
net present value (NPV) analysis, 9, 23, 35, 51,
  92–93, 99, 170; expanded "strategic" NPV,
  25–26, 83, 87, 90–91; of forecasted cash
  flows from a single transaction, 76; traditional NPV method, 34
Netherlands, 75
"New Economy" firms, 70, 164

opportunism, 2–3, 13, 15, 32, 99, 119, 152,
  164, 170. *See also* strategic opportunism/
  opportunities
option bidding game, designing and solving
  of, 124; Step 1: determine the players of,
  124–25; Step 2: determine the sequence of
  play, 125–26; Step 3: determine the choices
  and information of rival bidders, 126; Step
  4: estimate the payoff structure for each
  player, 126–27; Step 5: look forward and
  reason backward to determine the most
  likely outcome, 127–29. *See also* Nash equilibrium; sequential move game; simultaneous move game
option game valuation of acquisition opportunities, 130–32 (box); backward option valuation of growth opportunities, 131–32;
  dominant strategies and the Nash equilibrium, 131; payoffs in the 2 x 2 matrix, 130–
  31. *See also* option game valuation of acquisition opportunities, effective application of
option game valuation of acquisition opportunities, effective application of, 147: experi-

mentation with game assumptions and specifications, 148–49; realistic game layout, 148; subdividing complex strategy into simple building blocks, 147

option games, 70, 123–24, 171–72; and acquisition strategy, 75–76, 78; limitation of the option game approach, 149; options game theory, 97 (box); quantification of, 161; use of to overcome bidding pitfalls, 65–66. *See also* option bidding game, designing and solving of

option value, 79, 81, 94; competitive interaction and growth option value, 81n5; growth option value, 13

options: avoiding options that inflate hot deal valuation, 27–28; call real options, 27, 30; "exchange" option, 38n20, 78–79; exit options, 86; long-term favorable options to exit at the horizon, 29; merger options, 86, 106; minority stake/staged investment options, 27; the option to defer, 27; the option to exit or divest early, 27; the option to expand at or before the horizon, 29; option interaction, 86; option value characteristics, 79–80; potential options, 102; put real options, 27, 30, 32; strike price of, 30–31; ubiquitous nature of, 152–54; underlying value of, 30. *See also* acquisition options, classification of under competition; call options; growth options; option value; real options

overconfidence, 47–48, 47n10, 151, 154–55, 156

overoptimism, 20, 47n10, 154, 156, 172

overshooting, 93–94, 99; avoiding overshooting in top-of-the-cycle frenzies, 94–95

overvaluation, 24, 45, 57, 158, 160, 162; suppression of, 61; of the telecom industry, 70, 164

Pearle Benelux, 75

pharmaceutical industry, the: and the acquisition of R&D ventures, 35; drug development in, 30

Phelps Dodge, 125, 133, 134, 145–46, 147

Phelps Dodge Inco Corporation, 146

Philips Corporation, 171

platform acquisition option, example case of, 136–39 (box); Scenario 1: bidders' consideration of acquisition simultaneously, 141–42; Scenario 2: preemptive commitment using first-mover advantage, 142–43; Scenario 3: minority stake and flexibility, 143–45; Scenario 4: new players that raise the stakes, 145–47, 146n20; Step 1: payoffs in the 2 x 2 matrix, 136, 144nn17–18; Step 2: dominant strategies and the Nash equilibrium, 138, 144; Step 3: backward option value of acquisition games, 138–39. *Politics* (Aristotle), 8

present value growth opportunities (PVGOs), 13–14, 79, 100, 102–3, 113n7, 114–15, 161, 165, 167–68; estimation of from present value of growth options and the adjusted market value of a firm, 64; "implied PVGO," 62, 62n27, 113, 162; PVGO-to-price ratio, 63, 63n29; strength of top-down PVGO methodology, 119; top-down PVGO valuation, 69, 70, 160

price, 66, 75; commodity price uncertainty, 143; estimating the fundamental price (P), 64–65n33; price competition, 89; price-earnings ratio, 14, 51. *See also* mispricing; value, of a target company

private equity fund(s), 14, 19, 35, 51n20, 154

private equity investment/investors, 9, 13, 14, 38, 44, 51, 51n20, 82; investors as opportunists, 35

private equity partners, 13, 15, 35, 147

procyclical acquisition waves, 19, 91, 97

profitability: average profitability, 25; top-of-the-cycle profitability, 24

psychology, 20; applications of testing managerial biases in business situations, 4–5; psychological experiments highlighting vulnerability to deception, 3–4. *See also* behavioral theory

quantitative options models, 100

rationality, 47, 66, 94; bounded rationality, 3, 12, 127, 157, 161, 169; deviation from, 4–5; economic assumptions of, 169; rationality-irrationality dichotomy, 170. *See also* rationality, in dealing with personal bias, financial markets, and "irrational" rivals

rationality, in dealing with personal bias, financial markets, and "irrational" rivals, 163; mitigating comparable valuations distorted by mispriced industries, 164–65; mitigating irrational price escalation in multibidder contexts, 165; mitigating overcommitment

rationality, in dealing with personal bias, financial markets, and "irrational" rivals (*cont.*)
to a suboptimal strategy, 163; mitigating suboptimal timing over the business cycle, 163; mitigating valuation influenced by a biased mind-set, 164; mitigating the winner's curse, 166

real estate, 30, 38, 171; option to exit real estate, 39 (box); real estate bubble, 170; real estate prices, 154–55

real options, 3, 8–9, 29, 58, 61, 63, 93, 101–2, 123n2, 124, 159; analyzing of prevents uncertainty neglect in strategy, 9; analyzing of prevents uncertainty neglect in valuation, 9–10; behavioral real options, 20; and the mitigation of bias, 60; as platform investments, 80n4; purpose of real options analysis, 26; real options exercise bias, 93–94; real options theory, 20n6, 102, 123. *See also* real options input parameters; real options thinking, examples of in hot and cold markets; real options valuation

real options input parameters, 29–32; estimated volatility (endogenous or exogenous), 30; option term or maturity, 31; strike price, 30–31; threshold levels, 32; underlying value of the options, 30

real options thinking, examples of in hot and cold deal markets, 32; exit opportunities in hot and cold markets, 35, 38, 39–40 (box); looking for growth opportunities beyond the nearby in cold markets, 34–35, 36–38 (box); using minority stakes to exercise caution, 32–34

real options valuation, 12, 57, 79, 96 (box), 152, 164, 166

"reference group neglect," 47n9

research directions, 169; behavioral option games to operationalize strategic management theory, 169–70; descriptive theory of behavioral real options, 169; embedding of behavioral theory in new valuation tools, 170–71; empirical research using top-down decomposition, 170

restructuring, 15, 24, 27, 162; restructuring of fragmented markets, 120; restructuring strategies, 14, 75, 162

Rio Tinto, 116, 117

risk, 45, 53, 60, 116; of comparative mispricing, 164; downside risk, 8, 30, 62n27; estimation of, 46, 156; evaluation of, 46; geographic risk, 117; of intense competition, 89–90; of overconfidence, 47; parallel risk mitigation, 8; perception of, 46–47, 68, 155–56; risk-adjusted probabilities, 132 (box), 138 (box); risk preferences, 45–46n6; risk profile, 10; short-term risk, 41; systemic risk, 62n27; of underestimating the effects of option interaction, 164

Sender, Gary L., 31

sequential move game, 125, 127; and backward induction for the solving of, 128–29

serial acquirers, 22–23n11, 44n3, 168, 168n11

serial acquisitions (the case of Vodafone), 43–44, 44n3, 67, 75, 165, 166; acquisition price paid for Mannesmann, 65–66; acquisition strategy of Vodafone as a portfolio of real options, 58, 60; and buy-and-build principles, 43, 79; conclusions concerning, 68–70; as an example of global consolidation, 44; and managerial hubris, 45n5; and the mitigation of biases, 45; platform acquisitions of, 58. *See also* serial acquisitions (the case of Vodafone), overcoming potential pitfalls in serial acquisition strategy; serial acquisitions (the case of Vodafone), potential pitfalls in serial acquisition strategy

serial acquisitions (the case of Vodafone), overcoming potential pitfalls in serial acquisition strategy, 57–60, 69; overcoming Pitfall 1, 60, 60n26; overcoming Pitfall 2, 61; overcoming Pitfall 3, 63; overcoming Pitfall 4, 64–65; overcoming Pitfall 5, 66–67; overcoming Pitfall 6, 67–68

serial acquisitions (the case of Vodafone), potential pitfalls in serial acquisition strategy, 44–45; Pitfall 1: overinvestment or overconservatism in consolidating industries, 45–46; Pitfall 2: judgment biases resulting in overinvestment, 46–48; Pitfall 3: relative valuation with insufficient adjustment, 50–51; Pitfall 4: multiple variations in financial markets, 51–53; Pitfall 5: entrapment in an escalating bidding contest, 53–55; Pitfall 6: the "winner's curse," 55–57, 57n23; potential valuation pitfalls, 48, 50

Shakespeare, William, 151

shareholder value, 68, 88, 106, 113, 120, 169

short-termism, 22, 120

simulation, 86. *See also* Monte Carlo simulation

simultaneous move game, 125, 127; finding the dominant acquisition strategy in, 128

Smit, J. T. J., 127

Sony Corporation, 171

Sophocles, 19

strategic opportunism/opportunities, 2–3, 15, 32, 152, 153, 163; and education strategy, 153–54; the value of synergistic opportunities, 83–87

strategic value, 13; strategic preemption value, 90; strategic preemption value of investment timing strategies, 91–93; strategic reaction value, 90

"sunk cost fallacy," 34n16, 55, 95, 155

synergies, 5, 6, 44n3, 47n10, 79, 84, 87, 92, 142, 144n17, 146, 156; interasset synergies, 11, 12, 101; intertemporal synergies, 12, 117, 154, 160; overestimation of, 168; potential synergies, 21, 124, 133; realization of, 25, 127, 134, 135; significant synergies, 135; unique synergies, 51, 53, 67

Teck Cominco, 125, 146; market value of, 115

terminal value estimates, 23

Thaler, Richard, 51n19

Thales of Miletus, 8

threats, credible and noncredible, 129n8

Time Warner, 171

timing strategies: determination of, 161; preemption value of investment timing strategies, 91–93

Tintaya copper mine, 101, 107

Tong, Tony, 12n13, 103n4

top-down framework: application of beyond the mining industry, 117–18; and the mining industry, 112–17; strength of top-down PVGO methodology, 119; top-down PVGO valuation, 69, 70

Toshiba, 171

transaction multiples, 25, 157

Trigeorgis, L., 127

tulip mania (1636), the, 6, 6n8, 7

Tversky, Amos, 22n9; prospect theory of, 45–46

UMTS (3G) licenses, auction of, 56–57, 158

uncertainty, 2, 3, 5n6, 27, 153; adapting to, 8–9; commodity price uncertainty, 143; endogenous uncertainty, 5, 5n6, 148; executive perception of, 155–56; exogenous uncertainty, 5, 5n6, 34; and groupthink, 21; impact of, 76; macroeconomic demand uncertainty, 6; market demand uncertainties, 148; perceptions of uncertainty (inner distribution) differing from true volatility (outer distribution), 5. *See also* uncertainty, valuing of; uncertainty, visualizing/seeing of; uncertainty neglect

uncertainty, valuing of, 11–12, 163; and bottom-up option games valuation, 12–13; goal of, 3; use of top-down valuation to mitigate executive valuation biases, 13–15

uncertainty, visualizing/seeing of, 3–5; seeing the intended strategic path as uncertain, 5–6; the target value is more uncertain than perceived, 6–7; winning the bidding process as more uncertain than perceived, 7–8

uncertainty neglect, 25–26; and the caution argument (staging, deferring, or recouping an investment), 26–28; and the venturing argument, 29

United Kingdom, 57

United States, 46

urban land development, 171

valuation, 19–20, 164–65; compound option valuation, 85–86; dual valuation of growth option to avoid irrational infection, 61–63; high-market valuations, 50n16; relative valuation with insufficient adjustment, 50–51, 157; value of an options portfolio in consolidation, 87. *See also* valuation analysis; value, of a target company

valuation analysis: avoiding irrational infection of, 22–23; checking DCF overvaluation in hot markets, 23–24; potential pitfalls in, 156–57

value, 75; acquisition value, 79, 82–83; flexibility value, 84–85; heuristics of relative values, 50; relative values, 51, 62, 64, 87; stand-alone value, 83; of a target company, 10–11, 12, 12n13, 13n14, 102n2; target values, 50. *See also* option value; strategic value

Vasotec, 77

venturing, 26, 29–30, 32; cautious venturing, 35

Verizon, 43

Vodafone. *See* serial acquisitions (the case of Vodafone)

Vodafone Libertel (Netherlands), 58, 63

Vodafone-Panafon Hellenic (Greece), 58

Vodafone Telecel-Comunicacoes Pessoais SA (Portugal), 58
volatility, 3, 5, 8, 10, 15, 25, 65, 94; cash flow volatility, 113n7; estimated volatility (endogenous or exogenous), 30, 31; historical volatility, 30; implied volatility, 30; oil price volatility, 35; price volatility, 116; project volatility, 31 (box)
Von Clausewitz, Karl, 123

Walkling, R. A., 168n10
war games, 148–49
"War of Attrition" experiment, 53, 54
Warburg Pincus, 76
weighted average cost of capital (WACC), 23, 116

winner's curse, the, 7, 11, 55–57, 57n23, 158; mitigation of, 166; severity of, 67; Winner's Curse experiment, 54
WMC Resources, 107n5, 141

Xstrata, 75, 95, 117, 125–26; and the acquisition of Falconbridge, 133–35, 136 (box), 141–43, 143n16, 144–47, 146n20; bid of for WMC Resources, 107n5; classification of Xstrata's acquisition options, 106–7; consolidation strategy of, 110, 134; growth of in market value, 104; listing of on the London Stock Exchange, 101; specific acquisitions of in the mining industry, 101, 106–7, 110. *See also* dual real options valuation (the case of Xstrata)

CPSIA information can be obtained
at www.ICGtesting.com
Printed in the USA
BVHW04s2027040618
518199BV00004B/78/P

9 780691 176413